THE ANCIENT STONES
OF ENGLAND

COMPANION VOLUME

The Ancient Stones of Scotland   W. Douglas Simpson

TUDOR EDWARDS

The Ancient Stones of England

ROBERT HALE · LONDON

© *Tudor Edwards 1972*
First published in Great Britain 1972

ISBN 0 7091 3331 6

Robert Hale & Company
63 Old Brompton Road
London, S.W.7

Printed in Great Britain
by Ebenezer Baylis & Son Ltd.
The Trinity Press, Worcester, and London

CONTENTS

ILLUSTRATIONS

7

PICTURE CREDITS

Department of the Environment: 1, 5, 6, 7, 17, 18, 19, 21, 29; G. Sherren: 2, 3, 4; Aerofilms Ltd.: 8, 25; A. F. Kersting: 9, 10, 11, 12, 13, 14, 15, 16, 20, 22, 23, 24, 27, 28, 30, 32, 34; J. D. Sherren: 26; *Country Life*: 31; Barnaby's Picture Library: 33, 35.

PLANS

1

Introduction

On Cotswold there are primitive slab bridges across the Leach and the Windrush, and on the wolds above them are slab tombs, galleried and sealed and overladen with ramparts of earth. These uplands are hedged with stone, cunning solid walls set up without mortar beside the lonely sheep-walks. In the valleys or tucked into the roots of the hills, snugly fitting the rise and fall of the land, are village compositions of manor house, church, tithe barn, farmstead, bridge and wayside cross. Houses of honey-coloured limestone are felicitious with stone gables, mullioned windows, high-pitched stone tiled roofs and kneelers. The churches are likely to be overpeering deep and wide combes or merging into adjacent farmyards, and they probably resemble architectural palimpsests, being compounded of fabric that is Saxon, Norman and Gothic. In a clearing ringed by mounting woods lies the tesselated pavement of a Roman villa, and but a league or two away rises the stark broken keep of a castle and a high tangle of Gothic tracery remaining from a medieval monastery. Here within a small circumscribed area may be seen to perfection the work of man in his organic relation to the earth, whence comes his building material and his means of livelihood.

The pattern is repeated, with regional variations, over the length and breadth of the country, from Dartmoor up through the High Peak to the North Yorkshire Moors trenched by the glacial canyon of Newton Dale, its heights of Levisham Moor and Wardle Rigg straddled with round barrows and cairns, and its surrounding moorlands spiked with no less than thirty crosses, their exact function and purpose now forgotten. All this was not created overnight but evolved out of the strains and stresses of thousands of years, from the precarious struggle for survival of the early primitive hunters, through pagan fear and the refining influence of the Cross to the crude experiments in crafts and building technique and the gradual dissemination of learning and the arts.

Our remote past is still a matter for incredulity and wonder. More than that, it is for many an intangible nether world, completely amorphous and uninhabited. An American acquaintance, returning from a day's jaunt in the Shakespeare Country, pronounced Kenilworth Castle to be "just a bunch of rock all busted up", and one can understand the feeling of frustration. Certainly one can stand before the gaunt shapeless cliffs of Kenilworth with the same sense of baffled bewilderment that one feels before Knossos. And already the battlefield of Cassino seems as unreal as Bannockburn.

It is perhaps something like half a million years ago that primitive man first began to make tools of stone in southern England and Wales. He has been dubbed Lower and Middle Palaeolithic man, and his age was followed by the long succession of Upper Palaeolithic, Mesolithic, Neolithic, Bronze and Iron Ages. The last overlapped the Roman invasion of A.D. 43. For four centuries Britain was part of the Roman Empire, and colonnades and temples and Corinthian capitals (all borrowed from Athens) were reared in English valleys. "What Regions boast of more Antiquity and genuine Reliques of it of all sorts? What Earth throws up so many Roman Coyns, Medals, Urns etc. that one would think Rome it selfe was transplanted in to Great Brittain?" demanded the youthful William Stukeley at the end of his first expedition in 1710.

Then the Saxons landed on these shores, and their centuries saw the growth of a vigorous Christian Church and the creation of the kingdom of England as a political unit. They also produced Beowulf, the Lindisfarne Gospels and the high crosses of Ruthwell and Bewcastle. Our art history is complex. Strange cross-currents from Gaul and Byzantium, from the Middle East and the Scandinavian North went to the making of English art destroyed by the Danes. Under the Norman occupation England entered the main stream of Romanesque art, and the land was starred with castles and newly-blooded monasteries which had their fountain-heads across the Channel. Fortification and the arts of war developed side by side with a new piety and a new culture, and the sacred and the profane were for once easy bedfellows.

The end of the thirteenth century brought art into the castle, and soon, instead of castles, we were building manor houses and country granges, still mildly fortified, for peace had not come with the Plantagenets. Soon too the impetus of the monasteries had weakened, and the foundation of colleges and hospitals was in favour. From the Gothic of the Ile de France we evolved our own peculiarly national style, ushering in Chaucer's golden age of Gothic genius, though it spent itself out in barely two centuries and was finally extinguished by the new humanism of the Reformation.

The Renaissance was a tardy arrival to these shores. After 1500 we borrowed from Italy and from Flanders to form the cross-bred Elizabethan and Jacobean styles. It was G. K. Chesterton who suggested that Shakespeare and the great Elizabethans throw "a gigantic shadow back" upon all that went before. The Elizabethans fondly imagined that they had done with the Middle Ages. Yet their houses were virtually Gothic shells tricked out with Classical details, the tournament persisted, and their greatest poet, Spenser, fostered archaisms inspired by the similar vogue for Chaucer. Another medieval survival, though it was a crude distortion, was the transference of devotion to Our Lady to a Virgin Queen, a natural response to the Reformation. Gloriana reigned supreme, worshipped with an almost blasphemous adulation, so that mansions newly built were as shrines ready to receive her, often untenanted by the owners "until that holy saint may sit in it, to whom it is dedicated".[1]

So we come to Wren and Vanbrugh and Hawksmoor and the glories of their baroque megalomania, and, as the eighteenth century progressed, to a return to Palladio and the whimsies of the new Rococo. Robert Adam reintroduced us to echoes from Athens before English architecture entered a confusing world of eclecticism in which the vernacular genius of our craftsmen was allowed full play. It was long the practice to attribute much of our best architecture to apparently omnipresent and incredibly prolific celebrities, and our plastic arts to foreigners, and it is only during the last few decades that the honours have been bestowed where they belong, to obscure but highly-talented regional

[1] Letter from Sir Christopher Hatton to Sir Thomas Heneage dated Sept. 1580, quoted in E. St. J. Brooks, *Sir Christopher Hatton* (London, 1946). See also John Buxton, *Elizabethan Taste* (London, 1963).

master-masons, sculptors, woodworkers and plasterers. Even the architects of our Gothic masterpieces have now been identified by a band of devoted specialists, of whom Mr. John Harvey must be singled out. Anonymity is gradually being banished, and in the Renaissance and later fields writers of Sitwellian calibre (and we must refer specifically to Sir Sacheverell Sitwell) have done much to interpret and evaluate.

There, if not before, we must call a halt, for while this is briefly the preamble to our story, our concern is with 'ancient stones', and we may conform, though loosely, to the arbitrary date limit of 1714 which until recently was rigidly imposed by the Royal Commission on Ancient Monuments.[1] Indeed our original aim was to examine those sites and buildings which are either in ruins or are no longer in normal use, but here we face a dilemma, for apart from prehistoric and Roman sites, castles and monasteries, extremely few significant houses and churches are abandoned, and one must refer to still functioning buildings if only for purposes of continuity, development and comparison. In the vast assembly of English parish churches we have a legacy unrivalled elsewhere in Europe and indeed anywhere on this planet, while our domestic architecture is, with prose and poetry and painting, the highest expression of our native genius.

Despite development and destruction, history yet lies beneath teeming streets and the lonely furrow, and it seems almost certain that much will come to light that will radically change many of our preconceived notions. In 1969 alone some eighty-five sites in England were excavated and recorded, and this book can, therefore, be no more than an attempt to introduce and to indicate the riches that lie about us. The terminology of antiquity is full of quirks and contradictions, and we are constantly being exhorted to change one 'label' for another. It is, perhaps, of little consequence.

The Englishman, except by concession to foreign usage, will not call his Anglo-Saxon period 'protohistory', he calls it 'early history', and has as much right to keep the phrase as the Germans have to keep their *Frühgeschichte*. 'Prehistoric', on the other hand, is his standard broad term for everything in his country that is generally or generically Pre-Roman, from Eoliths to Druids. . . . Terminology is of two kinds: common or everyday, and learned or scientific. . . . The word 'Norman', for the style of architecture, was at first only

[1] The survey period is now extended to 1850.

used by the learned, but with the spread of education it has been adopted into common speech. All of us know a Norman church; and if the more refined specialist of today were to tell us we ought only to call it Post-Conquest Romanesque, we should say he had forgotten the difference between his specialist vocabulary and our everyday one. It is the same with 'prehistoric'. The word, denoting everything in Pre-Roman Britain from Eoliths to Druids, has passed into common speech; we can today only accept the situation, and be thankful for the spread of education that has caused it.[1]

Finally, as Sir Mortimer Wheeler has reminded us, the archae-ologist is not digging up *things*, he is digging up *people*. Our purpose, then, is to show man in his changing environment, in life and in death, in war and in peace, in castle keep and monastery cloister and stalled church quire, in town house and rural farm-stead, and how he progressed from such a primitive cave dwelling as Wookey Hole in the Arthurian country to the palatial halls of a Seaton Delaval, now derelict, in far Northumbria.

[1] Professor Christopher Hawkes, *Proceedings of the Prehistoric Society*, 1951.

2

Primitive Hunters

When the north of Britain was a frozen glacial world its inhabitants were nomadic hunters, moving from place to place in small family groups, following the wild animals and searching for edible plants and wild vegetables. Since it is improbable that they had any permanent camp sites (and if they had these would have been destroyed by later climatic conditions) all that has survived of these people are the tools they made from pieces of flint and animal bones, often preserved in caves and the gravel of river terraces. With the later Palaeolithic age we can be certain that modern man, *homo sapiens*, had appeared on the scene. He too lived in the mouths of caves, lighting his fires to drive away the wild beasts who were rival claimants for occupation, but he also made lightly constructed shelters of branches and skins. He and his family used fur and leather for clothing, and they decked themselves out with necklaces and trinkets made from small carved bones, shells and perforated animals' teeth, while their more specialized tools were fashioned not only from flints but also from bone, antler and ivory.

One cultural group of these people, known as Aurignacian after a site in France, has been traced in Wales, notably in the Paviland caves below the golden lichenous heights of the Gower Peninsula. Here was found the celebrated Red Lady of Paviland, no voluptuous siren but the osseous residue, stained red by the action of iron oxide, of a Cro-Magnon man. Only one group, the Creswellian (named after the Creswell Crags in Derbyshire), can be readily identified in England. These people flourished in many cave sites, including caves at Creswell, the Victoria Cave in the Attermice Cliffs near Settle in Yorkshire (discovered in the year of Queen Victoria's coronation), and several of the caves which honeycomb the Mendips in Somerset. The Hyaena Den at Wookey, so named by Sir William Boyd Dawkins, who as a young man explored this cave as his first venture in the field of geology, has yielded the bones of mammoth, lion and bear but no human relics beyond man's flints and the ashes and burned stones of his fires. In nearby Gough's Cave at Cheddar, however, a skull and human bones were accompanied by flint scrapers and blades and a rare deer antler, pierced and decorated. This last implement was probably used for straightening the shafts of arrows (the Esquimos still have a similar shaft-straightener), and it is known from the caves of France, where it was long regarded as a prehistoric wand of office and given the name of *bâton-de-commandement*. The only specimens of Palaeolithic art yet found in Britain, engravings on bones which include a horse, reindeer and stylized human figure, were discovered in the Creswell caves.

As the ice finally receded from Britain and the climate became warmer, the tundra gave way to steppe-like vegetation, which in turn was replaced by light woods and then dense forests. Here lived the Mesolithic hunters, a European people who had moved westward into Britain from Denmark and the Baltic. They lived in forests and along the marshy edges of lakes and streams, and they hunted, fowled and fished with antler spearheads, arrows with minute flint tips and barbed harpoon-heads of bone. They had tools for wood working and parallel-sided flint axes and adzes for felling and shaping tree trunks. Since they were still largely nomadic their huts were of an impermanent nature, merely oval scoops in the gravel screened with branches and skins, such as have been found at Abinger and Farnham in Surrey.

These people were often watermen, travelling by the waterways, then more extensive than today, in canoes hollowed-out from tree trunks and perhaps of birch bark like those of the North American Indians. Consequently they were often lake or lake-side dwellers. The most important Mesolithic settlement found in this country is at Star Carr near Scarborough in Yorkshire, where excavations revealed a platform of birch trunks and branches on the shore of a prehistoric lake, together with a comprehensive collection of tools and other objects. Unfortunately nothing is now visible of this site. The platform appears to have been occupied in the winter months only by a small group of perhaps twenty individuals, engaged primarily in fishing and hunting red elk and deer. Among the objects found were the crowns of red-deer skulls with antlers still attached but perforated, probably used as head-dresses in magico-religious practices, but possibly put to the more prosaic and functional purpose of enabling the hunter to approach more closely to his quarry. Other significant survivals were elk-antler mattocks, beads of perforated amber, rolls of birch bark from which containers were made, and large quantities of bracken fungus for tinder.

Remains of similar platforms have been discovered not far away in the broad alluvial Vale of Pickering, which in Mesolithic times was the Lake of Pickering. Here parallel rows of piles or stakes driven into the marshy ground, together with human and animal skeletal remains, tools and other objects, indicate lake dwellings roughly contemporary with Star Carr. Such dwellings must have been almost identical with those of Lake Neuchatel in Switzerland, and they provide a transition to the later crannog and the more elaborate lake village of Glastonbury.

These are the first human habitations known to us. Even so, they were of an impermanent character, for man was still a wandering hunter leaving no durable marks on the landscape, no effect on the natural forest environment. Until he learned to harness natural forces to his purpose and to develop improved tools his choice of habitation was dominated by the physical features of his territory.

According to H. Peake and H. J. Fleure, "A number of lines of evidence . . . lead us to suspect that most of the essential elements of civilization developed before 5000 B.C. in some region within 200 miles of Aleppo", and the epochal discoveries are characterized as "the cultivation of wheat and barley, the shaping of stone implements by grinding, the making of pottery, the invention of spinning and weaving, and the discovery that the ores of metal could be melted and cast into a mould. It seems likely, too, that the erection of permanent houses dates from about the same time."[1]

It was only with the Neolithic period, a little over 3000 B.C., that a people from Brittany and the north-west, from Spain and Portugal, able to adapt the local outcrops of stone to their use and build more durable habitations, came to these shores. Skilled in grinding and polishing stone tools, these people represented the Mediterranean and Megalithic phase of the New Stone Age

[1] *Peasants and Potters.*

culture. At first they settled on the chalk downlands of southern England, and here they raised crops of wheat and barley and grazed their herds. Pioneers in the domestic arts of grain-growing, stock-rearing and pottery-making, they were the founders of our agrarian economy and the first to change the landscape, creating an open country of crops and grassland. Thus there came about the slowly developing nuclei of village communities with all the monumental constructions of communal life.

3

Houses and Tombs of Stone Age Man

One of the very earliest (possibly *the* earliest) Neolithic stone-built settlements ever to be discovered is that above the Danube near Donji Milanovac in northern Yugoslavia, where some forty trapeze-shaped houses with solidly constructed hearths were discovered. Their date is believed to be anywhere between 8000 and 6000 B.C. Remains of well-preserved houses of much the same date, possibly a little later, have recently been unearthed in Cyprus, on the coast near Kyrenia. Here some of the house walls have survived to a height of over 7 feet, and in at least one of them the walls are corbelled in their lower parts. Internally there are stone and clay benches set against the walls with hearths in front set on clay platforms or in pottery bowls let into the floor. Between the houses were passageways and drainage channels.

There are no such monuments, certainly not of such an early date, in the British Isles, but in the far north is one settlement of singular importance. Here, the most complete specimens of the Neolithic domestic dwelling, even to their equipment, are to be found at the celebrated prehistoric village of Skara Brae on the western shore of the mainland of Orkney. Erosion and the sea carried away much of the village, but seven stone huts were discovered in 1850 after a storm had blown away the top covering of sand under which they had lain concealed throughout the centuries of recorded history. This Stone Age village was later excavated by Professor Childe, who found that the houses were connected by paved galleries or alleys, and that each was provided with a central hearth and inbuilt stone furniture. This furniture, dresser, shelves, cupboards and bed, recalls the built-in furniture of seventeenth-century farmhouses in the Lake District and has some affinity with the slate fittings of Welsh houses. The masonry throughout is of fine quality, and the whole construction displays a sense of architectural form which is not seen again for many centuries. Indeed this type of house seems to have no immediate successors. Isolated phenomenon or not, it is a unique monument affording a vivid illustration of the domestic economy of a Neolithic community.[1]

Skara Brae has no counterpart in England, and indeed no prehistoric dwellings survive with any such degree of completeness until we reach the Iron Age. Dwelling sites of Neolithic people of the Windmill Hill culture have been identified at a few places like Haldon and Hembury in Devon, but there are no tangible remains. There is little evidence to suggest that people lived in the so-called causeway camps—large hilltop enclosures formed by one or more concentric rings of quarry ditches with internal banks, broken by causeway gaps of undug subsoil—of which the most well-known is Windmill Hill itself, near Avebury in Wiltshire. Such enclosures were probably used for congregating for some social, religious or economic purpose, and for sheltering cattle at stops in a persisting nomadic existence. A possible permanent camp has been identified about the marshy source of the river Lea at Luton in Bedfordshire, where a massive bank with external ditch apparently defended an area of many acres.

The Neolithic age is chiefly characterized by collective tombs, and these are among the most imposing monuments of prehistory. There were then two streams of civilization from southern Europe by sea to the north and north-west. Each movement was responsible for the erection of huge megalithic or stone tombs to receive their dead, and these are found with little variation emanating from the Mediterranean to Spain, France, the British Isles and Scandinavia. In general they are of two types, gallery graves and the later passage graves.

The gallery grave was a long gallery or stone passage with little or no distinction between entrance passage and chamber, and this was covered by a long barrow or mound of earth. The most imposing groups of these graves are distributed over the Severn-Cotswold area, on either side of the Severn estuary, in South Wales, the Mendips, north Wiltshire and Berkshire. Of these the most interesting is probably that at West Kennet near Avebury

[1] For a full account of Skara Brae see the official guide by V. G. Childe and also his detailed study *Skara Brae: A Pictish Village in Orkney* (1931).

in Wiltshire. One of the largest long barrows in Britain, it is
350 feet long and 8 feet high, although the burial chamber at its
eastern end is only 40 feet long. Two side chambers lie on either
side of the passage, which ends in a rectangular chamber. Three
enormous stones blocked the entrance when the last burials had
taken place. Excavation showed that some thirty adults and child-
ren had been buried in the tomb, together with pots similar to
those found at Windmill Hill.

The Cotswold limestone country is richer in chambered long
barrows even than Wiltshire; no less than eight can be located
on the wolds above the village of Lower Swell. The best preserved of them is Belas Knap, lying high on the tilted plateau of
Cleeve Cloud above Saxon Winchcombe. The true oolite, to be
found only on Cotswold, is here, sensitive alike to light and
chisel. It lies only inches beneath the soil, and with the eighteenth-
century enclosures it was extracted and set up in stone hedges,
dry-walled, with copings or 'cock-ups' of flat stones set edgewise.
Honey-coloured fragments litter the ground, soft to the touch
and set with tiny fossils. It is an apt place for a megalithic monument, and Belas Knap lies bellied upon the ground, stretched out
like a hog's back and covered with gently stirring grass, for the
mound of earth laid upon the stone framework is intact. One of
the last of the Neolithic galleried tombs to be built, it has asym-
metrical burial chambers, and at its eastern end is a recessed false
entrance with incurving ramps or horns built up with perfectly
fitting wafers of stone, the prototype of all the art of Cotswold
dry-walling. Only three of the Cotswold long barrows have
this curious false entrance, though it is to be found in the tomb
of Capel Garmon on the Denbighshire moorlands. It may have
been devised to mislead marauders, and a similar feature is built
into the Egyptian *mastaba*, a rectangular stone or brick tomb.
When the Victorians rifled Belas Knap they found the skeletons
of thirty-seven people buried with their tools, amulets (some
made of perforated boars' tusks), beads and pottery vessels containing food and drink for the last journey. Some powerful
religious impulse must have prompted the great labour involved
in such an elaborate tomb, but of their ideas and hopes we can
know nothing.

The line of hills from here to the mouth of the Severn is
crested with these tombs, though none is as elaborate as Belas

Knap, unless it be that known as Hetty Pegler's Tump near Uley on the edge of the Jurassic cliff, with its five chambers, two now blocked. A few more of these galleried graves on Cotswold may be noticed. That at Notgrove is double cruciform in plan with an ante-chamber, central passage and five chambers, formed, like the others, with alternating slabs of stone and dry-stone walling, the whole being roofed. It is approached from the east end by a horned entrance with double walls. It is of unusual importance because it has a central dome which contains a cist in which were found the bones of an adult male, in whose honour the entire construction may have been built.

The tomb at Nymphsfield is single cruciform in plan, with an ante-chamber that is wider than the passage, and, again, this was approached from the east end by a horned entrance. It was here that the necked jar, which is without parallel in this country, was found. Similar jars have been found in France, and this one may well have been brought into this country by the builders of the tomb, who in all probability came up the Severn in hollowed-out canoes. Rodmarton is the same type as Belas Knap, with one small chamber on each side and a false entrance at the east end. The chambers are approached from the top of the mound, and three steps lead down to tiny passages and porthole entrances. One of these porthole entrances still retains the sealing-in stones which were placed there by the last users of the tomb, a rare feature. Haematite has been found in the Rodmarton and Nymphs-field tombs, showing that the Palaeolithic practice of painting the body continued into the Neolithic period.

The technique and labour employed in building these tombs are impressive, to say the least of it. The hornwork and the masonry in general are superb, there are often stone-corbelled roofs of domical type, and a tomb like Rodmarton contains some 50,000 tons of stone and would proably have taken 100 men two years to build. Related groups of gallery graves survive in north-west Wales, the Peak area of Derbyshire, Cornwall and the Isle of Man, and these probably gave rise to similar tombs in Ireland and south-west Scotland.

The chambered tomb, which has been called the ancestor of the modern family vault, was designed for communal burial over a long period, so that it naturally developed various forms and characteristics in different areas. Several centuries after the first

Windmill Hill people settled in Britain other groups of immi-
grants began to arrive on the west coast from the mouth of the
Loire and southern Brittany, and it was these who built the
passage graves, the expression of a new religious mystique involving, perhaps, ideas of a Mother Goddess. The constructional
form of these tombs seems to have originated in the Western
Mediterranean, whence the idea was carried round the Iberian
peninsula, up the coast of Brittany and thence to Cornwall,
Wales and central Ireland. It is in these areas that the finest passage
tombs are to be found. The normal type consists of a round or
rectangular burial chamber with corbelled roof, entered by a
long narrow passage, the whole covered with a round barrow or
circular mound of earth.

The finest groups of passage graves are undoubtedly in Ireland,
where over 150 survive, of which the greatest is New Grange in
County Meath. A small group exists in North Wales, however,
and of these two on Anglesey are quite remarkable. Bryn Celli
Ddu is a mound 90 feet in diameter containing a short passage
at the end of which is a polygonal chamber. Standing in the
chamber is a single, upright stone which may be of phallic significance. Human remains found here indicate that burial was by
both inhumation and cremation, unless it was the scene of human
sacrifice on a large scale. The other Anglesey tomb is Barclodiad
y Gawres, in which the chamber at the end of the passage is
cross-shaped. Five of the wallstones of this chamber are decorated
with stylized carvings of spirals, lozenges and chevrons, motifs
which occur in a number of Irish and French passage graves.

In Cornwall a grave near Sennen called Chapel Carn Brea was
originally unusually high with retaining stone walls and three
concentric inner walls. Another passage grave near Zennor,
Zennor Quoits, has lost its barrow. Cornwall is noted for its
'quoits' and 'dolmen', as they are locally termed, former round
barrows of which the mounds have gone leaving only the table-
like standing stones of chamber and ante-chamber with massive
capstone. On the Scilly Isles there is a notable concentration of
'entrance graves', a variation on the passage grave. Here the
burial chamber opens straight out of the circular mound, and in
many cases the mound itself has gone. Finally mention must be
made of a small group of burial chambers set at the extreme end
of long narrow rectangular barrows, apparently related to

North German and Scandinavian tombs. There is a sparse concentration of these close to the Medway in Kent, of which the best known is Kits Coty House near Aylesford, though only two standing stones and a capstone survive.

Late in the Neolithic period the Windmill Hill folk began to dig mines to obtain better flint for their tools, sinking shafts through the upper chalk and then cutting out galleries. Several flint mines have been found in Sussex, notably at Cissbury, and the Chilterns, but the largest known group, some 360 shafts covering an area of about 34 acres, is located near Brandon in Norfolk. These are known as Grime's Graves, a name deriving from an earlier popular belief that this curious area might be the Devil's (or Grim's) burial place. Ostensibly a confused mass of mounds and hollows, the shafts are now difficult to identify, but two of them, one containing a fertility shrine, with galleries, have been preserved and are open for inspection. Tools used in the mining included wooden or scapula shovels and red-deer antlers, and seven antler picks are embodied in the fertility shrine.

During the 1,400 years or so of the Neolithic period the Meso-lithic hunters, the Windmill Hill farmers and the passage-grave builders slowly merged and developed as one unified late Neo-lithic culture, characterized by the production and organized distribution of polished stone axes, though there were regional variations in such things as pottery styles. A little after 2000 B.C., however, another wave of new explorers, who arrived on the eastern and southern shores of Britain from the area of the Rhine delta, quickly overran the rest of the British Isles.

The Beaker people, probably the first Celtic race to invade our island, were so-called, for lack of any generic name, from the distinctive pottery vessel known as a bell-beaker which we find buried with their dead. They were a dominant restless people little inclined to agriculture, though they grew barley. They wore clothes of woven woollen fabric or skins fixed with buttons or pins, they hunted with copper knives and bows and arrows, they imported metal goods from Ireland at a time when metallurgy was unknown here, and they made the first attempts at trepaning. They buried their dead singly in a crouched-up position beneath a small round barrow.

Few Beaker settlements or earthworks have been found in

Britain, and it seems that they took over and developed existing late Neolithic sites. They did, however, introduce three types of religious monuments: the stone circles, stone rows and henge monuments with two or more entrances (these were built with a single entrance before the arrival of the Beaker people). Henge monuments were ceremonial circular banked enclosures with internal ditches and settings of posts or stones. Stonehenge and Woodhenge are not typical examples of henges. Woodhenge contained six concentric rings of wooden posts with a ditched enclosure 250 feet in diameter, evidence of roofed circular wooden temples of a type distinct from the unroofed circles that have endured in stone at Avebury and Stonehenge. Recent excavation has shown that the enclosure at Durrington Walls in Wiltshire was of the same type, and as late as 1969 excavations at Marden, about 10 miles upstream from Durrington Walls, produced postholes and other evidence of a circular wooden temple and established the importance of yet another major ritual site within the great temple series of Late Neolithic Britain.

Unlike comparable sites the Marden enclosure is not even roughly circular but is of irregular half-moon shape, with one side lying open to the Avon which forms a natural boundary. The pottery recovered is of a type known as grooved ware and, with the flintwork, is closely comparable with the finds from other sites of this type and is probably to be dated to the period 1700–1600 B.C. Picks of red-deer antler were clearly used as tools in the construction.

Stonehenge itself underwent three distinct building periods. The first has been dated by Professor R. J. C. Atkinson as being between 1900 and 1700 B.C., and it represents the first phase of a series of developments and alterations which were spread over many centuries. By about 1600 B.C. the Beaker people set up a double circle of bluestones within the old henge monument and constructed the avenue which is now barely visible. It is remarkable that these bluestones had been quarried at Carn Meini in the Prescelly Mountains of Pembrokeshire, dragged to the coast, floated on rafts to the mouth of the Bristol Avon, then upriver and along the Frome tributary, hauled overland to the Wylye river, by raft again down the river, and so up the Wiltshire Avon to the great plain.

Three hundred years have passed since young John Aubrey,

out hunting from Marlborough Castle, was led by the chase "through the village of Avebury into the closes there, where I was wonderfully surprised at the sight of those vast stones of which I had never heard before, as also at the mighty bank and graff about it . . .". Thus was discovered that mighty megalithic monument, more than twenty times the size of Stonehenge, to which, beneath the open sky, people came from far and wide with a religious compulsion which we cannot measure. It was at Avebury that the Beaker people constructed a great four-entrance henge monument around the stone circle, throwing up a massive circular rampart and ditch round an area of 28 acres, and adding three smaller circles with a common axis along a diameter of the main circle. The Kennet Avenue, a ceremonial avenue of two rows of upright stones, links the circles with a double stone circle on Overton Hill, well over a mile away to the south-east. All these standing stones are of unhewn sarsen stone, a local sandstone once occurring naturally on the downs, though most of it has now been cleared away by farmers. Burials and fragments of pottery found in some of the stone holes suggest that the henge was built by Beaker people and native Neolithic slaves. Many of the stones have disappeared, filched by local builders, but this must have been almost the largest complex of prehistoric standing stones in the world—almost but not quite, for the great series of *alignements* at Carnac in Brittany consists of no less than 2,730 menhirs.

Many stone circles and alignments survive in the West Country, the Pennines and Cumberland, but they cannot be accurately dated and, in general, they are more characteristic of the Bronze Age.

4

The Bronze Age and its Monuments

The Bronze Age lay within the period called Sub-Boreal, cool, dry and becoming steadily warmer with long summers. Woodlands, mainly of oak, alder, lime and ash, marched over the hillsides, and moorlands were dry and firm. Most people continued to lead a pastoral life, cultivating grain and increasing their herds and flocks, and the increasing population spread over a greater area of the highland zones. Metallurgy steadily developed to produce new and better implements, and this and the impact of foreign traders brought the palstave, the typical axe-head of the mid Bronze period, the looped spear-head and the rapier.

In the earlier years the people of Wessex worked and controlled the export of Irish copper and gold and Cornish tin and bronze, and they pushed trade routes across Europe to barter their metal ores for necklaces and pendants of Baltic amber, decorative pins from northern Germany, ceremonial jadeite axes from Brittany and faience beads from the Mediterranean. Amber and gold cups and fine gold inlay decoration on hilts of bronze daggers suggest links with Mycenae in southern Greece. While such ornaments have been found in substantial quantities, little has survived in the form of human habitations.

The predominating monuments continue to be sepulchral, either directly or by association. Round barrows continued to be built, usually over a single burial, though some are found to contain a number of burials. The vicinity of the ancient Ridgeway track on the sea-heights of Dorset is studded with over 100 barrows, with the Poxwell stone circle as the miniature Stonehenge of this vast burial ground. Burials of the wealthy Wessex families were placed in groups or cemeteries of round barrows of different types. Men were usually interred in bell-barrows, the mound separated by a wide flat margin from a surrounding ditch and outer bank, while the richer women were buried beneath the tiny mounds of disc-barrows. Other Wessex barrows included saucer-barrows, low mounds surrounded by a ditch, and the simple bowl-barrow, a mound with or without a surrounding ditch.

The great mound of Silbury Hill near Avebury was originally an early Bronze Age barrow built of layers of turf and gravel, its edge perhaps contained by stakes surrounded by a broad deep ditch. Soon after its construction it was enlarged to its present enormous size, the largest artificial hill in the country. It may have been rebuilt as a token of prestige for some Wessex family. Was it, perhaps, the family responsible for the redesigning of Stonehenge? Since the eighteenth century a number of attempts have been made to ascertain the purpose of this gigantic earthwork; a duke, a dean and several professors have directed incisions into its smooth flanks, or have tunnelled deep into its heart, but the mound still withholds its secret. Early Victorian antiquaries believed that Silbury Hill was Roman, since it seemed to stand on the Roman road from Bath to Marlborough, but Sir John Lubbock (later Lord Avebury) traced the ditches along the road and found that they curved abruptly southward to avoid the hill.

There were regional variations in the north and west, where the barrows are often constructed of stones, the ditch of the south being replaced by retaining kerbs or dry-stone walls. In the centre stone slabs often form a cist or stone coffin. In the north the barrows are usually spaced out in prominent positions along a high ridge or over a moorland summit. On the North Yorkshire Moors the larger barrows are called 'howes', and many have individual names, e.g. Lilla Howe, Green Howe, Loose Howe. Loose Howe on Danby Moor is 60 feet in diameter and 7 feet high, and excavation revealed the burial of a body fully clothed and with a bronze dagger, placed in a wooden dug-out canoe with a second canoe as cover and a third one alongside. A second burial here was of cremated bones in an urn, accompanied by a stone battle-axe and bronze dagger; this can be dated to about 1600 B.C. when cremation had begun steadily to replace inhumation burials.

Earlier burials in Yorkshire often contained vase or bowl-shaped pots known as food vessels, which have evolved from beakers and later Neolithic pottery forms, though more elaborately ornamented. Many examples of these vessels from round barrows are to be seen in the museums of Scarborough and Whitby. Some of the most interesting food vessel burials were found in split tree-trunk coffins, like that from Gristhorpe. The Gristhorpe burial, excavated as far back as 1834, contained a short cist skeleton, wrapped in hide fixed with a bone pin, with a bronze dagger and other objects. Jet necklaces are also a feature of this 'Food Vessel' culture in Yorkshire. Jet working was an active industry in the area at this period, and many ornamental jet wares were distributed throughout the country and exchanged for the gold and bronze of Ireland.

There was intensive habitation, both by the living and the dead, of the high windswept moorlands from the top of York-shire all the way down to Bodmin Moor in Cornwall. In the North Riding of Yorkshire alone there are estimated to be over 10,000 cairns and round barrows. Most of them are concentrated on the North Yorkshire Moors, that lonely high plateau trenched with dales and haunted by the red grouse, golden plover and curlew. The cairns are mostly small heaps made almost entirely of small stones rarely more than a few feet in diameter. Many of them are grouped into cemeteries of several hundred sites, and most belong to the full Bronze Age period, though the majority of excavated examples have yielded no information with regard to date or even function. It may be assumed that they were sepulchral and covered inhumation burials which have been completely destroyed in the acid soil conditions. A number have, however, yielded cremations, some accompanied by a food vessel or contained in a collared urn, and these at least may be dated roughly 1600–1400 B.C.

Certainly some of these cairn groups are associated with small fields and banks which are characteristic of some Bronze Age areas. The largest of these Yorkshire moorland cemeteries is John Cross Rigg on Fylingdales Moor near Whitby, where there are over 1,200 closely grouped cairns associated with a double ditch. At Danby Rigg there are over 800 cairns on the 'Rigg' or ridge and the remains of a stone circle in which two urn burials were excavated. At Harlyn Bay in Cornwall, there was unearthed in 1900 an unusual cemetery containing some 200 cists with a great many skeletal remains. These burials, without any protection for the body unless it had perished, were in three layers a few feet below the surface of hard sand. No pottery or other objects were unearthed, and indeed the site is undatable.

Stone circles and rows are associated with a cult of the dead and must be regarded as combinations of temples and tombs, shrines and sanctuaries. On Dartmoor there are about ninety small circles as well as sixty short stone rows. Some of the alignments lead away from barrows, but others stand alone, and in some of them a single block marks the end of the row. The plan at Merrivale near Princetown is of particular interest. On the south are two parallel stone rows running almost east to west. The north row runs from a circle to a standing stone and is 590 feet long. The south row has a standing stone placed at each end, with a stone circle surrounding a cist half-way along it, and this is 850 feet long. Slightly south of this row, near another stone circle, is a fine stone cist, one of the largest on the moor. Such a complex construction must be pregnant with a significance which escapes us.

Another important group is that of Shovel Down near Chagford. One stone avenue leads to the centre of a barrow which consists of four concentric circles, and north-west of this is another avenue unconnected with a barrow or standing stone. South-west of the barrow circles is yet another avenue running to the centre of a barrow at the south end. Obviously another complex of importance. The longest row of standing stones on Dartmoor is at Stall Moor near South Brent. It runs from a circle (the retaining wall of a lost barrow) for 2 miles to a barrow on Green Hill, and there are over 700 stones in the row.

Briefly, we can notice a few circles ranging right across the country. There are the Rollright Stones in Oxfordshire, "corroded like worm-eaten wood by the harsh Jaws of Time", as old William Stukeley put it, standing beside the ancient road which passes the dolmen called the Whispering Knights. There is Arbor Low and the Bull Ring high in the stony country of Derbyshire, both henge monuments containing stone circles (though the stones of the Bull Ring were removed last century). At Stanton Drew in the pastoral orchard country of Somerset are three large circles and two rows leading to the river Chew. This is often termed 'druidical', like the so-called Druid's Circle at Keswick in Cumberland, with its thirty-eight stones, all of the Borrowdale volcanic series, in the outer circle and ten in the quadrangular enclosure within the eastern rim of the circle.

One may or may not agree with Dr. Johnson that when a man has seen one 'Druidical temple' he has seen enough, but certainly the dramatically sited Stonehenge conditions most of our minds as to the appearance and character of such megalithic monuments. The excess wealth of the Wessex culture may have influenced the remodelling of Stonehenge about 1500 B.C., when the double circle of bluestones was dismantled and the great lintelled stone circle and five sarsen trilithons (literally three stones, two uprights and one across the top) were erected. These trilithons have some curious architectural refinements, including groove and tongue and mortice and tenon joints for attaching lintel stones to one another and to their uprights. All the upright stones are carefully smoothed and have an entasis, like a deliberate swelling, half-way up the stone. This was a device used in classical architecture to counteract the effects of perspective. Such a refinement would only be expected where contact with Greece existed. A carving on one of the trilithons represents a hilted Mycenaean dagger. Could it have been the trade-mark of a Mycenaean architect or overseer brought to Britain to supervise the final building of Stonehenge?

The temple is on a ritual axis with its climax towards the south-west, and it has been suggested that Stonehenge was used for astronomical purposes on the position of the Heel stone, which stands about 40 yards outside the outermost circle, between the two earth banks to the east of the horseshoe of arches. Many archaeologists believe that this Heel stone was used to mark the position of the midsummer sunrise, but its position slightly south of the axis passing through the centre of the Great Trilithon arch is difficult to explain because the rays of the midsummer sun do not strike it until the sun is clear of the horizon. It has now been suggested that the stone was placed to mark the rising point of the moon in midwinter in years when an eclipse is likely to take place. On the other hand the axis and the passage between the earth banks to the east of the great arch were oriented towards the midsummer sunrise.

The Stonehenge people first placed marker stones to indicate the rising and setting points of the sun on midsummer and mid-winter days. It has recently been established that if the full moon closest to midwinter rose slightly south of the midsummer sunrise marker a lunar eclipse was likely to occur, but there was never any eclipse when the midwinter full moon rose much to the north or south of the summer sunrise. Then they observed the north and south limits of the winter full moonrise, and placed the Heel stone midway between those limits.

The more settled farming life of the later years of the Bronze Age is indicated by the fairly substantial remains of settlements consisting of stone huts and low rectangular walled enclosures. These huts were almost invariably circular in plan, of rough unmortared masonry, with walls of a compatible thickness. The hearth was either in the middle of the floor or against the wall, and close to it was a 'cooking hole' some 15 inches deep. Across part of the floor was a dais, probably for the beds. Originally each hut would have had a central wooden post or a timber framework of conical design, covered with skins or branches and turf. Such settlements have survived on the uplands of Cornwall, Devon, Yorkshire, Cumberland and Northumberland. A few are to be found on the Mendips in Somerset, and their scarcity here is partly explained by the fact that many people lived in the caves and rock shelters of these hills, where Bronze Age burials and stone hearths have been found. Indeed there is a visual record of the occupation of the Mendip caves from Palaeolithic times right up to the Romano-British period.

One area prolific in settlements of round stone huts is the mist-laden Bodmin Moor in Cornwall, below the granite crowns of Brown Willy, Brown Gilly and Rough Tor. Dartmoor was also thickly populated by the later Bronze Age dwellers, and no less than thirty settlements have been identified and have tangible remains. The largest of all the pounds or enclosures is Broadun Pound near Postbridge, where an almost continuous wall encloses some 12 acres and a score of huts. The most important surviving settlement, however, is Grimspound, 2 miles north-east of the above. It is enclosed by a circular wall or pound, about 10 feet wide and, originally, just under 6 feet high. The enclosed area is 4 acres, and there are remains of twenty-four huts. These were circular, and about half of them had fireplaces and raised internal platforms. The walls stand in places to the original height of 3 feet. The entrances are on the south-west, and some doors are complete with jambs and lintels, and they have shielding wind-break walls. Those huts without hearths and other evidence of human habitation were probably cattle-stalls or storehouses. A stream runs through the enclosure (a rarity for pounds), and the fields outside are marked by low walls in a fair state of preservation.

On the slope of Little Trowlesworth Tor is a pear-shaped pound with enclosing wall, and the half-dozen hut-circles here are unusual in that they embody stones arranged to form short tunnels over a yard in length, originally vermin traps with shutters to trap the rodents in the tunnels. There are large clusters of huts on Brent Moor and in the vicinity of Princetown, and on Standon Down near Lydford there are over seventy hut circles scattered over the slope and not confined within an enclosure. There is another large settlement near Postbridge, and this has led some people to ascribe the clapper bridge at Postbridge to a Bronze Age date.

These huts, like the stone circles, can rarely be accurately dated, and the new science of radiocarbon dating must inevitably change many preconceived notions. Certainly the use of terms like Neolithic, Early, Middle and Late Bronze Age and Iron Ages A, B and C has become obsolete. As Professor R. J. C. Atkinson so succinctly puts it,[1] ". . . since such development does not take place uniformly, even in an area as small as Britain, it is inevitable that at one and the same time there will be a community, say, in Wessex which, in virtue of the possession of certain diagnostic types of bronze weapon, must be assigned to the Middle Bronze Age, while another in northern England, less advanced, belongs to the Early Bronze Age, and a third in northern Scotland, retarded through geographical isolation, will still be in the Late Stone Age."

Progressive and scientific excavation also upsets accepted theories. The so-called lake villages of Meare and Glastonbury in Somerset have hitherto been attributed to the final phase of the Iron Age, about 200 B.C. Certainly they were occupied at that period. In 1969, however, digging through the foundations at Meare revealed the first positive evidence of earlier occupations. What was discovered was a succession of well-preserved timber structures built and rebuilt on the same site, consisting of substantial tree-trunks, some with joint holes that could have supported wattle and daub superstructures. These remains are certainly of Late Bronze Age date, but even earlier occupation

[1] *Stonehenge* (London, 1956).

The interior of West Kennet Long Barrow, Wiltshire

Two views of the east side of the burial chamber of Belas Knap, Gloucestershire: (*left*) the entrance and (*right*) the interior

cannot be excluded, and one is reminded of the Mesolithic crannog at Star Carr. These new discoveries might also establish a link between the lake village and the ancient track across the peat moors near Meare, dated by radiocarbon to 2800 B.C.

5

Fogous and Hill Forts

The transition from the Bronze Age to the Age of Iron was a gradual process, and no close date can be given as to the first arrival in Britain of men who used iron for their weapons and tools. The period was one of upheaval and shifting of peoples, partly due to further climatic changes and pressure on land. From somewhere in the fifth century B.C. successive groups of people showing distinctive features in their culture and using iron for their implements reached this country from areas as far west as Brittany and as far east and north as the Rhine mouths. Iron became progressively used for a wide variety of purposes, and with the passing of time metal styles, as with pottery, indicated influences from the Continent and introduced a native sub-Celtic culture. The use of the lathe was discovered, and wheels for ploughs, carts and chariots appeared.

The country lay within the sub-Atlantic climatic period, extremely wet and cold, and the people congregated on well-drained and sheltered sites on the hill slopes, avoiding the boggy moorlands and marshy valley bottoms. Agriculture continued to form the basis of daily life, wheat tended to replace barley, and the plough came into common use, in the south anyway, though cereal production was probably of minor importance compared to cattle herding. Wool for clothing was produced all over Britain, and few farmhouses were without a vertical loom.

Little remains of the small farmsteads which must have existed fairly widely over the country. These were almost invariably circular, constructed of different regional materials and varying in size. Usually four central posts, surrounded by a ring of smaller posts, supported a wide conical roof. The walls were often of wattle daubed with clay, or a continuous circle of posts set in a palisade trench. Smoke from a central fireplace escaped through a hole in the roof, while a porch may have given added protection from draughts and driving rain at the door.

At Little Woodbury near Salisbury a chance photograph taken by a pilot officer of stone crop-markings revealed a settlement a little over 3 acres in area enclosed within a wooden palisade, not for defensive purposes but merely to give protection against animals. Within the enclosure were two circular dwelling-houses of which the larger was some 50 feet in diameter, the smaller rather more than 30 feet. The framework of the houses consisted of massive upright timbers. The infilling of the walls was not of clay or cob but may have been of planks, wattle or straw, while the roof was roughly thatched with straw. Also in the enclosure were large numbers of pits dug in the chalk, post-holes, shallow depressions, primitive ovens made of cob and quantities of burnt flints and ash. What was established beyond doubt here was that the pits were used as storehouses in which the grain could be kept underground, dispelling once and for all, it is to be hoped, the popular notion that these were underground dwellings. Little Woodbury may be regarded as representative of the large number of similar farms on the chalklands of southern Britain during the Iron Age. Little Woodbury itself is believed to have been abandoned in the first century B.C. after an occupation of some three centuries.

We can see another example at the other end of the country, at High Knowes on Alnham Moors, in Northumberland. Here is a circular enclosure some 150 feet in diameter, formed by twin trenches over 6 feet apart, designed to support a double fence of close-set wooden posts. Within the enclosure lie the floors of four circular houses, two of them 50 feet in diameter, the timber walls being originally set in trenches and their conical roofs supported on concentric rings of internal posts. About 100 yards to the east is another and more extensive settlement of similar form containing the distinctive grooves and floors for some fifteen round timber houses.

The same type of dwellings translated into stone existed in the highland parts of Britain, continuing and developing Bronze Age house types and such walled villages as Grimspound. It is now clear, however, that some of these settlements of round stone houses must belong to a period almost immediately preceding the Roman occupation and even to the Romano-British period.

Such is that at Greaves Ash in Northumberland where two groups of round stone houses, with twenty-seven huts in one group and thirteen in the adjoining group, spill out from the bounds of an Iron Age hill-fort.

Cornwall is particularly rich in villages of the later Iron Age people who arrived here from the Continent after 250 B.C. The type of house built at Skara Brae seemed to have no immediate successors, and we find nothing comparable before the building of Chysauster behind Mount's Bay. Despite the fact that Chysauster is some fifteen centuries later than Skara Brae it lacks both the amenities and building technique of the Orkneys village. The eight large rectangular houses so far excavated (one of which is 90 feet long) are arranged in pairs on either side of a fairly wide street. The massive dry-stone walling, in places 15 feet thick, has survived to the height of about 6 feet. The entrance is through a deep passageway, giving on to a central, presumably unroofed, court, from which the rooms, built in the thickness of the walls, open out. There is here some affinity with the Scottish broch. Each house, which has drains and pavements, consists of two apartments, a living-room with a hearth and a granite basin built into the floor for use as a mortar, and a byre for cattle. Here then is the forerunner of the medieval longhouse housing men and cattle under a single roof, which has survived among pastoral peoples in wild and mountainous regions to the present day. The smaller rooms were roofed with stone ceilings of domical type, and the long narrow byres were probably thatched. At Bosporthennis near Zennor is another of these village sites. The best-preserved house is 25 feet long inside, and it has two rooms, one round and one oblong, which are connected by a doorway. It is roofed by overlapping courses of stone, resembling the Irish bee-hive hut.

We find in Iron Age Britain the beginnings of a form of feudal society where the wealthier farmers assumed the lead over local groups and virtually became chieftains. Then they set up defences, initially a single line of rampart and ditch ringing a hilltop to enclose perhaps a dozen acres. Where natural features of the terrain were inadequate for defence deep external ditches were dug, the materials from them being piled into a stout timber and stone-faced rampart set with a wooden stockade. These were the first hill-forts. The chieftains would set up their huts within the forts while the rest of the community continued to farm outside, though in many places the entire community would be housed within the defensive enclosure. The number and close proximity of these forts suggests that the age was characterized by periodic warfare as this or that tribe or dynasty sought to establish its authority.

Chysauster lay near the hill-fort of Castle-an-Dinas West, and many other Cornish hut-circle villages were sited near such forts. There are three villages below Chun Castle and another near Caer Bran. The first two are later Iron Age forts of the multi-vallate type, Castle-an-Dinas West having three concentric granite ramparts and Chun Castle having two rings of ramparts, each with a ditch outside. The fort at Carn Brea near Redruth is of the early univallate type with a single rampart and ditch enclosing an area 1,100 feet long. This hill-top was intensively occupied over many centuries, and within the enclosure are some 200 stone huts which are pre-Iron Age. Excavation has revealed Neolithic axe-heads, arrow-heads and pottery. An elaborately decorated Bronze Age urn, some 20 inches high, complete with handles and containing remains of burnt bones was recovered from a cairn on the site.

We shall notice the later development of the hill-fort, but a feature associated with the Cornish forts deserves our attention. This is the underground retreat known as a *fogou* which is known elsewhere in Britain only in Ireland and Scotland, where it is generally termed a *souterrain* or earth-house. William Borlase, the eighteenth-century antiquary, termed it a 'hedge cave' and discounted any strategic purpose. *Fogou* is the Cornish name for a cave, but it usually applies to artificial subterranean passages which are adjuncts to a hut-circle village or a hill-fort. In characteristic form it is a tunnel entered by a tiny doorway and a downward sloping stone-lined passage, opening out into underground chambers or fairly lofty galleries. The tunnels are built of dry masonry, corbelled inward and roofed with enormous slabs of granite.

The remains of a *fogou* can be seen at Chysauster, but the feature is more rewardingly to be examined elsewhere. The largest *fogou* in the duchy, in an excellent state of preservation, is that called Halligye at Trelowarren. It is 90 feet long and 6 feet high, and somewhat complex in design. The main tunnel leads to a microscopic doorway which opens onto a narrower passage. Near this doorway is a ridge of rock stretched across the main tunnel to a height of 2 feet, an effective stumbling block to an enemy groping his way through the darkness. At the eastern end the tunnel dwindles sharply into a small passage which opens through a stoutly-built doorway into a gallery over 6 feet high. From this gallery another minute doorway leads into a low passage made only for crawling. Finally this passage leads upwards to a ditch protected by two ramparts of the hill-fort which stands above the *fogou*.

In the *fogou* at Chapel Euny near Sancreed, now partly fallen in, the main tunnel, 66 feet long, leads through a low passage into a large circular chamber about 15 feet in diameter and perhaps 12 feet in height, paved and drained, and built of beehive construction with large blocks of granite, corbelled inward and rising originally to a domical roof, though now open to the sky. Branching from this passage chamber was another long chamber, according to Borlase. Quern's whetstones, grinding stones, an iron spear-head, a fragment of enriched pottery, blocks of tin and animals' teeth have been found here. Here, again, the *fogou* was strategically sited on the edge of an Iron Age village and in close proximity to the hill-fort of Caer Bran. Other *fogous* are to be seen at Boleigh in the Lamorna Valley and at Pendeen. At Boleigh the passage is now 35 feet long but was said to have been so large during the Great Rebellion that Cavaliers were in hiding there for some time. The exact function of the *fogou* remains problematical. Tacitus, the Roman historian, in his description of Germany, describes how some of the inhabitants of Celtic stock dug caves in the earth to which they retired in winter, so that the *fogou* may have been purely domestic; certainly the paving and draining of the chamber at Chapel Euny points to this, though the absence of a hearth may be significant. On the other hand the direct linking up of the *fogou* at Trelowarren with the hill-fort above it indicates a strategical retreat or escape.

Little or nothing remains of the celebrated 'lake villages' at Meare and Glastonbury in Somerset, the only known sites in this country, though the crannog has been discovered and excavated in several places in Scotland. It may have been a fugitive tribe that settled on the marshes of the Somerset plain that lies north of the Polden Hills, building villages by driving piles into the quaking peat bog and layering it with tree-trunks filled in with brushwood, stones and clay, thus forming small islands. On these platforms they erected round huts of wattle and daub, floored with clay. The platforms were stockaded with wattle and daub, and each had a landing-stage with walls of grooved oak planks driven into the peat and filled in with horizontal boards. Excavation of the Glastonbury site showed that there were some sixty huts housing a few hundred people. The strange circumstances of hearths being piled one above the other, as many as ten deep, indicates the sinking and compression of the bog over a long period. It was at first thought that the village was occupied somewhere between 200 B.C. and the coming of the Romans, but, as we have earlier noted, recent excavations indicate tenure during the Bronze Age and possibly even earlier.

An extraordinarily comprehensive range of Iron Age objects was found buried in the preserving peat during the original excavations (which were carried out uncritically with results that are often infuriatingly baffling). Wooden vessels were obviously lathe-turned, bone combs were clearly used for weaving, and the rotary quern was in use for grinding corn. These people smelted iron, made pottery of graceful Celtic design and went fishing in dug-out canoes. They kept horses, for harness has been found, as also the wheels of carts or chariots. Bill-hooks and sickles signified that they had cornfields and pasturage on the mainland. Further, there were iron currency bars, wheat cakes, fireclay crucibles, lead net-sinkers, brooches and pins, bronze finger-rings, coloured glass beads and dice marked from one to six. The lake village people were clearly superior to their kith and kin not far away in the great cave of Wookey Hole, though some artefacts, the stone spindle-whorls, the decorative pottery and the bone weaving combs were common to both communities.

In the more remote northern areas the changes of the Iron Age which are so clearly marked in southern England had little noticeable effect. Here the Bronze Age lingered on until the Roman occupation. In the north-east of what is now Yorkshire, however, there lived the Parisi, a people who had come from the north-eastern parts of Gaul, and their culture suggests a fighting aristocracy having some affinity with the Iron Age people of the south.

These are known as the Arras culture after the Yorkshire village where one of their richest known cemeteries has been found. Their method of burial differed from that of other Iron Age people, interments being under small round barrows surrounded by ditches forming a square. The remains of 200 Arras culture barrows can be seen at the Danes Graves near Driffield in the East Riding. The graves of their chieftains were notable for the accompanying two-wheeled carts or chariots, either complete or dismantled, horses and shields. Such chariot burials have been found at Cawthorn, Pexton Moor, Hunmanby and elsewhere. The great hoard of metalwork from Stanwick, the vast complex of defensive earthworks finally overthrown by the Romans, illustrates the wide range of decorative metalwork associated with chariots.

It was in the violent last phase of the pre-Roman Iron Age, when the Belgic tribes of the Aylesford culture who had arrived here from northern Gaul sought to subdue the native non-Belgic population, that the hill-forts were developed into complex defensive sites. They formed no part of a general strategic scheme, such as the chain of forts which the Romans later devised in the northern and more unruly parts of the country, but each was an isolated stronghold designed for the protection of the adjacent community, on much the same principle as the feudal castle dominated England during the Middle Ages. These forts varied in plan, size and elaboration. Hill-forts that were never completed, like that at Ladle Hill in Hampshire, illustrate various stages in the construction of such sites. Shallow marking-out trenches first circled the hill top. Then deep ditches were dug and hundreds of timbers cut for facing the rampart. Once the wooden posts were in position along the inner edge of the ditch, a second row of timbers was set 10 feet or so behind them. The two rows were bonded together with cross-timbers and the gap between filled with rubble. In stone country masons trimmed and laid dry-stone rampart facings. Building the entrances was more intricate, involving guard chambers and sentry walks. The average hill-fort would need rather more than 10,000 timbers, and since there are about 1,400 forts in England and Wales the amount of forest clearance in the Iron Age must have been comparable with that of Elizabethan times.

We have seen that the earlier forts were of univallate type, consisting of single rampart and ditch. Now, however, both existing and new forts became multivallate with an increasing number of defences. "A fort seldom had more than two entrances, since these were always a point of weakness, and elaborate efforts were made to strengthen them. Wooden gates at angles to the ramparts, gates in inturned barbicans, gates protected by claw-like outworks, gates with footbridges for sentries over the top— all were tried with varying degrees of success."[1] The intricate entrance pattern of the west gate of Maiden Castle in Dorset, the Celtic Mair Dun, at the time of the Roman attack between A.D. 43 and 47 shows to what Vaubanesque lengths the builders carried their design. The ramparts here enclose an area of 45 acres and in all extend over a space of 115 acres. The earthworks cover the flat summit of a natural hill and the ramparts are in places three deep, over 60 feet high and extremely steep, while four entrances are surrounded by a network of banks. Maiden Castle stands on a site which was occupied as early as Neolithic times. The eastern third of the site was fortified about 300 B.C. and the fortifications were extended to their present dimensions about 100 B.C. The fort covers an oval area on the crown of a hill 432 feet above sea level. Excavation has shown that the ramparts consist of earth, chalk, clay and rubble, faced on the inside with stone, with the facing itself buttressed at intervals by upright timber posts. On the summit are a series of post holes spaced out from 4 feet to 2 feet 6 inches apart. These holes belong to a defence of a later period; the original wall, of which a portion still remains, was of stone.[2] Hod Hill, enclosing more than 200 hut buildings, similarly had an entrance masked by cross ramparts involving sinuous passages of approach. Badbury Rings, also dominating the landscape of Hardy's Dorset, is another fortress with triple vallum and fosse, and so is the mountainous Eggardun. From all these eyries the furtive Celt anxiously scanned the land for the glint of a Roman breastplate.

These *oppida* or fortified hill settlements of the south-west were very different from the simple forts of the south-east, as the Romans were now to find out. They were to encounter almost equally stubborn defences in the north. Juvenal, describing

[1] James Dyer, *Discovering Archaeology* (1969).
[2] Dr. R. E. M. Wheeler, "The Excavations of Maiden Castle, Dorset", *The Antiquaries Journal*, vol. XVI, 1936.

the avocations of the Roman legionary of his day, mentions among them '*diruere castella Brigantum*'—to destroy the castles of the Yorkshire Brigantes. Thus it was that the great hill-fort of Stanwick fell. In Northumberland the chief of these forts is that at Yeavering, a minor *oppidum* with a substantial stone wall enclosing the sites of some 130 huts over 13 acres.

Yet even when the Roman legions overran the forts and the Glastonbury lake villages were abandoned, the cave-dwellers held their own. With the dawn of Christianity, out of the darkness of the cave floor at Wookey Hole appeared the bold monogram of Christ, forming the reverse of the coins of the Christian emperors of Rome.

6

The Roman Occupation

It would be inaccurate to say that the Iron Age was extinguished by the Roman invasion which began in A.D. 43, but this event does mark the transition from the prehistoric to the historic period.

The advance of the Roman legions over southern Britain was fairly swift. As Gibbon wrote: "Neither the fortitude of Caractacus, nor the despair of Boadicea, nor the fanaticism of the Druids, could avert the slavery of their country, or resist the steady progress of the Imperial generals." Within a very few years the southern part of the country was so successfully subdued that the building of forts and the maintenance of troops became unnecessary, and the Romans were able to concentrate their military formations in the northern, and more obdurate, areas of the country.

Roman roads were predominantly strategic in purpose, designed to provide quick transit from one important settlement to another, and this system of road communications, considering its purpose and function, has never been surpassed. It covered a network of some 6,000 miles. The major roads were probably built in the early stages of the conquest. Among these were Ermine Street, the great northern road running from London to Lincoln and then on to York; Watling Street, running through the midlands to Wroxeter and Chester; the Fosse Way from Lincoln to Exeter and the Devon coast; and the Kentish network linking the harbours at Lympne, Dover, Richborough and Reculver with Canterbury and thence to the fords across the Thames where London was beginning to grow. Many of these roads now lie beneath our tarmac highways, but exposed sections remain in several places. A notable stretch can be seen on Stane Street, running across the South Downs of Sussex, where iron-slag was used for metalling. Another section shows the remarkable paved surface of the road up the steep slope of Blackstone Edge in the southern Pennines, with complete paving and a central trough-stone for drainage or, more probably, to act as a brake on the wheels of Roman carts. One of the best preserved roads of Roman Britain, probably little known, is the so-called Wade's Causeway flung across the bleak North Yorkshire Moors. It runs north-east from Malton (the Roman *Derventio*) to Whitby, and for some 5 miles from Cawthorn Camp its line is very clear. On Wheeldale Moor the road is uncovered for about a mile. It is 16 feet wide, made with flat stones laid on gravel, with side gutters and culverts. The *agger* or embankment for the metalling is a little under a foot high, but the upper layer of metalling has disappeared. On each side of the road was a marking-out ditch, separated from the *agger* by a *berm* or flat space.

The needs of the Roman roads were threefold—military, administrative and commercial—and much the same reasons gave rise to three groups or classes of town. The *colonia* made provision for veteran Roman soldiers who had completed their term of service and also aimed to establish a highly Romanized form of life which might influence local native communities. There were only four *coloniae*—Colchester, York, Lincoln and Gloucester. The *municipium* was an important commercial centre with special privileges conveyed by charter. Such was St. Albans. A third type of town, the *civitas*, was founded as the successor to an Iron Age settlement and was usually the capital of an area still occupied by the old British tribes; the inhabitants did not enjoy the rights of Roman citizenship. Such were Silchester, Wroxeter and Leicester.

Despite the fact that Londinium was the largest city of Roman Britain and a great commercial centre (Tacitus writing of it as it was in A.D. 60 refers to it as a great market-place), there is no evidence that it enjoyed a titular dignity under the style of *colonia*, *municipium* or *civitas*, though by the fourth century its importance was recognized by the distinguished title *Augusta* which was con-ferred upon it. Londinium with an area of about 330 acres was of considerable size by western standards, but most towns were small. The next largest, Cirencester, contained 240 acres. St. Albans and York had about 200 acres each. Wroxeter with 120 acres and Silchester with 100 were still larger than most towns. Even Roman Bath was a small lodging town owing its existence to a large suite of baths and at least two shrines. Despite the fact

that, as Tacitus tells us, Agricola gave both private encourage-
ment and public assistance in the raising of public buildings,
squares, temples and private mansions, these are not, in general,
either monumental in scale or particularly ornate, and it is perhaps
the schoolroom that has left us with an exaggerated vision of
Roman Britain. Certainly there was nothing to vie with Antioch
and Alexandria or with the Roman cities of France and North
Africa. Yet the Roman legacy is remarkable enough.

Early in the eighteenth century William Stukeley, the most
perspicacious of our early antiquaries, was able not only to trace
the foundations and general layout of every Roman town he
visited but found himself confronted by a wealth of Roman lesser
objects lying about in a casual profusion that now seems incredible.
Today it is possible to see these sites only as palimpsest, as fragments built over by medieval and modern buildings. Of Romano-
British towns which remain still easily accessible beneath open
fields only one, Silchester, has been fully excavated. The greatest
and most tangible structural remains of the occupation are
Hadrian's Wall, the bath buildings at Bath, the theatre at St.
Albans, the amphitheatre at Caerleon, the Mithraic temple in
London and the ruins of many spacious villas, though clearly a
great deal else has survived.

At the end of the first century when Londinium was still an
open city a small legionary fortress was built in what is now
Cripplegate. Detected by Professor W. F. Grimes's excavations
in 1950, it was laid out on the standard rectangular plan for such
a fortress, with a small square stone turret in one of the corners.
When the town was walled about a century later the wall
embodied two sides of the fort. The wall, which followed an
almost semi-circular course, was not much more than 15 feet
high—where sections survive the upper portions are medieval in
date and the Roman courses are often buried in up to 12 feet of
silt that separates the Roman street level from our own. The wall
was built almost wholly of Kentish ragstone with brick bonding
courses at intervals of 5 feet, and it was punctuated by gateways
and, later, with at least twenty-one bastions. It can be studied in
detail in several surviving sections, notably at the Tower of
London and in the street appropriately called London Wall. As
befitted its size and status Londinium possessed a number of
imposing buildings. The largest of them was the Basilica, whose

structural remains on the site of Leadenhall Market give us some idea of its original size and splendour. Its dimensions were so vast that it dwarfed most of the basilicas in Rome itself. In design it was a vast aisled hall, probably as much as 505 feet long and 150 feet wide, with apses at its eastern end. In places the walls go down nearly 30 feet below modern street level and appear to belong to two periods. The earlier walls are of ragstone with thick bonding courses, the later entirely of brick. The early walls were probably part of a basilica destroyed by Boudicca in A.D. 61 which were later rebuilt. The larger apse at the east end appears to have belonged to the earlier building, which was 90 feet longer than its predecessor. The basilica was obviously surrounded by a densely distributed complex of buildings and outbuildings, including rows of shops. Facing it on the riverward side was a great forum or public square, 500 feet across, with two-storey shops and houses along the sides. Clustered round the forum and basilica were the large and opulent residences of the city merchants and officials, and such administrative buildings as the Treasury and the Mint.

The opportunity for excavation in the aftermath of bombing revealed not only the Cripplegate fort but also the temple of Mithras by the banks of the Walbrook. Discovered on a site in the City in process of being cleared for the erection of an office block, it is a basilican-type temple with the bases of classical stone columns forming a nave and two aisles, a rectangular ante-chamber at the east end and a triple apse at the west end. Oak piles supported beams for timber floors. Only three other Mithraeums are known in Britain, and they are all on the Hadrianic Wall. All are small, no more than 35 feet by 12 feet, so that the London temple, 60 feet by 20 feet, is extremely large and important. Here was found a marble head of Mithras, wearing a Phrygian cap, and figures of other pagan deities.

York (*Eboracum*), unlike London, is known to have enjoyed the highest grade of civic dignity which could be bestowed by Rome, that of a *colonia*, and it was one of the three permanent legionary bases of Roman Britain. We do not know the date of its foundation, though the fortress on the other side of the Ouse was set up in A.D. 71 by the Roman Governor of Britain, Quintus Petilius Cerealis, a relative of the reigning Emperor Vespasian. Nor have we yet been able to identify the circuit of its defences.

It is almost certain that it was built on the rectangular grid plan, with its principal streets intersecting at their centres. The street plan survives where today Petergate (*Via Imperialis*) intersects Stonegate (*Via Praetoria*). The remains include parts of a suite of public baths, but the most striking survival is the Multangular Tower, a polygonal bastion built at the western corner of the curtain wall when the defences were reconstructed about the end of the third century. The upper portion is medieval but the remainder is built with courses of small dressed stones alternating with courses of brick.

The first *colonia* to be established in Britain was at Colchester, where it was founded in the year 49 by Ostorius Scapula and given the title Colonia Victricensis, although it continued to be known as *Camulodunum*. Senate, temple and theatre all perished in the destruction of A.D. 60, and a new town was built upon the ashes of the old. It was planned in the customary Roman style with numerous streets intersecting one another at right-angles and subdividing the whole into about forty separate *insulae*. The town was not walled until well into the second century. The walls, enclosing an area of about 108 acres, had a circumference of nearly 2 miles, broken by six gates and two posterns, and strengthened at convenient points by square and semicircular towers. A considerable portion of the wall remains almost to the full height, as well as four semicircular towers and the lower parts of the towers of the west or Balkerne Gate with its four wide portals. This monumental gate probably had no peer in Roman Britain. Through it passed the road to London along whose sides lay the chief cemeteries of the *colonia*. Two notable tombstones, one of Favonius Facilis, a centurion of the Twentieth Legion, and the other of Longinus, a trooper in the regiment of Thracian cavalry, both thrown down in Boudicca's rebellion, survive.

That *Camulodunum* was a wealthy and highly Romanized community is clear from the rich tombs, mosaic pavements and sculptures found within the walls, and from temples and a theatre found outside the *colonia*. Little remains of the great temple of Claudius built *c.* A.D. 50 to serve as the chief centre in this country of the official religion, the worship of the Emperor. Its superstructure has all but vanished, but the vaults, originally filled with rammed earth, which served as its supporting podium, still survive beneath the Norman castle. This is an impressive relic of

what was probably the earliest and certainly one of the largest
stone buildings of Roman Britain. It had a deep colonnaded
portico and colonnades running along each side, and a monumental altar flanked by statues stood in a forecourt which formed
the southern approach.

The other two *coloniae*, Lincoln and Gloucester, followed the
rather formal semi-military pattern to be seen at Colchester,
though both were late foundations and originally half the size of
the latter. Lincoln (*Lindum Colonia*) was founded in the 90s. It
was from the first a walled town with four gates. Little remains
above ground but a section of wall and a fragment of the north
gate now called Newport Arch. Gloucester (*Glevum*) was founded
a year or two later. It had a quay and the rare feature of a river
dock. Fragments of the forum and of buildings which had
Corinthian capitals to their columns have been recovered, as well
as tesselated pavements and tombs with sculptured reliefs. The
original street plan can be traced, most tangibly at the Carfax or
crossing of four streets in the middle of the city, but nothing
remains of the walls or indeed of anything above ground.

Since most Romano-British towns are buried deeply beneath
later building, the most revealing sites are those of Caerleon,
Silchester, Wroxeter and St. Albans. Caerleon, as its Welsh name
implies, represents 'the camp of the legion', in particular of the
Second Augusta Legion which made its home there somewhere
between A.D. 50 and 75. This legion had formed part of the
original Roman army of conquest when it was led by a future
Emperor of Rome across the South of England, and, in one place
or another, it remained in Britain until the fourth or perhaps the
beginning of the fifth century. We do not know how long it was
actually stationed at Caerleon, but the arrival on the banks of the
Usk (whence the new fortress received the name *Isca Silurium*)
was of twofold significance. It virtually marked the beginning of
history in western Britain, and it marked the establishment of the
final frontier of the Roman Empire in north-western Europe.
With Chester and York, it formed the permanent base of the
system of lesser forts and military roads whereby the richer lowlands of England were shielded from the mountaineers of Wales
and northern Britain.

Caerleon is one of the few places where considerable areas of
the fortress still lie beneath open fields, and some 60 acres of

Grimspound hut circle on Dartmoor

Chysauster, Cornwall: (*above*) the aerial view and (*below*) a close-up at ground level

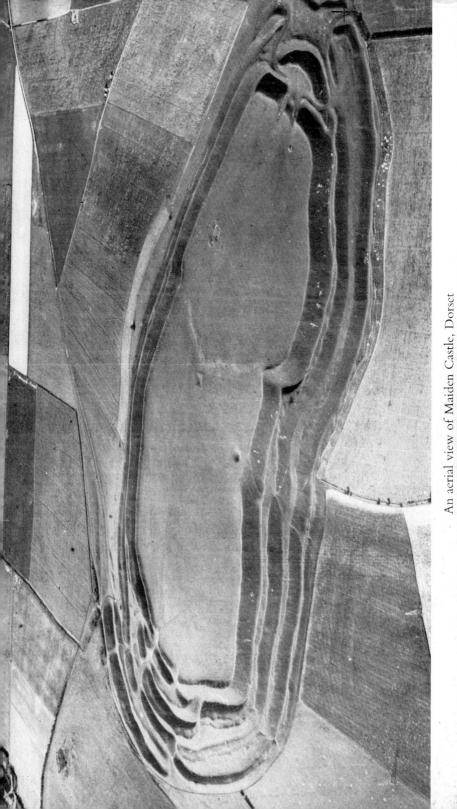

An aerial view of Maiden Castle, Dorset

St. Albans Roman theatre, an aerial view

vacant land are known to contain remains. The dimensions of the fortress were roughly 540 yards by 450 yards, enclosing a rectangle of some 50 acres. At the southern corner the wall stands to a height of 10 feet. The gateways have vanished but their positions are marked by four roads converging upon the centre of the fortress, where, under the present churchyard, stood the *principia* or headquarters building. Unscientific excavation long ago destroyed the main bath building of the garrison outside the eastern corner of the defences, but other baths lie beneath nearby fields. Remains of the barrack blocks and their ancillary buildings have been unearthed, and sculptured fragments suggest the existence of a temple of Diana. The chief building so far excavated is the great stone amphitheatre with no less than eight entrances, built late in the first century outside the walls.

Silchester (*Calleva Atrebatum*) today provides a picture of a Romano-British town as it was during the third and fourth centuries, and one which may be held as representative of a tribal capital of that age. On the original somewhat unscientific excavations Sir Mortimer Wheeler had this to say:

> I am not of those who scorn the horizontal excavation (in the nineties) of the Roman town of Silchester. True it was dug like potatoes, without a shadow of the scientific nicety of the contemporary excavations in Cranborne Chase; and the resultant plan is the uncritical synthesis of a varying urban development through more than three centuries. But it gave at once, and with a rough accuracy, the general impression of a Romano-British town such as fifty years of subsequent and often more careful work have failed to equal. More exact vertical and horizontal digging on both this and other similar sites has indeed begun to reveal the sociological evolution essential to our historical perspective; but who amongst these later and wiser excavators has not constantly referred back with profit to the crude primitive assemblage of Silchester?[1]

In size Silchester was much the same as Colchester, but its shape was an irregular polygon. Lying at its centre and covering nearly 2 acres of ground was the chief of its public buildings, the forum, which served both as a civic centre and as a market place for traders. It was colonnaded on all sides, the pillars clearly supporting a pentise roof, and it was entered from the east through a monumental gateway over which was placed a dedicatory

[1] *Archaeology from the Earth* (Oxford, 1954).

4

inscription in large lettering cut on polished slabs of Purbeck marble. Within the gateway was a large open courtyard surrounded on three sides by colonnaded porticoes. On the fourth side lay the great basilica, over 230 feet in length and almost 60 feet wide, divided into a central nave and side aisles, with *tribunalia*, raised platforms for the magistrates, at either end in apsidal recesses. Beyond the basilica was a further range of rooms with the *curia*, the meeting-place of the cantonal senate, centrally placed. The floors of the basilica were of red tesserae, its walls were frescoed and its columns were made of Bath stone with Corinthian capitals. There was a prodigal use of marble, both native and imported, and the *curia* was lined with white Italian marble. Among the statuary were an immense stone image of the guardian deity of *tutela* of the Atrebates, a bronze representation of an emperor and a bronze eagle with wings outstretched for flight. Other public buildings included temples, a suite of baths and a large *mansio* or guesthouse for important visitors (resembling that of the great temple of Nodens settlement at Lydney). There was no theatre within the walls, but (as at Caerleon) an amphitheatre, so far unexcavated, lay outside the east gate.

The excavations at Wroxeter (*Viroconium Cornoviorum*) were facilitated by a large open site unhampered by later development. The forum here is seen to be on a scale even more massive than that at Silchester, and its dedicatory inscription dates it to the reign of Hadrian in the years 129–30. Public baths, shops and even a smithy, all clinging to Watling Street, have come to light, as have some tombstones of the Fourteenth Legion.

St. Albans (*Verulamium*) was one of the first Roman sites to be excavated on any scale, but there are gaps in our knowledge of its development still waiting to be filled in. The area of Roman occupation lay in close proximity to a Belgic *oppidum*, and this site was early abandoned for a new one, largely prompted by the passage of Watling Street along the floor of the valley (there was a similar shift from Maiden Castle to Dorchester). Like Colchester and London, St. Albans was sacked at the time of the Boudiccan rebellion, and it was then built on a more lavish scale. The town was originally laid out on the grid plan along the southern bank of the river and enclosed within defences, of uncertain date, comprising an earthen bank and ditch embracing about 150 acres. Later, not before the close of the second century, the town appears to have been extended to some 200 acres and the great stone walls and gates erected, as they were in many other towns at about the same date. Two monumental gateways, each with double roadways flanked by footways and great projecting drum towers, marked the passage of Watling Street through the walls. The forum dates from Agricola's time—it is dated exactly to the second half of the year 79 by fragments of an inscription bearing Agricola's name coming from a massive gateway—and stood in the centre of the town, with a temple enclosure on its western side. Later in the Hadrianic period the theatre that is now fully excavated was built on a site adjacent to the temple. As originally constructed this temple consisted of the typical square *cella* surrounded by an external verandah, the enclosure measuring 300 feet by 160 feet, but both temple and enclosing wall were twice modified by reconstructions, the second occasion being at the end of the fourth century, when the neighbouring theatre had long since fallen into disuse.

The remains at Cirencester (*Corinium Dobunnorum*) suggest that outside London it was the most prosperous city in the country. Like Silchester and Wroxeter (and like Leicester and Aldborough, among others), it was a tribal or cantonal capital on a site previously occupied. Five Roman roads converged upon it. The modern town almost overlies the Roman one and there has been little organized excavation. The walls, where they remain, have lost their stone facing, and the only spectacular monument is the amphitheatre, which, however, has little stonework to show. The grand scale of the original public buildings can be seen in the Corinium Museum, where the sculpture includes a notable group of the Celtic triad of Mother Goddesses, sometimes known as the Matres Campestres—there may have been a temple to them here, as there was at Benwell in the far north. Fragments of a great column dedicated to Jupiter suggest the existence of a temple in his honour.

Canterbury (*Duroverum Cantiacorum*) and Winchester (*Venta Belgarum*) are representative of moderately sized tribal capitals, both of them a little over 100 acres within the circuit of their walls. Canterbury was sufficiently secure geographically to remain without a stone wall or any other protection until about A.D. 270 when the threat of Saxon incursions was growing. This was another town built on an extensive Belgic settlement. The site of the basilica can be deduced only from the remains of the gravelled courtyard of the forum, but its magnificence can be gauged from the marbles imported from Greece and Italy, Egypt and Asia Minor. Nor do we know when this basilica was built, but it is reasonable to assume that it was during the first century since the town already had a theatre by the third quarter of that century, a theatre rebuilt on a more imposing scale about a century later.

Roman Winchester is so overlaid by medieval and later building that very little had come to light before the excavation of the Saxon cathedral, adjacent to the medieval cathedral, begun in 1961 and now in its final stages. Other excavations in Castle Yard, an area which lay in the south-western quarter of the Roman town, may be equally revealing. On the slope of the hill there are traces of occupation dating from the middle of the first century, with a substantial section of the Roman defences, a massive earth rampart of the second century, to which a stone wall was later added. Below the Saxon cathedral lie parts of the forum and a Roman street, and there are also important levels of what should perhaps be called post-Roman occupation.

We have so far said little about that important centre of social life, curative and recreational, the public bath-house, remains of which have been found on most civilian and military sites. Here, in addition to swimming, immersion and gymnastic exercises, the full ritual of the Roman bath was taken by methodical progress through a series of interconnected rooms heated to varying degrees. The heat was produced in a furnace whence it was carried beneath the floors by a hypocaust system, and upwards through the walls in box-shaped flue tiles. The most celebrated bath establishment is probably that of the West Country spa later named after the establishment itself, Bath. Here beside the Avon the Romans found hot water ready made—about A.D. 150 the Alexandrian geographer Ptolemy referred to it as 'Hot Springs'. About a century later the place acquired its more celebrated name of *Aquae Sulis*, the waters of Sul.

The city covered only some 23 acres and was purely a civilian town. The baths, however, though lacking the scale of the great contemporary Thermae of Caracalla at Rome, were considerable by any provincial standards. They ran from west to east for about 350 feet, all the buildings roofed (in what manner is uncertain) with the exception of the great swimming bath which may always have been open to the sky. Round the plunges were corridors and apsed recesses, some for dressing and foregathering, with hypocaust chambers to give an even warmth. The chief spring was that which supplied—and still does—the Kings Bath just below the south wall of the Pump Room. Conduits led the water to the series of shallower circular and rectangular pools which we see today. Most of the ground plan, the actual plunge baths, the hypocausts for central heating the nearby rooms, and some of the superstructure of walls and columns remain. The original splendour of the great central plunge, the oldest swimming bath in the British Isles, can be deduced from the steps and column bases and the thick floor of Mendip lead all remaining *in situ*.[1] A great deal of finely tooled and sculptured stones have been assembled, and the order favoured here was clearly Roman Doric.

The other great monument of *Aquae Sulis* was the temple of Sul Minerva, where the Roman Minerva merged with Sul, the local patron deity, as the presiding goddess. Remains of this temple were unearthed in 1790, but none is now visible above ground. Fragments of it indicate that it was a small temple with a frontal portico of four Corinthian columns, carved cornices and a triangular pediment surmounting, and there may have been a kind of colonnaded precinct. A dramatic piece of sculpture, one of the finest left in all the Western province of the Roman Empire, which has survived was clearly part of the entrance pediment and depicts the 'Gorgon' Sul-Minerva. A reconstruction of the temple in a public park is probably near enough.

The Romans adopted the architectural forms of the Greeks, that is to say they adopted the three Greek orders, Doric, Ionic and Corinthian. On these they made variations, so that we have a form of Doric known as Roman Doric, and a curious combination of Ionic and Corinthian known as Composite. The order that they used most often and with most success was the Corinthian. They often used the column and entablature structurally, as the Greeks had used them, though they frequently used them merely as decoration. The arch in one form or another was a

[1] The foundry for making the lead was discovered, in 1970, beneath the Pump Room.

dominant feature in their architecture, as was the vault, though few characteristic vaults have been noted in Britain. It may be that the Roman was essentially an engineer and a planner, but it is a libel to maintain, as has been maintained, that his art was always coarse and often brutal. Certainly he was a master of utilitarian works, but his sense of proportion and balance in basilicas, public buildings and palaces, his sculpture, mosaics, tesselated pavements, wall frescoes, glazed windows, doors on hinges and the further refinements of his house declare his talents as architect and artist. He had too an extraordinary knowledge of materials, and his mortar and concrete have become almost proverbial.

It should be realized that the homes of the people remained virtually untouched by those civilizing influences which are among the characteristic features of the estates generally called Roman villas. The more prosperous Iron Age farmers, could afford to replace their wooden huts with farmhouses in the Roman style, but their tenant farmers and slaves and indeed the mass of the native population continued to live in round wooden huts. Villas were only infrequently, and not generally, bought as country retreats by wealthy Roman officials, and they were rarely built all as a piece as we see them today. Often the villa occupies a site inhabited since before the Roman occupation, and the building in the final form in which we see it may have evolved over three or four centuries. The number of villas whose history can be traced in detail throughout the period of their occupation is extremely small. Two of these deserve special attention. They are Park Street, near St. Albans, and Lockleys at Welwyn, some 10 miles north-east of St. Albans.

At Park Street artefacts from both the Bronze Age and the early Iron Age have been discovered. There were no structural remains of these periods, but three separate successive structures of the first century A.D. could be distinguished, all Belgic in character, all circular and constructed of timber with floors of clay or rammed chalk. The new villa was a Roman rebuilding of c. 65, built above the earlier huts to a simple rectangular plan with five rooms and a cellar. The lower walls were of flint bedded in mortar, with brick quoins, the upper parts of the walls were of timber-framed construction. Windows were glazed, the internal walls were covered with decorative plaster, and some of the

fittings were made of native marble. Somewhere in the middle
of the second century a corridor was built along the entire
length of the house, and blocks of rooms were added at each end.
A hypocaust found here was almost certainly used for drying
corn rather than as domestic heating. Nor was this the end of
development, for there was yet another rebuilding early in the
fourth century.

The development of Lockleys, not far away, shows a markedly
similar pattern. Here the first settlement on the site is represented
by a Belgic circular hut, probably occupied during the first
quarter of the first century A.D. This was superseded by a second
hut inhabited both before and shortly after the Roman invasion.
Somewhere about A.D. 65 a new house was built upon the old
site. In plan and construction it resembled the contemporary new
villa at Park Street, but along the south-western front there was a
verandah supported by timber posts resting on flint bases. In the
middle of the century, approximately at the same time as the
rebuilding of Park Street, it was rebuilt, the timber verandah
being replaced by a stone corridor, and projecting wings being
added. It seems that the villa sustained damage from fire towards
the middle of the fourth century, when there was a final rebuilding.

The historical sequence revealed at these two villas indicates
the possible similar development on other villa sites, but our
present knowledge in this field is limited. Such development was
compatible with an increasing prosperity under the *pax Romana*,
and with this prosperity the amenities and refinements of the
villas as we see them today gradually came into being—but not,
clearly, all at once. The most significant feature of the early villa
was the transition from the round to the rectangular plan, but the
luxuries of baths, heating systems and tesselated floors were yet
to come.

There are over 600 sites at which Romano-British villas or
farms have been identified with certainty, and more than 100
others at which remains suggestive of villas have been found.
The great majority lie south of the Humber and east of the
Severn (the most northerly villa yet discovered lies near Durham).
About seventy of them have been identified on or about the
Cotswold plateau.

The most common type of villa was that on the 'winged
corridor' plan, consisting simply of a range of rooms planned as a

long and rather narrow rectangle, with a corridor along the length of one side and projecting wings at each end. Such are the villas at Lullingstone, Kent; Ditchley, Oxfordshire; Brading, the Isle of Wight; Bignor, Sussex; and Woodchester, Gloucestershire. These are among the most completely preserved examples, the homes of wealthy men with large estates and outbuildings, and they will repay careful study. At Lullingstone the original villa of flint and mortar was remodelled late in the second century by the addition of a large suite of baths, and early in the fourth century another remodelling provided an apsidal dining-room raised upon a platform or dais and opening from one side of a large central room (a similar semicircular dining-room may be seen at Aldborough in Yorkshire). The elaborate mosaic pavement flooring the two rooms portray Bellerophon killing the Chimaera and, in the dining apse, the abduction of Europa by Jupiter in the guise of a white bull, with a Latin couplet alluding to the first book of the *Aeneid* (scenes from Virgil have been recovered on wall plaster at Otford, another Kentish villa). The most remarkable feature of Lullingstone, however, is that the property in its final form was adapted for Christian assemblies, and this part of the interior recalls the arrangement of the rooms in the Roman house beneath the church of SS. Giovanni e Paolo in Rome. The wall frescoes of praying Christian figures were without parallel in Britain until the recent discovery (1969) of a similar portrait group on the wall of a mausoleum unearthed in a Romano-British cemetery at Poundbury, Dorchester, Dorset. This latter group consists of three figures drawn in cement paint, with mineral colourings, and is contemporary with the Lullingstone frescoes.

The villas of Brading, Bignor, Chedworth and Woodchester were on an even grander scale, for excavation here shows that each stood on one side of a large square courtyard with other buildings grouped about it. At Bignor there were no less than sixty rooms and substantial *ergastula* or quarters for the slaves or native serfs. Here the pavements show Ganymede carried off by an eagle, Medusa with snaky locks of hair, and the Seasons. At Brading the pavements have mosaic scenes from the Eleusinian mysteries. The Seasons occur again in corner panels of the main floor at Chedworth, where the principal design is a formal pattern of flowers and foliage. Terracotta and glass were not used here, and incredible skill must have been required to fit together the tesserae which would have come from the local Cotswold hills, oolite to give the light browns, cream and grey; lias to give the darker slate and green; and sandstone the various shades of red. At Chedworth the main block contains the *urbana* or living-rooms, including the *triclinium* or main apartment, its walls perforated with hollow flue-tiles to convey heated air from the furnace below the floor. The south wing approximated to the *rustica* or servants' and kitchen quarters, the north wing, with its furnaces, dyeing and tanning chambers, to the *fructuaria*, which more normally housed the cellars, granaries and storehouses. There were rebuildings and extensions at Chedworth, notably in the long north wing, which is detached from the east wing. The bath wing here was on an elaborate scale, and including the hot bath and cold plunge there were six rooms. In such large villas the bathing complex consisted of the *frigidarium* or cold plunge (the swimming bath), a *tepidarium* with warmer water, a *caldarium* or hot-air room, possibly a *sudatorium* or Turkish bath and *apodyteria* or dressing-rooms. Behind the north-eastern corner of the Chedworth villa and directly under the rising ground is an elaborately designed reservoir which supplied the large quantity of water needed. The importance of the bath suite was clearly universal. Even at Well in the North Riding of Yorkshire a separate bath house lay 25 yards east of the villa; it consisted of five rooms, two of which had hypocausts, and south of this in a cobbled court was a large cistern or plunge bath 40 feet by 15 feet.

Woodchester, on the other side of the Cotswolds, was on the lavish scale of Chedworth; and one of its mosaic floors, depicting Orpheus with his lyre charming birds and beasts, is almost 50 feet square. These Cotswold villas were invariably built of stone—at Witcombe the walls stand to a height of 6 feet with Roman plaster still on them—though many, like Chedworth, were timber-framed in the upper portion, the roofs constructed of tie-beams and king-posts and stone slated, as they were not to be again until the Middle Ages.

The first occupation of northern Britain was made by the Governor, Julius Agricola (A.D. 77–84), whose legions reached their limit at the battle of Mons Graupius, somewhere to the east of Inverness. The occupation of Scotland was temporary, and

Hadrian established his famous frontier wall between the Tyne and the Solway in 122–3. This is the greatest monument to Roman achievement in Britain. Running from Bowness to what is still called Wallsend, a distance of some 73 miles, it rose to a height of some 20 feet, with a thickness of about 10 feet, though the western sector was originally of turf before being rebuilt in stone shortly afterwards. The wall was punctuated at every Roman mile by a milecastle, a small fortlet for the patrolling garrison, and between each of these were two small turrets or signal stations. Later sixteen substantial forts (*castella*) were added to house regiments of auxiliaries, some of them infantry, some cavalry. Normally a fort was garrisoned by a cohort, a unit nominally consisting of some 600 men. Each legion was divided into ten cohorts, so that at the time of the occupation a legion comprised roughly 6,000 men plus 60 centurions, to which was attached a squadron of cavalry numbering 120 men.

To the south of the Wall a banked and ditched earthwork known as the *vallum* was dug, about 10 feet deep, 20 feet across at the top and some 8 feet at the bottom. The north and south banks were each 20 feet wide, and each was set back 30 feet from the ditch, so that the total width of this tremendous *vallum* was 120 feet, the Roman surveyor's unit known as the *aetus*. There were gated causeways to the forts and revetted causeways to the milecastles. This formidable obstacle marked the southern boundary of the great military zone which cut across the country from sea to sea. In close proximity to the south of the wall and *vallum* lies Stanegate, the road built by Agricola through the Tyne gap between Corbridge and Carlisle, a Roman road older than the wall and incorporated in the first design. This was of marked strategic value and was well defended by terminal forts at Corbridge and Carlisle and intermediates at Chesterholm and Nether Denton.

The forts on the wall conformed, more or less, to a standard plan, and the most impressive of them is undoubtedly Housesteads (*Vercovicium*). First scientifically excavated in 1822 by John Hodgson, the historian of Northumberland, the well-preserved remains lie in one of the most dramatic landscapes to be seen in Britain. Rectangular in plan, it covers almost 5 acres, with four main streets interconnecting with the four gateways of massive masonry at each side. The main gate was on the east. The lie of

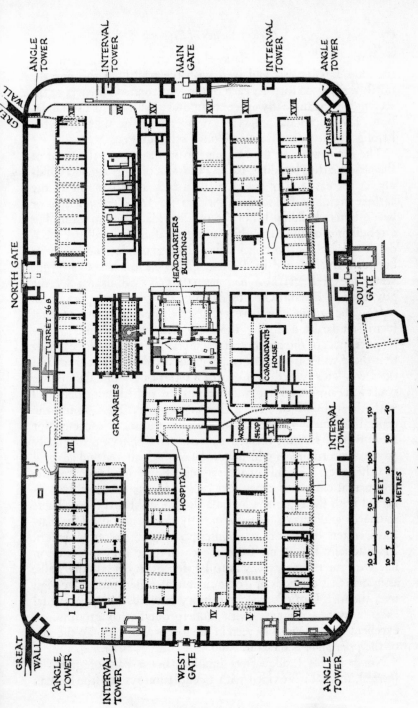

Housesteads after a survey by A. C. Dickie and R. C. Bosanquet
(*courtesy of the Department of the Environment*)

the ground dictated the relationship of the fort to the wall, and the long axis lay east and west with the wall itself forming the north wall of the fort. At each of the four rounded corners of the rectangle is an angle tower, contemporary with the fort's foundation. The occasional interval towers along the sides probably belong to one of the later periods of rebuilding.

The main street of the fort runs from the gate to the front of the headquarters building, passing to south of an elongated building, at the east end of which a small bath suite was one of the earliest buildings rediscovered within the fort. The *principia* or headquarters building is not the original Hadrianic structure but a rebuilding of the early third century, after the wall had been destroyed by the northern tribes during the internecine strife between rival would-be Roman emperors on the Continent, when the wall garrison had been largely withdrawn by the governor of Britain, Clodius Albinus, to fight in support of his claim. The *principia* here, as at Chesters, typifies an architectural form standardized during the early Empire. Responds at the front corners of the building and a solitary pier in the street show that there was a front portico. A pillared colonnade at front and sides was later walled up to form a series of rooms. Behind the court a monumental doorway led into an arched judgement hall with the tribunal or official dais at one end. Then comes the central regimental chapel (*sacellum*), its threshold socketed for monumental screens, flanked by two pairs of rooms originally pay and record offices which were later much altered and adapted to other uses. The cult of the reigning Emperor dominated the regimental chapel of every fort, where it was inextricably connected with the regimental standards also enshrined there. These standards and images were frequently displayed on a low platform, often decorated with inscriptions and coloured reliefs. Traditionally this shrine faced the enemy and was so placed in line with the main gateway as to be seen from beyond the walls, assurance that the gods of Rome maintained their protective vigil over the fort. From the second century onwards most regimental chapels were equipped with underground strongrooms—an excellent example is to be seen in the fort at Chesters. To the side of the *principium* is the commandant's house (*praetorium*).

North of his headquarters building lies a pair of granaries (*horrea*), the floor provided with a ventilation system (the Roman army lived mainly on grain, which, like wine and lard, was supplied in bulk). Opposite these is the barrack block, which clearly shows how the occupying force, the First Cohort of Tungrians, was housed. This force was organized in ten companies or *centuria* of eighty men each, and each unit of eight men had its own room for eating and sleeping, with an ante-room for arms and kit, while at the end of each row of ten such rooms lay the larger centurions' quarters. Beyond the granaries lies the north gate. A well-preserved feature is the latrine building in the south-eastern angle of the fort, the rows of seats, without subdivisions, facing one another across a central passage, the whole being flushed by the overflow from a large tank built against the back of the south-eastern angle tower and supplied by rainwater from the tower's flat roof. Below the fort the sloping hillside is seamed by a series of agricultural terraces which have largely obliterated the Roman extramural settlement, formally recognized as a *vicus*, some remains of which may be seen in the shops and taverns, the latter with open fronts which could be closed by shutters sliding in grooves that are still seen in some of the stone thresholds. Beyond this settlement are the burial grounds and temples, among them a Mithraeum and a small semi-circular shrine built to house a triad of unnamed deities, hooded and enveloped in long cloaks. Roman soldiers worshipped a complex pantheon of deities and spirits, and a wealth of sculptures and religious dedications have been found in the wall forts and military temples.[1]

Westward along the wall a short distance from Housesteads may be seen the best preserved of the milecastles (number 37). It measures 57 feet wide by 47 feet long internally, with portals 12 feet wide to north and south linked by an axial roadway. The gates are uniform in plan, and at the north gate the lower stones of the actual arch are still in position. The north gate was crowned by a tower, to match the turrets along the wall, and each gate had an inscription, commemorating the milecastle as Hadian's, built by the Second Legion when Aulus Platorius Nepos was governor, or soon after A.D. 122. West of the road lies the site of a small building which had quarters for eight men, together with stores and depository. Allowing for reliefs there would have been a garrison of sixteen men. This is a country of crags and rising cliffs

[1] See I. A. Richmond on the religious cults of Roman legionaries at Corbridge in *Archaeologia Aeliana*, Fourth Series, Vol. XXI (1943).

with bare moorlands sweeping to the north, and one is here sharply aware of the Roman tactical brilliance and of the unerring sense for terrain.

The fort at Chesters lies in the softer landscape of the Tyne valley, where the lie of the land allowed the fort to be built athwart the wall, so that three gates gave access to its northern side. The excavated and well-preserved remains here duplicate some of the features at Housesteads, the headquarters building and commandant's house being particularly notable, while the museum is lavishly rich in sculptured and inscribed stonework, altars, etc.

A late interpolation between Chesters and Housesteads was the fort of Carrawburgh, of which little remains, but there is here one of the most interesting extramural buildings visible on the wall, the Mithraeum or temple of Mithras. It measures only 35 feet by 15 feet. A small ante-chamber or vestibule (*pronaos*), containing a crude little mother-goddess, was divided from the main hall by a wooden screen. Beyond this is the hall itself (*triclinium*) with a central arcade guarded by statues of attendant deities and flanked by the stumps of posts which once supported the roof. Along the line of posts stand small altars, at the front edge of low benches revetted in wattle-and-daub. At the end of the building is the sanctuary. Here there remain three altars, dedicated by successive commandants of the First Cohort of Batavians, the garrison of Carrawburgh in the third and early fourth centuries. One altar of late date has an engraved inscription and a relief of Mithras as the sun god. Peculiar to the ritual was a lamp-niche cut in the back of the stone to illuminate the pierced rays of the crown. Behind the altars a shallow flat niche contains a projecting stone sill which supported the relief common to all Mithraic temples commemorating Mithras slaying the bull and so releasing the beneficent creative forces of Nature. The effigy of Mithras, like those of his torch-bearers, Cautes and Cautopates, was destroyed and removed, and it seems almost certain that this was a systematic desecration during the tenure of a Christian commandant. In any case Mithraism was officially outlawed by Rome in 395. As Sir Ian Richmond so succinctly puts it: "The Mithraeum at Carrawburgh thus provides a valuable glimpse not only of one of the most disciplined and principled of pagan cults, but of open battle by the Church triumphant at a time when the formulation of orthodoxy was the condition of stable survival for an oecumenical church."

North of the wall are several outpost forts and a series of temporary camps. Among the most interesting of these is the Roman station of *Bremenium*, into the framework of which the village of High Rochester is now fitted. Here, as at Chesters, the fort lies athwart the wall, and here is the third known site of a Mithraeum —traces of Mithraism in Britain seem to be confined to the northern military area, though found also in London and Caerleon. This fort guarded the approach from the high moors and the junction of a cross-road into eastern Northumberland. Excavations have shown that it was first occupied in the Flavian period under Agricola (A.D. 78–84), but it was rebuilt by Lollius Urbicus, who reoccupied Scotland in 139–40. In its heyday the fort was equipped with spring-guns whose firing emplacements (*ballistaria*) have been found and are commemorated in two inscriptions. Of the terminal forts on Stanegate south of the wall that of Chesterholm is of more interest, since its gates, headquarters building and long narrow-fronted shops lining the curving street, all of the third and fourth centuries, can be seen in tangible form.

The Antonine Wall across the isthmus between the Forth and the Clyde, built *c.* 143 by Quintus Lollius Urbicus, then Governor of Britain, was abandoned a few decades after its completion, as were the forts in the southern parts of Scotland. The Hadrianic Wall held out for close on three centuries. It was overthrown on four occasions, in A.D. 196, 297, 367 and 388, and after each of the first three destructions it was immediately reconstructed. After that it simply petered out. Changing conditions brought withdrawal of the garrisons, and the forts and civil settlements that had grown up outside their walls took on a civilian and domestic character.

During the last century of the Roman occupation attention was diverted from the northern frontier to the southern coastline. The threat of Saxon attack against the eastern and southern shores of Britain was met by the building of fortresses at commanding points along the coast between the eastern side of the Wash and the Isle of Wight. Extensive remains of these forts, the so-called forts of the Saxon shore, still exist, notably at Burgh, Reculver, Richborough, Pevensey and Porchester. Only one of them, Richborough (*Rutupae*), has been extensively excavated. It occupies the site of an early defensive work, and its rectangular enceinte covers over 6 acres. Its walls, built of chalk clunch and sea-polished nodules of flint with brick lacing courses, are 11 feet thick and rise in places to a height of 25 feet. They are strengthened by round towers at the angles and square towers at the sides. A remaining gateway on the west has a single entry 11 feet wide, flanked by square towers. The labyrinth of subterranean passages and chambers may perhaps have been the *ergastula* or slave quarters such as we have noted in the villas of Bignor and Chedworth. Pevensey is oval-shaped, and some of its walls still stand to the height of the wall walk, 28 feet above the ground. Here, as at Porchester (in each case the Normans built a castle within the Roman walls), the wall towers now project on the outside of the curtain, instead of on the inside as in the forts on Hadrian's Wall, a disposition which gave greater range to the ballistae mounted on the towers, especially at the corners. Forts similar to Richborough were built at Dover and Lympne, and these three, together with a fourth at Reculver, built early in the third century and slightly different in character, formed a compact group commanding the narrowest part of the Channel and the approaches to the Thames estuary. Other forts were built along the East Anglian coast as far north as the Wash, and of these Burgh Castle has extensive remains.

The last phase of Roman fortification in Britain was the extension of the Saxon shore defences northward, towards the end of the fourth century, when serious Saxon inroads coincided with inland raids by the Picts from Scotland. When Theodosius rebuilt many destroyed defences he extended the old system by planning a series of signal stations on the headlands of the Yorkshire coast. Five stations were built between the Tees estuary and Filey Bay, each consisting of a high watch-tower of stone or timber, placed within a massive protective wall still further protected by a wide ditch. From the towers watch was kept for sea-raiders and messages could be passed inland and relayed to the Roman fleet and army. Pictorial representations of such signal stations can be seen on the sculptured panels of Trajan's Column and the Column of Marcus Aurelius in Rome.

These stations were set up at Huntcliffe Goldsborough, Ravenscar, Scarborough and Filey. That at Scarborough, on Castle Hill, is completely revealed and preserved. The watch tower was 50

The pavement of a room in the Roman villa at Chedworth, Gloucestershire

The Roman baths at Bath, Somerset

feet square and must have been about 100 feet high. The enclosing wall had rounded corners and projecting angle towers and the whole site was enclosed by a ditch. The station at Goldsborough, also preserved, is similar in plan to Scarborough. The Huntcliffe station is identical in plan with Goldsborough, but it stands on the edge of a precipitous cliff and has lost much of the original site by erosion; evidence was found in the well that the station was violently destroyed in a piratical raid in which the garrison and their families were put to death. Indeed there is sufficient evidence to suggest that all these stations were destroyed before the end of the century and that they functioned for barely a score of years. With the collapse of these coastal defences the Roman occupation of the North was drawing to its close. When, in A.D. 383, Magnus Maximus made a bid for the imperial throne it marked the beginning of a series of troop withdrawals by imperial contenders which steadily drained the country of its military strength. By the year 410 there were no legions left in Britain.

7

Early Christian Monuments

The extent to which Christianity was established in Roman Britain is still somewhat problematical, but it may well have been more firmly rooted than one might infer from the paucity of Christian remains. Christianity is believed to have reached Britain by way of Gaul during the third century, and Tertullian could claim *c.* 208 that parts of Britain still untouched by Roman rule had been conquered by Christ. Early in the following century bishops are recorded as being established in such cities as London, York and Lincoln, and we know that a bishop from Britain was present at the Council of Arles in A.D. 314. At Poundbury in Dorset the largest Christian cemetery of Romano-British yet discovered, containing 150 graves of the fourth century, was recently unearthed. Beyond such cemeteries the visual physical evidence is limited to a few well-known sites—the supposedly Christian church at Silchester, the Christian wall-paintings at Lullingstone and Poundbury, and the Christian monograms on a mosaic pavement at Frampton in Dorset and on a stone slab at Chedworth. This monogram is the distinctive Christian Chi-Rho sign, the initial letters in Greek of Christ's own name, and the sign adopted on all his standards by Constantine after his traditional vision before the battle of Milvian Bridge. And there are, of course, a number of early inscribed stones.

The only remains of what was almost certainly a Christian church are those at Roman Calleva, now Silchester. This was clearly designed as a miniature reproduction of a Roman basilica, and in plan it has decided affinities with the Mithraeum at Carrawburgh. Only its foundations now survive, but from these we have a fair idea of its form. It lay east and west and was probably built of long thin Roman bricks roofed with rust-red tiles.

Across its east end was a narthex or portico with a pentise roof and three wooden doorways. Short arcades of three stone columns of classical type divided the nave from the aisles. The west end had a central apse containing the altar, the position according with general classical practice. A square with a pattern of black, white and red tesserae marks the site of the altar. The church paving, where it remains, is a mosaic of tesserae made of red tiles cut into 1-inch squares. To the east of the church there was a laver at which the worshippers washed before entering, and near it was a well. There are no distinct remains of the atrium which, it has been suggested, surrounded the church instead of lying to the east of it as usual. There must have been other Christian churches in Roman Britain (quite apart from the wattled church of Glastonbury, which was old when St. Paulinus, Archbishop of York, cased it over with wood and lead early in the seventh century), and indeed the church which we now know as St. Martin's in Canterbury was believed by Bede to have been built during the Roman occupation. This embodies a great deal of Roman fabric, which, however, was re-assembled here in the seventh and eighth century, and no part of the building can be regarded as of Roman construction. As we shall see at Reculver and elsewhere the Saxons used Roman bricks and other materials whenever possible.

Christianity had probably not long survived the withdrawal of the Romans. Renewed missionary work was therefore necessary, and this was done from Ireland and Wales, chiefly after the fifth century. Increasing Saxon conquests after A.D. 550 spread across Britain until the whole country was reduced to a series of Saxon kingdoms, independent states of which the chief were Northumbria, Mercia, Wessex and East Anglia. The south-west and Wales lay outside this development, and here, as in Ireland, Celtic culture was preserved. So there was clearly a practising Christian body in these islands when the Roman monk St. Augustine, prior of the monastery on the Coelian Hill, undertook his missionary expedition to Britain at the close of the sixth century. Indeed the Celtic monk Columba of Iona, who worked in the North of England and the Lowlands of Scotland, died in the very year of Augustine's arrival, A.D. 597.

The immediate result of the Roman mission was the foundation of the abbey of SS. Peter and Paul (later St. Augustine's) at

Canterbury, to be followed by the building of a number of smaller churches now known as the Kentish group. Each of these churches, with the exception of that at Reculver, consisted of a rectangular nave with a chancel at the east end terminating in an apse and separated from the nave by a triple arcade carried by lofty columns. A porticus or square chamber that served as a sacristy or possibly a chapel projected from each side of the building at the junction of nave and chancel, and there was a small west porch. All were of masonry, often re-using Roman material, and built by craftsmen imported from Gaul. This was by no means the general practice, for Bede writes of churches being built *"more Scottorum non de lapida"*, that is of oak timbers with a thatched roof. All these churches were orientated, an arrangement by no means common in Europe at that time.

The church of St. Peter-ad-Murum at Bradwell-on-Sea, Essex, was built, soon after 653, almost entirely from Roman masonry in one of the gateways of the 'Saxon shore' fort known to the Romans as Othona. Here the chancel, the *portici* and the west porch have disappeared, but the nave, about 50 feet long, still stands. The springing of one of the three arches that opened into the chancel can be seen in the blocked east wall, and the foundations of the semi-circular apse can be traced. This church was, in fact, built by Cedd, brother of Chad, who came from Lindisfarne in the far north half a century after the arrival of Augustine, and who, despite his upbringing in the Celtic tradition, constructed his church in almost exact accordance with the churches of Augustine's Roman mission. It is the only one of the eight churches of the Kentish group which lies outside Kent.

The last of these churches was that at Reculver, built in 699 and pulled down in 1805, though the foundations remain and the stone columns of the triple chancel arches are preserved in the undercroft of Canterbury Cathedral. The foundations clearly illustrate that Reculver approximated to the basilican plan of the Early Christian Churches in Italy. The full basilican plan appeared *c.* 670 with the church of Brixworth in Northants. This is the only seventh-century monastic building which has survived in the Midlands. Originally it had a west porch, a square hall or nave aisled with arcades of round-headed arches springing from massive oblong piers, triple arches leading into the presbytery or chancel and, beyond that, an apsidal sanctuary. The arches of the arcades were turned in double rows of Roman brick and a similar technique was used in the clerestory windows of the nave. The aisles were taken down and the arches of the nave filled in, but the rest of the fabric remains, including the oldest clerestory in England. Another rare feature is the ambulatory of a crypt, begun but never finished, beneath the sanctuary. Little wonder that this church has been described by a leading authority as "perhaps the most imposing architectural memorial of the 7th century yet surviving north of the Alps".[1]

Meanwhile pressure from the East forced the British or Celtic Church to retreat into its two strongholds of Lindisfarne and Avalon (Glastonbury). This church had its roots in Ireland, with outposts in Iona and Galloway, while in Wales there was a strongly independent church resembling a tribal organization. Celtic Christianity differed in many respects from the Roman type which Augustine had established in the south. It was largely monastic in its organization, its buildings were based on a different plan, it practised asceticism in solitary and remote places, it had a more fervent missionary zeal and it differed on questions concerning the shape of the monastic tonsure and the method of calculating the date of Easter.

The history of Lindisfarne opens in 635 when the monk Aidan left Iona to set up his bishopric at Lindisfarne, on that spit of land separated from the mainland by a strait of flat sand over which the tide ebbed and flowed twice daily. We have no evidence of what his monastery looked like, but from our knowledge of Iona and similar sites in Ireland it is not difficult to reconstruct the main features of a typical Celtic monastic settlement, which had more in common with the lauras of Egypt than the western coenobium. It was probably surrounded by a cashel or stone wall or by a fosse or ditch. The church was the main building, generally placed in the middle of the enclosure. A refectory and guesthouse were the only other buildings of any size, and the cells of the monks were no more than detached huts. At first these cells would be built of wattles but these were very soon replaced with stone. There were often other cells occupied by anchorites either within or without the enclosure. Many such, built of flat stones

---

[1] A. W. Clapham, *English Romanesque Architecture before the Conquest* (Oxford, 1930).

without mortar and shaped like beehives can be seen in Ireland, notably on the island of Skellig Michael. The eremitical life was considered more perfect than the cenobitic, and it was common for Celtic monks to leave their monasteries for remote hermitages in much the same feverish spirit as the Nile dwellers stampeded into the silence of the deserts. Thus it was that St. Cuthbert, prior of Lindisfarne from 664, fled to the rocky sea-girt solitude of the Farne Islands amid the seals, fulmar petrels, kittiwakes and puffins, where he, in the words of an eighteenth-century historian, "built a cell with a small oratory and surrounded it with a wall which cut off the view of every object but Heaven". The austere practices of Cuthbert on his Farne island and Guthlac at Croyland in the Fens were western survivals of the ideals of St. Anthony and Simeon Stylites. Early in the eighth century Cuthbert's cell or *mansio* was rebuilt and a succession of hermits dwelt on the site (the existing chapel is medieval).

From what remain of the first churches of the Northumbrian school it is clear that their planning differed greatly from that of the Kentish group. In its simplest form the oratory was a rectangular building of wattle and daub or wood, with an altar at one end, and a little later a small square chamber or sanctuary was added at the east end. The prototype of this two-celled Celtic church may have been the dwelling of the Saxon chieftain, consisting of a hall for the household and retainers with a private chamber at one end separated from the hall by a partition with a central doorway. By the close of the seventh century some of these churches were being built in stone. Escomb church in Durham, one of the few Celtic churches in the north that was not of monastic origin, is our earliest surviving stone version of the typical Saxon nave and chancel plan, and it must be of late seventh-century or early eighth-century date.

Escomb church remained in normal use until 1860 when a new church was built nearby, but the old church having fallen into disrepair was later carefully restored. Its rectangular nave is of great height in proportion to its length. A tall narrow arch opens into a chancel no more than 10 feet square. Most of the fabric is built of Roman masonry, and it is possible that the chancel arch formed of radial voussoirs is a Roman arch removed from the nearby fort at Binchester (in the church of Corbridge the entrance from what was the west porch into the nave is a Roman

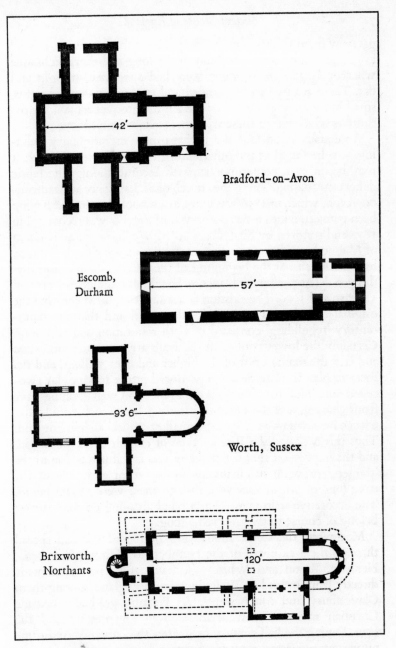

42'

Bradford-on-Avon

Escomb,
Durham

57'

93' 6"

Worth, Sussex

Brixworth,
Northants

120'

Saxon Churches (*Brixworth after plan in* The Victoria County
History of Northamptonshire, *Volume IV, the others after Banister Fletcher*)

gateway from Corstopitum). The jambs of the doorways, as well as of the chancel arch, are built in the long-and-short technique whereby large slabs of stone were laid alternately upright and flat. There are two round-headed and two square-headed lights, small but widely splayed inside. Even the grooves remain for the shutters which closed these windows against the elements.

An equally important and perhaps more extraordinary building is to be found at the other end of the country in Wessex. It may be, in part, contemporary with Escomb though the fabric defies exact dating. This is the church of St. Lawrence at Bradford-on-Avon, which in 1856 was in use as a school, the chancel having been converted into a three-storeyed cottage. It was recovered in 1872 and restored by Sir Gilbert Scott. We know from William of Malmesbury that there was an early monastic church founded by St. Aldhelm at the beginning of the eighth century, and that this was destroyed by the Danes, to be rebuilt somewhere between A.D. 950 and 1000. The existing fabric suggests, however, that the original church was not wholly destroyed and that the tenth-century 'rebuilding' consisted of both restoration and additions. Certainly the lower courses of the walls are extremely primitive and lack the mason-craft of the higher and later walling, and the Escomb plan is more or less reproduced in the rectangular two-celled unit. The chancel arch is cut in the solid wall dividing nave from chancel, and the opening is only 3 feet 6 inches wide and 9 feet 9 inches high, probably the smallest chancel arch in England. Thus this is basically a Roman type of church of Celtic origin, and the impression that the building was cruciform is due to the 'transept' or wing originally projecting from each side of the nave (one of which survives), though these were in fact *portici*. The decorative strip pilasters and blind arcading on the exterior belong of course to the later rebuilding.

Meanwhile the Celtic monachism of Lindisfarne had spread through the area north of the Humber, to Melrose, Gateshead, Hexham, Ripon and Whitby. A few settlements were made directly from Ireland or Wales in western England, among them Glastonbury and Malmesbury. As England gradually became Christian monasteries were founded in Lincolnshire and the Fens. During the half century or so after the arrival of Augustine numerous monasteries arose, deriving in one way or another from the monasticism of Iona or Gaul, and at this stage only the group in the Kingdom of Kent followed the Rule of St. Benedict with its Roman traditions.

The pattern began to change in the second half of the seventh century, after the wrangling of the Synod of Whitby in 664, which with the exception of a few outposts brought the Celtic Church in England in line with the customs and usage of Latin Christianity. The primitive pattern of Celtic, as of Oriental, monachism was out of place in western Europe, and it was inevitable that the Rule fashioned by the sane realistic Roman mind of St. Benedict should prevail. It is most likely that the Rule drawn up at Monte Cassino was expressly designed for Benedict's own communities, though it has been suggested that it was written at the command of Pope Hormisdas for the monks of the Empire. As a legislative document it owes more to Pachomius than to any other, though Benedict's conception of the cenobitic ideal, the family life, largely derives from Basil. In its wisdom and sincerity it is one of the masterpieces of the Middle Ages, prescribing a common life of absolute regularity and strict discipline and catering for all its practical contingencies. Among other things, St. Benedict, well over 1,000 years before Karl Marx, had cut out the pride of personal possession and had established a community on the lines of a naturally developed collectivism.

It was Wilfrid of York, himself a monk of Lindisfarne, who after a journey to Rome introduced the Rule of St. Benedict into the north, and under his influence the Rule was established at Hexham and Ripon. Another monk, Benedict Biscop, returned from Lérins and other monasteries in Gaul and Italy to found Wearmouth (674) and Jarrow (685) and plant the Rule there, and, incidentally, to reintroduce stone building into Northumbria. Canterbury was now revitalized by a new wave of the Roman monasticism, and new monasteries blossomed in the south, the Midlands and the Severn and Thames valleys.

Nothing remains of Celtic Lindisfarne, and the ruined abbey is a pale echo of Norman Durham, which refounded it. Biscop's churches at Monkwearmouth and Jarrow, now blackened by the dust of the coalfield, can still be identified, though later building has replaced or submerged most of the original. Of the former there remain the high narrow west wall of the nave and the two-storeyed west porch (the lowest stage of a tower of five stages of varying Saxon dates) with baluster shafts supporting an enriched outer arch and a stone barrel vault to the lower story. At Jarrow, the home of the Venerable Bede, there is not much more. The small chancel of the existing church is the original monastic choir in which Bede chanted the Office, and south of the church are a few unidentifiable ruins. Of unique interest is the original dedication inscription of 23rd April 685, the earliest written record of the Anglo-Saxon period in Northumbria which can be accurately dated, set above the west arch of the tower. It is possible, however, that in Bede's time there were two churches on this site built upon the same axis and with only a few feet between them. This is suggested both by the awkwardly planned tower between the old chancel and the modern nave and by plans and drawings made before the nave was rebuilt. There is a parallel in St. Augustine's at Canterbury.

At both Hexham and Ripon medieval churches have replaced the originals, but in each instance Wilfrid's crypt has survived. These are the earliest crypts in the country, bearing little or no relation to those of the basilican churches of Italy, and that of Hexham is built entirely of Roman dressed stones. The crypt at Lastingham on the North Yorkshire moorlands dates from *c*. 1080 and must be the earliest of the Norman period surviving in an English parish church. It is mentioned here because the monastery of Lastingham was founded from Lindisfarne by St. Cedd in 654, and after its destruction by the Danes was refounded in 1078 from Whitby. Most of the church was rebuilt by the time that, before 1086, the site was abandoned. It is a remarkable work, with four short columns, having massive capitals with coarse volutes and primitive carved foliage, dividing the crypt into nine low compartments with groin vaults.

Substantial traces of the domestic buildings of a Celtic or early Anglo-Saxon monastery are conspicuously absent. The abbey of Whitby, a double house of monks and nuns, was founded in 657 by St. Hilda, abbess of Hartlepool and a kinswoman of King Oswy of Northumbria. This was the home of the poet Caedmon and the scene of the Synod of Whitby. It was destroyed by the Danes in 867, and the existing ruins belong essentially to the thirteenth century, but excavations in 1924 revealed to the north of the abbey remains of the original settlement (unfortunately not left exposed). The foundations of a number of buildings were recovered which were almost certainly the cells (*domunculae*) occupied by individual monks or nuns. Each was similar in plan, measuring about 18 feet by 11 feet, with structural details suggesting division into two rooms, one serving as a living-room with a hearth and the other as a sleeping room with a lavatory in one corner connected to an external drain. No trace was found, however, of an early church or any other communal building, though there was a rich yield of sculptured stones and funereal monuments with runic or Latin inscriptions. The only other site in England where such buildings can be traced is at Tintagel in Cornwall (see below), though they are to be seen at Iona and on other Scottish islands.

The climax of Anglo-Saxon sculpture, which strangely enough was at its beginning, is also best seen in the old kingdom of Northumbria. When there could be no provision for a resident priest, preaching crosses would be set up to provide convenient points of assembly for the people. In a life of St. Willibald, who was born *c.* 700, it is stated that "It is the custom of the Saxon people that on the estates of noble and good men they are wont to have not a church but a Holy Cross dedicated to our Lord and reverenced with great honour, lifted up on high." The Anglian motifs on the earlier cross shafts were dominantly panels of interlacing bands linked with figures in high relief, and these were being cut at the end of the seventh century along with scrolls of leaf and vine with birds and beasts among the scrolls, all inspired by the Early Christian art of the Eastern Mediterranean. Style changed with Danish influence, and, as we shall see in the next chapter, the bulk of the crosses which have survived are Anglo-Danish or Anglo-Norse of the tenth and eleventh centuries. Few of these remain *in situ*, since they have been largely removed to churches and museums for safe keeping.

Among the finest of these crosses with narrative carvings from the Gospels, of late seventh to early eighth-century date, is part of the splendid cross at Rothbury in Northumberland, where part of the shaft is now used as the stem of the font in the parish church. One face shows an Ascension scene with, below, a group of Apostles. The other broad face is ornamented with a basket plait. One narrow side depicts the inhabited vine scroll, and the other a savage scene which presumably represents Hell. Other fragments of this cross are now in the Museum of Antiquities at Newcastle. Outside the church of Masham in Yorkshire is an early ninth-century shaft, round as are its contemporaries at Wolverhampton and Dewsbury, carved under Mercian influence with arcaded tiers showing the Ascension and Apostles, legendary stories and grotesque animals. In the crypt of Lastingham's church is the head of a monumental cross which must have been about 24 feet in height, carved with a loose interlace pattern. At Hackness, not far from the above and also in the church, are two important pieces of an early cross with a large runic inscription and a Latin memorial to an early abbess of the nunnery (a foundation from Whitby) which existed here between 680 and 869. The sculptural motifs include a head of Christ.

In a category of its own, to be compared only with the equally celebrated cross which it resembles at Ruthwell over the border in Dumfriesshire, is the Bewcastle cross in Cumberland. One of the most beautiful and sophisticated monuments of the Early Christian period anywhere within the bounds of the Western Empire, it stands *in situ* in the parish churchyard. The cross head, alas, is missing, but the shaft carved from a single block of stone tapers up to a height of some 15 feet. On its west face are carved three full-length human figures, in the bottom panel a falconer and his falcon (possibly representing John the Evangelist with his eagle), above it the figure of Christ, and in the top panel John the Baptist carrying the Agnus Dei on his left arm. The east face is wholly covered with a flowing vine scroll with birds and beasts. The Scotic or Irish archetypal element is revealed in the panels of interlaced pattern, but the feeling of both the figure sculpture, the mantles draped in classical tradition, and the vine scroll is quite Byzantine. Indeed both this and the Ruthwell cross have always presented a puzzle, for their ornament was a century or more ahead of anything of its kind in Western Europe. The main runic inscription suggests that this was a funereal monument. We know from a twelfth-century Northumbrian source that the grave of Acca, Bishop of Hexham, who died in 740, was marked by two sculptured crosses, and what is believed to be the shaft of one of them is preserved at Hexham. But certainly the Bewcastle cross is one of the great luminants of the age which produced the Lindisfarne Gospels, the poetry of Caedmon and Bede's *EcclesiasticalHistory*.

In Cornwall, the south-western limit of the country, a Celtic Christian civilization of great spiritual power survived up to the

Saxon invasions from Wessex and its final conquest by King Athelstan in 930. The origins of this culture date back to the fifth and sixth centuries when missionaries arrived from Ireland and Wales. This was the golden age of Celtic saints, and there is a whole hagiological literature rich in stories of such Welsh saints as Petroc, Gulval and Madron, of Cleer Morwenna, Nectan and Tudy (all daughters of the Welsh King Brychan), of the Irish saints Breaca, Gwithianus and others, of Non, mother of the Welsh David, and of Gunwalloe who came from Brittany (which had been colonized and christianized from Cornwall about 450). Most of the minor saints wandered from place to place, leaving behind them a hermitage or a chapel or a well. Old Fuller says they were born under a travelling planet, "neither bred where born, nor beneficed where bred, nor buried where beneficed". The major saints left behind them monastic settlements, half cenobitic, half eremitic, which were centres of learning, the off-spring of such celebrated South Welsh cradles of Christianity as Llantwit Major, Llaniltud, Llangarvan and Caldey Island (which became another Lérins).

Architecturally there is little enough to speak for this period. Most of the hermitages that survived were rebuilt as medieval chapels, and most of the holy wells were rebuilt in or around the fifteenth century. There are about twenty-five inscribed stones, ranging from a fifth-century specimen with a Latin inscription at Hayle to Saxon examples of the tenth century. Some of these stones are partly inscribed in Ogham lettering, as at Lewannick, St. Kew and the cross at St. Clement, which has the sign of the cross in a circle. The coming of the Saxons does not seem to have broken the tradition. Crosses are ubiquitous—there are well over 300 of them in Cornwall, though many of them are medieval with the wheel-cross predominating.

Among the best of the wheel types are those of Phillack, with a Crucifixion and plaitwork decoration of Hiberno-Saxon type, Lanivet, Constantine, St. Buryan, Merther and Lanherne, the last an elaborate cross with a Crucifixion, interlacing and an inscrip-tion. At Sancreed there are two crosses with unusual heads, one having sumptuous interlace work and a key pattern, and both having a Crucifixion. At Cardinham is a fine high cross with four-holed head, knotwork on the front face and a shaft in three panels with inscription, plaitwork, interlacing and scrolls. Mylor

has the tallest cross in the Duchy, over 17 feet, with sparse ornament limited to incised circles and concentric circles.

Most of the churches in Cornwall were founded during the
Celtic period, that is roughly A.D. 500–800, but all appear to have
been completely rebuilt by the Normans in the twelfth century.
Yet one has survived, albeit in ruins reduced almost to the foundations, revealed by the shifting sand dunes at Perranzabuloe. It is
reputed to be the little oratory or cell of St. Piran, a disciple of
St. Patrick, who came over from Ireland. Its date must be late
sixth or early seventh century, and it is thus the earliest religious
building in the south-west of England and a memorial to the
Christianization of Cornwall. It is just under 30 feet by 16½ feet
by 19 feet in size, of granite, porphyry, slate and quartz rubble,
and coarse clay was used instead of mortar. A stone seat runs
round the interior of the building, and the altar is sited on the
east end. Originally it possessed a pitched roof and gabled ends
and only one small window on the south. In the eleventh century
a new church was built further inland, but this too was engulfed
by the sand. Excavation has revealed the plan of this later church,
which had fifteenth-century additions. Near it stands a plain cross
with four-holed wheel-head, which appears to have been mentioned in 960. A similar oratory to St. Piran's, that of St. Gothian
at Gwythian, was excavated from the sands last century but has
since been reclaimed by the dunes.

Tintagel, "Black cliffs and caves and storm and wind", as
Tennyson noted in his diary, is enveloped in the mists of Celtic
tradition and legend. The claim of Geoffrey of Monmouth (*c.*
1140) that it was the home of King Arthur has not found any
archaeological confirmation, but excavation has indeed proved
the site to be Celtic. On the tiny island across the narrow isthmus
remains of small rectangular huts, clearly those of a Celtic *clas* or
monastery, have been found. There are also the foundations of a
rectangular chapel dedicated to St. Julitta, close to the place of
the oldest of these cells, which was probably the saint's own cell,
later preserved as a sanctuary. Of the fragmentary castle in this
wild and evocative place there is nothing earlier than the twelfth
century, but, despite the sobering restraint of history, despite the
fact that Galahad and Arthur may never have walked here, this
will always be looked upon as the Utopia of chivalry, the symbol
of perfect knighthood.

8

The Saxon World

The most impressive monument of Anglo-Saxon antiquity is probably the great earthen dyke which bears the name of Offa. It is probable that the isolation of the British in Wales (the Welsh of today) had been completed by the end of the seventh century and that the boundary followed much the same course as the dyke. It is unlikely that it was designed for purely military reasons and there is no attempt at fortification, but it did become recognized as the border line, and at the same time it fairly accurately marked the limit of Anglo-Saxon power. There is no direct evidence that it was built by Offa but the English knew it as *Offan dic* and the Welsh as *Clawdd Offa*. The greater part of it probably dates from between *c.* 784, when Mercia was at the height of its power, and 796 when Offa died. The line of the dyke ran from the vicinity of Prestatyn, near the mouth of the Dee, to Chepstow on the Severn estuary, a distance of some 140 miles, thus stretching, as the historian Asser put it, "from sea to sea". It was not a continuous barrier but it blocked the most obvious possible points of entry in open country. Following an archaeological survey in 1925 some sections were scheduled as Ancient Monuments. Near Trefonen, a village some 3 miles from Oswestry in Shropshire, the rampart is about 12 feet high, and the ditch on the western side is 18 feet wide and 7 feet deep.

There is as yet little archaeological evidence of the homes and secular buildings of the Anglo-Saxon people. The evidence of place-names and cemeteries shows that the settlements of the early Anglo-Saxons were largely distributed in the east of the country between the Humber and the Thames. We know that many Roman towns continued to be occupied after the withdrawal of the legions, and it it not without significance that in the seventh century bishops and missionaries were particularly active in Romano-British towns, and that Canterbury, London, Rochester, Winchester, Dorchester (Oxon) and York were all episcopal seats before the eighth century. In this latter century Offa chose to have his coinage minted in Canterbury rather than in his own capital of Tamworth, and two centuries later Canterbury was so populous that the houses had come to be closely packed together. Excavation on war-damaged sites in Canterbury and London has produced evidence that there was some form of occupation between 400 and 600, but not on a scale to establish general conclusions. A comprehensive programme of scientific excavation now in progress at Winchester, virtually the capital of Saxon England, has so far revealed a Saxon street with seven successive cobbled surfaces, lined with timber buildings with cess pits. Meagre traces of domestic buildings have also been found in Thetford, Ipswich and Southampton. The small domestic houses of the early Saxon period seem to have been rectangular buildings with interiors sunk below ground level, the walls made of timber posts filled with panels of wattle and daub. Such buildings have been discovered at St. Albans and Sutton Courtney, Oxfordshire. Bow-sided boat-shaped wooden houses of the later Saxon period have been unearthed at Eaton Socon, Huntingdonshire; Buckden, Huntingdonshire; and Maxey, Northamptonshire. None remains to be seen. A Saxon weaver's hut recently found at Erringham, near Shoreham (Sussex), is to be preserved. At the lonely hamlet of Myndtown or Minton close in to the Longmynd in Shropshire the outlines and general arrangement of a Saxon village may be studied. Here church, manor house and a handful of cottages lie within their enclosing hedge atop a high elongated mound.

The difficulty in locating domestic sites must be obvious, since throughout the period even the most impressive secular buildings were constructed of wood and thus easily perishable, while even the defensive earthworks which must often have surrounded them have been obliterated by subsequent occupation. It is difficult to understand the recession or decline in secular building after the Roman example and precedent. The Saxons were excellent masons, their walling was often better than the Norman and their mortar was as good as the Roman. Until recent years evidence of the Anglo-Saxon use of window glass was limited to Bede's reference to Benedict Biscop's importation of glass-makers from Gaul and to Wilfrid of York's mention of the insertion of glass

Bewcastle Cross, Cumberland: (*left*) the south side, (*centre*) the east and north sides, and (*right*) the west side

The tower of Earls Barton Church, Northamptonshire, seen from the south-west

in windows previously fitted with linen or a fretted slab. We have now, however, discovered pre-Norman glass manufactories at Glastonbury, Thetford, Southampton and Old Windsor. Altogether one may wonder whether Saxon building was confined to wood to the degree which we have assumed.

The sites of several royal palaces of the period are known, and three of them have so far been excavated—Yeavering in Northumbria, Cheddar in Wessex and Hampton Lucy in Mercia. Yeavering in the north-eastern foothills of the Cheviots in Northumberland, the *ad Gethrin* of Bede, had been an area of Bronze Age occupation, and the landscape is dominated by the impressive Iron Age hill-fort of Yeavering Bell, and it was here in the seventh century that King Edwin of Northumbria set up a palace. The site was excavated between 1953 and 1957. The earliest structure on the site was a large timber fort, semi-circular with two parallel palisades, the inner one a formidable double palisade with a fighting platform. This is believed to date from the sixth century. The palace proper was probably begun towards the close of the century or early in the following century. The nucleus was a large timber hall and there were lesser buildings set about it, one of which may have been a pagan temple later converted to Christian use. To the west of the hall was a remarkable wooden amphitheatre built in concentric tiers to a height of some 25 feet, probably used for major assemblies when the king visited the area. The hall seems to have been replaced by another of more ambitious design and the amphitheatre enlarged, possibly in the reign of Edwin. At some time after this it would appear that there was a complete rebuilding of the main hall complex in a new architectural style, with the larger halls about 100 feet in length, and a Christian church and cemetery. Presumably the furnishing and decoration of these halls was akin to those described in *Beowulf*, the earliest important Anglo-Saxon poem. Bede tells us that this *villa regalis* was later transferred to Maelin, which is probably Milfield to the north-east. Milfield has not yet been excavated, but aerial photography has revealed there at least one building of the same shape as the later buildings at Yeavering. Another seventh-century royal estate lay at Catterick, which was the scene of a royal marriage in the eighth century.

At Cheddar in Somerset there was unearthed in 1963 a great complex of timber halls dating from the tenth to the fourteenth century, including the largest medieval timber hall so far known in the British Isles. The site of what was probably a palace of King Offa of Mercia has only now (1970) been discovered in the parish of Hampton Lucy near Stratford-on-Avon. Again aerial photography has led to excavation of a large complex of buildings. The excavations are now in progress and the results must be awaited, but the site has already yielded Saxon pottery which can be dated to the eighth century. The aerial photograph shows two groups of rectangular buildings, presumably originally of timber, on differing orientations, which may represent two phases. One structure is over 150 feet long by some 30 feet wide, and several others are nearly 100 feet long, including an apsidal-ended building. Another known site of an early royal estate is at Rendlesham in East Anglia, near to Sutton Hoo with its jewellery-filled ship cenotaph, where several mounds in all probability represent the royal burial ground.

What may perhaps prove to be the most important and significant site still awaits excavation, and that is the West Saxon royal palace in Winchester, which stood on an open site to the west of the cathedral. A wealth of Saxon material has recently come to light in Winchester, where at least two excavated churches have proved to be of pre-Conquest date. The most significant discovery is the *monasteriolum* (petty monastery) built *c.* 880–90 and traditionally founded by Alfred the Great. This monastery originally consisted of a dormitory and a wattled church, and it is the dormitory that has now been revealed in the foundations of a large stone building with a nave and two arcaded aisles. The building shows external signs of remodelling, with removal of the long arcades and the construction of a short arcaded hall across its central area, apparently an adaptation to serve as the south range of the claustral complex of new domestic buildings attached to New Minster after the fire of 1066. This vast building, which chronologically just comes into the Norman era, was nearly 160 feet by 50 feet, larger than the Norman halls of the bishop's palace at nearby Wolvesey.

Alfred's New Minster has yet to be excavated. It seems improbable that it will turn out to be a centrally planned church such as Alfred built at Athelney in 878 as a memorial of his victory over the Danes. Obviously directly influenced by the church of Germiny-des-Prés near Orleans, a well-known western Byzantine church of 810, the Athelney church was founded upon four great piers and was a quincunx, a square within a square, with a central lantern over it. According to an early record it was the first to be built upon this plan and thus gives a date for the introduction of the standard Byzantine plan into this country. The only centralized building to survive in any part is the great rotunda begun but not completed by Abbot Wulfric of St. Augustine's Abbey at Canterbury. The intention was to unite the two Augustine churches of SS. Peter and Paul and St. Mary by means of a great rotunda, but it remained unfinished at Wulfric's death in 1059. Later rebuilding obliterated the superstructure, but the lower stages remain (though little more than foundations), octagonal without, circular within, with an interior ring of eight massive rubble piers and massive half-round towers on north and south.

The tower was not originally merely an adjunct of the church but an integrated element. The turriform type of church, that is, the central tower nave, representing the western Byzantine style in Britain, is to be seen at a number of places. Here the nave was the ground floor of the tower, as may be seen at Barton-on-Humber, Lincolnshire; Broughton-by-Brigg, Lincolnshire; Earl's Barton, Northamptonshire; and Eastdean, Sussex, though later remodelling and eastward extension have changed the original plan. The best example is at Barton-on-Humber, supposedly tenth century but more probably of Canute's time (1017–35). Here the tower is round, of four stages, with long and short quoins and pilaster strip work. Earl's Barton has a square tower of four stages with long and short pilasters, some with gabled and round heads and the upper stage has an arcade of quintuple balusters. Cross-bracing or 'saltires' are shown, and even timber arches which recall the wooden stave churches of Norway. Most later Saxon churches have western towers, and among them is Barnack, Northamptonshire, which, like Barton-on-Humber and Earl's Barton, is elaborately decorated with pilaster strip work. Sompting, Sussex possesses the only surviving example of a tower with a 'Rhenish helm' roof, though there must have been others. This form consists of a tiled pyramidal roof resting upon the four walls each of which is carried up to a pointed gable. Certain structural details suggest that the original roof of St. Benet's at Cambridge was of a similar form. All these foregoing towers belong to what A. W. Clapham[1] called the English Carolingian group.

Another remarkable tower is that of the monastic church of Deerhurst, Gloucestershire, belonging to a small group (Jarrow, Monkwearmouth and Brixworth among them) of west porches on which towers were erected. This is a belfry tower of five stages of varying Saxon dates. The third stage has the visually striking and well-known massive double-gabled double openings with gabled projecting hood, massive stepped imposts and fluted jambs. There was here a polygonal apse (only a fragment remains), a rarity at that time, though it is to be found at Wing, Buckinghamshire, another significant church which was the first on the basilican plan, that is, with aisles, to be built since Brixworth appeared in the seventh century. Recent excavations beneath the chancel at Wing have given rise to a theory that the church was in fact founded earlier than its accepted tenth-century date, and that it may be ascribed to the mission of St. Birinus of Wessex early in the seventh century or to the missionary activities in the south of St. Wilfrid.

Something more must be said of Deerhurst. Its huge tub-shaped font is actually earlier than Ruthwell Cross (*c.* 680), so it is said, though this is problematical, and its ornate scrollwork and conjoined spirals are Celtic, resembling the true Celtic native metalwork. Another pre-Conquest building forms part of a farmstead south of the churchyard, and this was clearly a chapel consisting of nave and chancel, both rectangular, measuring just under 40 feet. The chancel arch is narrow with plain imposts. As long ago as 1675 an inscription was found on the site which stated that Duke Oddo built this royal hall and dedicated it to the Trinity in the fourteenth year of Edward the Confessor in memory of his brother Alfric (that is, in 1056).

By the end of the first milennium the cruciform church had developed, at least in embryo form. Rectangular nave and chancel were set out on the simple plan used by the old Celtic Church, but the external adjuncts to the nave, variously known as porch, porticus and chapel, became larger wings which in turn became transepts. Such transitional buildings may be seen at Worth, Sussex and Breamore, Hampshire.

Comparatively few Saxon churches remain today. A recent

[1] *Anglo-Saxon Architecture* (London, 1925).

monumental descriptive catalogue of them lists approximately 400.[1] The only surviving example of a wooden church is that of Greenstead in Essex, where the south nave walling is made of sawn tree trunks vertically placed together. The church is said to be the *lignea capella* which was built in 1013 as a resting place for the remains of St. Edmund, king and martyr, on their way from London to Bury St. Edmunds. It must be supposed that wooden churches were common in other forest areas. There are literary references to wooden churches as far apart as Wilton, Wiltshire; Lewes, Sussex; and Chester-le-Street, Durham. Essex has a group of churches which are almost wholly of timber except for their chancels, and they are probably of twelfth-century foundation on the 'fourposter' plan. That of Blackmore, however, is believed to be of monastic origin and has a central tower carried on six posts; over the crossing is an impressive network of timbering. In the formerly heavily forested area of Worcestershire there is a tradition of timber-framed religious buildings into the seventeenth century; timber-framed towers are numerous, and the church at Besford is wholly of fourteenth-century timber-framing.

Most of the later churches are to be found either on the limestone belt which runs southwards from the Yorkshire coast through Lincolnshire, along the western edge of the Fens and through the Cotswolds to the Dorset coast, or on the chalklands running from the top of Norfolk down to the Salisbury Plain with a long outlier through Sussex to Beachy Head. Most of the churches are in normal use, but a group of abandoned ruined churches is to be found in East Anglia. At North Elmham in Suffolk can be seen the plan of a small Saxon cathedral. This is of unknown date but probably early eleventh century and certainly before 1075 when the see was transferred to Thetford. This was a cruciform Carolingian church with an apsidal chancel and eastern transept of tau form (that is, having no presbyterial space between transept and apse), a tower in the angle between nave and transept on both sides, and a western axial tower. The function of the angle towers is not known but they may have been flanking towers or portici. There is pilaster strip-work round the apse. At nearby South Elmham are the ruins of the Old Minster. In plan this is a simple rectangular nave with an axial square

[1] H. M. and J. Taylor, *Anglo-Saxon Architecture* (Cambridge, 1964).

chamber on the west, probably a former tower and still standing to a height of some 14 feet, and the remains of an apse. At Weybourne in Norfolk the ruined church has an axial eastern tower with mixed quoining and occuli.

The characteristic features of Anglo-Saxon ecclesiastical architecture are pilaster strip-work (as Lombard bands and blind arcading), banded baluster shafts, quoining (especially the so-called 'long and short' quoins), primitive Byzantine *bifora* or openings in belfry towers, and occuli or round openings. Baldwin Brown thought that the pilaster work was derived from similar work in Germany known as *lisenen*, but later authorities favour the theory that the English form of wall decoration was derived from Armenia via Ravenna and the First Romanesque movement westwards. It seems that the importance of Armenia in its influence on the art and culture of western Europe is not yet fully appreciated.[1]

Two notable survivals, both in parish churches, may be noted here. In Breamore church in Hampshire, an early example of the completely cruciform church, an Anglo-Saxon inscription is cut on the head of the arch which opens below the south wall of the central towers and leads into the south porticus. In translation the inscription reads: "In this place the Word is revealed unto thee." The other feature is in the minster of Kirkdale in the North Riding of Yorkshire, largely rebuilt but retaining Saxon fabric, where an inscribed Anglo-Saxon sundial, now placed above the south porch, commemorates the rebuilding of the church during the latter part of Edward the Confessor's reign, c. 1060. The dial consists of a stone slab, 7 feet long, divided into three portions. The dial itself, in the middle, is divided into eight, which accords with the octaval system of time division common among the Angles. The outer panels contain the inscription. The inscription is in Old English, though it contains Scandinavian personal names, and it is a unique record of a purchase of the rights over a church under the parochial system. There are other Saxon inscribed sundials in the district, at Old Byland and Edstone. They are of far less interest, and they are clearly Anglo-Danish. All these places lay, of course, in the Wapentake, the Danish

---

[1] See R. Krautheimer, *Early Christian and Byzantine Architecture* (London, 1965) and E. A. Fisher, *Anglo-Saxon Towers* (David and Charles (Holdings) Ltd., Newton Abbot, 1969).

confederacy which grew out of the settlement of the Danish armies in these areas in the time of Alfred.

The Viking invasions which began in 787 gathered in momentum until towards the close of the ninth century the Danes were firmly established in the eastern side of the country from Teesside down to Essex. In the tenth century the Norsemen had planted settlements in Cheshire, Lancashire, Westmoreland and Cumberland, as well as in the Isle of Man and coastal areas of South Wales. With the sovereignty of Canute in 1016 the country was ruled by Danish kings for a quarter of a century until the old line of Wessex was restored in the person of Edward the Confessor.

The Viking invasions brought the wholesale destruction of the monasteries and the utter extinction of monastic life. Lindisfarne was sacked in 793.

Within the following hundred years all the monasteries of Northumbria had been destroyed or abandoned, and in the first half of the ninth century those of Lincolnshire, the Fens and the Kentish coast went also. At the same time, those of southern Mercia, Wessex and the Thames valley gradually fell into lay hands or became derelict. When Alfred began his reign no monastery was in being north and east of Watling Street, and regular life according to the Rule of St. Benedict had ceased to exist in the houses still calling themselves monasteries in the south and west, with the possible exception of St. Augustine's at Canterbury. So utter was the decadence that when Alfred wished, as part of his programme of reconstruction, to re-introduce the monastic life into his kingdom, he had of necessity to import a foreign community for his foundation at Athelney and to rely for its recruitment on foreign sources. In the event, Athelney would seem to have survived its patron by a few years only. Thus at the beginning of the tenth century regular monastic life was wholly extinct in England, and the ancient sites were either desolate, or in lay hands, or at best in the possession of a family of clerics.[1]

Yet the Vikings did not present a serious challenge to the continued existence of Christianity among the people, and indeed they came to accept Christianity and to set up churches as well as recognising several older church sites, giving them the name 'Kirkby', the church town. Guthrum, the Danish leader who became King of East Anglia, was baptised in 878 in fulfilment of

[1] Dom David Knowles, *The Religious Houses of Medieval England* (Sheed & Ward, London, 1940).

the peace terms made with Alfred, and within less than a generation Edmund (who had been killed by the Danes in 869) was being venerated at Bury St. Edmunds as a saint. Canute was a Christian, and throughout his reign he gave active help to the Church. Carved stone crosses and grave slabs remain as the most important Viking memorials.

The style of Anglo-Saxon sculpture changed after the Peace of Wedmore (878) and the establishment of the Danelaw. The Anglian motifs on the earlier cross shafts were dominating panels of interlacing bands associated with figures in high relief, and these were being cut at the end of the seventh century along with scrolls of leaf and vine and with birds and animals among the scrolls. With Danish influence dragons replaced animals, and finally in the Norse period the dragons became entangled in their own tongues and tails and became part of the linked interlacing. The bulk of the crosses and fragments now to be seen are Anglo-Danish or Anglo-Norse of the tenth and eleventh centuries, and on the whole they are inferior in quality to the earlier work. They are distributed in those areas in which Scandinavian influence was strongest, in the Wapentakes, notably the three Ridings of Yorkshire and the territory of the Five Boroughs (the shires of Lincoln, Nottingham, Derby and Leicester and the land formerly dependent on Stamford) and, of course, in the Norse settlement area of Lancashire, Cumberland, Westmoreland and the Isle of Man.

The crosses of Halton, Lancashire, and Gosforth, Cumberland, portray scenes from Scandinavian mythology. The latter, nearly 15 feet high, has a round shaft and a wheel head with interlacing patterns in the tight heavy Danish manner linked with scenes from the Norse *Edda* (at Kirk Ooslan in the Isle of Man is a cross with engraved scenes from the Sigurd epic). At Kirkby Stephen, Westmoreland, a fragmentary cross shaft depicts a barbaric devil who is probably Loki, the Scandinavian god of evil, bound and awaiting judgement. In the church of Middleton-by-Pickering, North Riding, there are crosses depicting bound dragons and Hugin, Odin's one-eyed raven, a warrior carrying a battle-axe (the Viking weapon) and a sword of Scandinavian type. Here we see the advent of Christianity and its clash with older beliefs. In the Isle of Man there are richly ornamented crosses at Ballaugh, Maughold and Kirk Braddan.

A peculiar feature is the 'hog-back' tombstone with naturalistic bears holding on to the ends, carved in the eleventh century under Norse influence. They are rectangular and solid in shape and roughly carved to represent a long low house, the ridged roof generally cut in a pattern resembling tiles. They are widely distributed in the north, especially in the Yorkshire North Riding, where they can be seen in the churches of Brompton, Pickhill, Levisham, Lastingham, Stainton-in-Cleveland, Osmotherley and Sinnington. At Brompton, near Northallerton, there are three perfect examples of a special form of these stones in which each gabled end of the 'house' is clasped by a bear, the two animals sitting up and facing each other. On the Pickhill specimen there is a beast in profile which is of the Danish Jellinge style, and a similar example at Levisham showing a large dragon is of the Ringerike style of *c.* 1100. The 'hog-back' can be found as far afield as Heysham on the Lancashire coast, a place of much Saxon activity, where a small ruined oratory on a rocky ledge overlooking the sea is certainly pre-Conquest and probably ninth century.

The last century of Anglo-Saxon England was a period of prosperity, richly endowed in the arts, in scholarship and learning, which took root in the new monasteries. If one man was responsible for the reflowering of monasticism when it had all but perished that man was Dunstan, who, in the mid-tenth century, beside the Tor rising sharply above Glastonbury, the Mount Tabor of the Somerset plain, restored his monastery and moulded his own community on the Benedictine model. Dunstan, Archbishop of Canterbury, was minister and counsellor to King Edgar, and in his work of reorganization he was assisted by Ethelwold, Bishop of Winchester, and Oswald, Bishop of Worcester. Ethelwold gave the Benedictine pattern to Abingdon and Oswald gave it to Ramsey in the Fens. A rich new stream of monastic life flowed through the Severn and Avon valleys, at Evesham, Worcester, Pershore and Winchcombe. Before the Conquest monastic life was firmly planted in other centres which were to become illustrious—St. Albans (soon to produce Mathew Paris and his *Gesta Abbatum*), Westminster, Ely, Peterborough, Coventry, Bury St. Edmunds (its *Chronicle* to be written by Jocelyn, a native of the town before he took the black habit), Gloucester, Winchester and elsewhere. In 1066 there were some thirty-five houses of men in England and nine large nunneries, all following the Rule of St. Benedict and the Customal drawn up by Dunstan and known as the *Regularis Concordia*.

There are written accounts of important monastic buildings constructed in the tenth century at Winchester, Abingdon, Worcester, Ely, Ramsey, Thorney, Peterborough, Durham and elsewhere, but beyond some fragments revealed by excavation there are no tangible remains of this period. When the Normans rebuilt they dug trenches for the continuous strip foundations, and in so doing they virtually obliterated the Saxon work and sometimes, as at York, the Roman. Remains of conventual buildings erected by Dunstan at Glastonbury have been identified. Little but foundations survive, and even these were found to be much mutilated by later work, but their extent suggests that Dunstan's monastery was on a scale comparable with the largest contemporary houses on the Continent.[1] It is doubtful, however, whether these early monasteries were laid out on any standard plan as were those of the Norman and later periods.

Of the monastic churches we have more recorded information and a little more in the way of visual evidence. None, however, is as complete as the tenth-century small monastic church of Deerhurst, where the Normans, instead of demolishing the entire fabric, as was their wont, merely reduced the length of the church by removing the apse and widened it by the addition of side aisles. Beneath the pavement in and near the south transept of Peterborough cathedral, originally a great Benedictine church, are the foundations of a small unaisled cruciform church, probably of the tenth century and of a type similar to that of Deerhurst priory. Christ Church chapel, the cathedral of Oxford, formerly the Augustinian priory church of St. Frideswide, was rebuilt from 1160. At the east end of the Lady Chapel, however, are three primitive arches which correspond with the foundations of three apses on the external side of the wall, so that here we have remains of the small church of *c.* 1004 with its eastern triple-apsical termination.

We have already noted the remains of the eleventh-century rotunda built by Abbot Wulfric in Canterbury. Some slight remains of the circular centrally-planned abbey church built at Abingdon by Abbot Ethelwold, *c.* 960, have been discovered,

[1] See C. A. Ralegh Radford, *Antiquity*, XXIX (1955).

though not enough to indicate the peculiar plan described in the abbey chronicle for it had a round chancel, round nave and round tower. The seventh-century predecessor of this church apparently had apses at east and west, the first record of double apses in western Europe—a century before the feature appeared in Carolingian architecture—and it may have influenced the design of Ethelwold's church.

9

The Norman Infusion

The Normans found England divided up into vills—each containing a group of houses surrounded by the common cornfields, grazing lands and woods, and each serving as a unit for purposes of law and taxation—and to this Saxon organization they added the organization of the manor and the manorial system of military tenure. They introduced the feudal castle, the private stronghold or fortified residence of a baron exercising seignorial jurisdiction over his tenantry. They introduced a comprehensive monastic system whereby episcopal sees were seated in monasteries, and churches associated with grammar schools came under monastic jurisdiction. After the Conquest there were four types of schools, and for official purposes and translation Norman-French was substituted for English (it was not until the mid-fourteenth century that English was reintroduced into the schools).

Before 1100 halls and houses were still being built of wood. Witness the immense timber hall excavated at Cheddar and the motte tower houses of the first castles. The earliest permanent domestic buildings in England belong to the twelfth century. Secular Norman stone architecture appears in four forms, the castle, the manor house, the town house and the living quarters of monasteries. Tradition ascribes a Jewish origin to the two-storeyed houses which appeared in certain towns, and it may be that Jews (brought into England by the Conqueror), wealthy and unpopular as money-lenders, needed the protection of substantial houses of stone with an upper floor. Certainly the well-known examples of Norman town houses are known under Jewish names—in Lincoln there are Jew's House, Aaron's House and Jew's Court; in Bury St. Edmunds there is Moyses Hall; and in Norwich there is Isaac's Hall, now much altered. Whatever the truth of popular belief this is an interesting group of houses departing from the prevailing single-storeyed, aisled-hall type.

They conform to a standard plan, rectangular, two-storeyed, each floor consisting of a greater and a lesser chamber with the most important room on the upper floor. The ground floor, normally a little under 40 feet long by some 20 feet wide, is invariably low in height with a vaulted ceiling, having, originally, narrow loop windows. On the first floor is the hall and a solar or smaller apartment. These chambers have larger two-light shafted windows, usually round-headed and set within a containing arch, though at Moyses Hall the arches enclose square-headed windows. The upper hall was usually entered by an external staircase, though at Isaac's House in Norwich the stair was enclosed in a forebuilding. The Jew's House has an elaborate entrance with interlaced chain-links or what is sometimes called an open heart pattern. The doorway of Aaron's House was originally similar, but the shafts have later crocket capitals and a heavy hood mould rests on a head and a caryatid bust. An enclosing arch above the doorway carries the chimney of the first floor fireplace. Originally there was probably a tall cylindrical chimney like those to be seen at Christchurch, Hampshire; and Boothby Pagnel, Lincolnshire. Jew's Court is believed to have been the Synagogue, but there are no medieval features on its front. Moyses Hall in Bury St. Edmunds was originally two Norman houses, one of *c.* 1140 and the other *c.* 1190.

There are ruined Norman houses at Christchurch and York. Of the latter only two walls remain in a court behind Stonegate. A window on the first floor has a shaft with a waterleaf capital dividing the two lights, and this ornament, a broad unribbed tapering leaf curving up towards the angle of the abacus, dates the building to *c.* 1180. The windows were rebated at the inside for shutters but were never glazed. It is thought that the undercroft here supported a wooden, not a stone-vaulted, first floor. In the Gloucestershire village of Sherborne is a cottage with a Norman doorway. These Cotswold valleys are remarkable for their Saxon and Norman churches, and H. J. Massingham wrote that Cotswold was remarkable for "Norman village architecture with its sense of gnomic mass in structure and richness in stone embroidery".

The manor house of Boothby Pagnell is of unusual importance, for though manor houses are held to have developed out of castles at the end of the thirteenth century this small house cannot be anything else. It has a moat, but it conforms to the late twelfth-century type and is the only house of its kind in England. It is rectangular, two-storeyed, with vaulted ground floor and hall and solar above, and it has an external staircase at the south end with a round-headed doorway on the first floor. There is a later wing and some later fenestration, but several original windows remain, some *in situ* and others reset. At Hemlingford Manor, Huntingdonshire, the same basic plan can be identified despite later accretions.

This idea of providing accommodation over more than one storey is also reflected in the great towers or keeps of the Norman castles. In the early Norman motte and bailey type of castle, to be seen on the Bayeux Tapestry, the tower house on top of the motte or earth mound was of wood. These mottes are still to be seen up and down the country, at Arundel, Lewes and Skenfrith, for example, and, where the castle has wholly disappeared, at Brinklow, Ellesmere, Haughley and elsewhere. Very few had, like the Tower of London, a stone keep or central tower from the beginning. Of eighty-five castles undoubtedly belonging to the eleventh century (and there were probably more) only a handful would appear to have been built of stone. From the close of the eleventh century, however, the owners of these first castles gradually replaced the wooden tower with a stone keep and the wooden palisades round the bailey or enclosure with a low stone curtain wall.

The first stone keeps were shell keeps containing all the buildings of the castle, which were placed on the inside of the large circular wall or shell, either occupying the whole space or enclosing a central courtyard. There are many such keeps, among them those of Arundel, Lewes, Carisbrooke, Restormel, Totnes, Launceston and Tamworth. Windsor Castle was originally of this type. The keep of Arundel, standing on a motte in the middle of a long and relatively narrow bailey, is built of good masonry strengthened by pilaster buttresses. A square tower projects from one side of it. The original halls and chambers have been cleared away, but they occupied the whole internal space, the roof timbers spring from a central wooden pillar and from corbels which still exist in the shell wall. Arundel Castle has been built up over the centuries, and it is obvious why a fortress was put

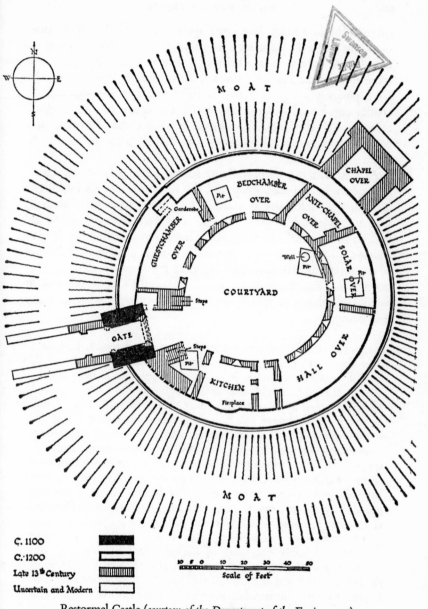

Restormel Castle (*courtesy of the Department of the Environment*)

there in the first place. It is built upon a spur of the downs commanding the river Arun at a point where there has always been a bridge. Where there is a bridge there is a road, where there is a river there is an avenue of attack from the sea, and where the river passes through the downs there is a gap through which armies can march inland. Similarly, the castle of Wallingford commanded the most important ford on the Thames, and Newcastle was placed to block the lowest ford on the Tyne river.

At Restormel in Cornwall the ruined castle presents an excellent example of a shell keep and the disposition of its buildings. Within the shell there is another ring wall, concentric with it, and surrounding a large court. The two-storeyed domestic buildings, great hall, kitchen, lesser hall, ante-chamber (leading to a chapel projecting beyond the shell), north chamber and the hall of the guard are contained in the space between the shell and the inner wall. The keep of Launceston, also in Cornwall, was so formidable that it is worth quoting Sidney Toy,[1] who describes it as being

composed of an ovoid-shaped shell and a round tower, built at a later date, probably about 1240, inside the shell. Here the shell, though smaller internally, is much more substantial than that at Totnes. It is 12 feet thick and 30 feet high, and has a deep battered plinth crowned by a round moulding. The wall walk was reached by two mural stairways, one near the gateway and one on the opposite side of the keep. A mural chamber with a barrel vault and having a ventilating shaft in one corner was probably a prison cell. The keep is approached up the steep mound, which investigation has proved to be a natural hillock, by a long flight of steps, formerly flanked by walls and covered in by a roof. The foot of the stairway was guarded by a round tower, and at the head stood the round-headed entrance to the keep which was later protected by a portcullis. The transformation of this building from a mere shell to a powerful keep was probably the work of Richard, Earl of Cornwall and titular king of the Romans. The work included the construction of the inner tower and of an embattled walk at the foot of the shell. Considering its commanding position, its three lines of defence and its magnificent middle platform, this keep when complete must have been amongst the most formidable in England.

[1] "The Round Castles of Cornwall", *Archaeologia* (Vol. LXXXIII, 1933).

The interior of Deerhurst Church, Gloucestershire, facing west

The south door of Kilpeck Church, Herefordshire

At Tamworth, first fortified by Edward the Elder and his sister Ethelfleda, Lady of the Mercians, the multiangular-shaped shell has a square tower on the east which projects slightly beyond the outside of the keep, and the wall walk was reached by two mural stairways in the thickness of the wall, as at Launceston and Totnes. On the east side of the castle mound is a moat bridged by a stone causeway built of herring-bone work. Herring-bone construction was used by the Normans (e.g. at Colchester) as well as by Romans and Saxons, and there is no reason to suppose that this causeway is any earlier than the late eleventh-century keep with which it is linked.

The twelfth century may be called the golden age of the Norman castles, the age of the massive lofty square or rectangular keeps, introduced from northern France but based on architectural patterns evolved in the eastern regions of the Byzantine Empire. These keeps provided well-designed and powerful dwelling-houses which were convenient and secure. From two to four storeys in height, the entrance was usually on the first floor and was reached by a stairway built against the side of the keep. The principal hall was generally on the entrance floor. There were fireplaces and garde-robes or lavatories, formed in the outer walls opening up from the main rooms. There was always a well; this often went down to a great depth and was carried up two or three floors, with a place at each floor to draw the water. There was almost invariably a chapel, either in the keep itself or in a building attached to it. At Dover there is an adjoining building with two chapels, one above the other.

Such keeps are distributed all over England from Bamburgh in Northumberland to Lydford on the borders of Devon and Cornwall. Among the most monumental of them are those of Castle Hedingham, Rochester, Castle Rising, Kenilworth, Ludlow, Norwich and Middleham. The well-preserved keep of Castle Hedingham towers from its high promontory overlooking the little town of that name in Essex. It was built *c.* 1135 by Aubrey de Vere, of flint rubble faced with Barnack stone, and its five storeys rise to over 100 feet. It is lighted by single and two-light round-headed openings. The flight of stone steps leading up to the first-floor entrance was originally covered by a fore-building. The hall is on the second floor, and it was heated by a wall fireplace, round-headed, ornamented with a double chevron

7

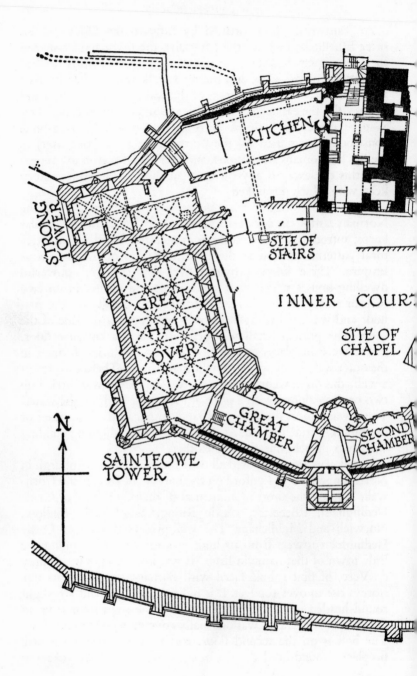

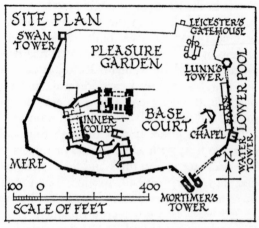

SITE PLAN

SWAN TOWER

PLEASURE GARDEN

LEICESTER'S GATEHOUSE

LUNN'S TOWER

BASE COURT

INNER COURT

CHAPEL

WATER LOWER POOL TOWER

MERE

N

100 0   400

SCALE OF FEET

MORTIMER'S TOWER

KENILWORTH CASTLE

■ LATE 12ᵀᴴ CENTURY

▨ 13ᵀᴴ CENTURY

▨ LATE 14ᵀᴴ CENTURY

▨ 15ᵀᴴ CENTURY

▤ 16ᵀᴴ CENTURY

▨ MODERN

FEET 10 0   50   100 FEET

SCALE OF FEET

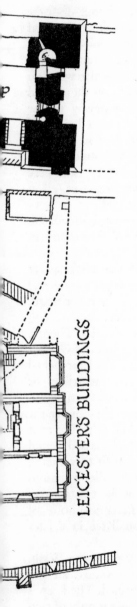

LEICESTER'S BUILDINGS

moulding and stone-canopied. The upper rooms are reached by a stair in the north-west angle turret.

Rochester's keep on the Medway—architectural tour-de-force or feudal monster—was built by Gundulph, monk of Bec and Bishop of Rochester, after the castle had been severely damaged when besieged by William Rufus. It consists of a square main building, bisected by a partition wall, and a rectangular wing on one side, the wing containing an entrance porch on the second storey and a chapel on the third storey; the stairway to the entrance has gone. It rises through four storeys to a height of over 100 feet, with angle towers or turrets rising 12 feet higher. The walls are 12 feet thick and they are lighted by round-headed openings. The great hall, arcaded, is on the third storey, and here there are two tiers of windows as well as two fireplaces, all in arched heads rich in chevron ornament and mouldings. In 1215 King John successfully besieged the castle, breaching both curtain wall and keep. The south-east angle of the keep was then rebuilt in its present form.

The keep at Kenilworth in the heart of the Shakespeare Country, known as Caesar's Tower, is of exceptionally powerful construction. It stands in the north-east angle of the inner ward. It is of two storeys, but these are of great height, rectangular, with massive towers at the corners and buttresses at the sides. There is a large hall on each storey. The entrance, before John of Gaunt's attentions in 1392, was on the second storey and was approached by a stone stairway against the west wall. The meutrières or loopholes here, *c.* 1130, are among the earliest existing medieval examples, and they survive in original condition. They pierce the 14-feet-thick walls below the battlements in line with the roof gutter and are approached from the walk which passed round three sides of the keep at this level. The keep was further altered in the time of Queen Elizabeth, when Robert Dudley's masons hacked away at the small original apertures for light to convert them into big mullioned windows. The metamorphosis of Kenilworth was long and complex, as we shall see in a later chapter.

At Castle Rising in Norfolk, almost within sight of the Wash, the Norman gatehouse and keep stand where almost all else (including the chapel in the courtyard) has vanished. The keep is low and massive, almost the twin of Norwich, and is only of two storeys and lacks its battlements. Here, as at Newcastle and Dover, the approach stairway is enclosed within and defended by a fore-building. The vestibule at the top of the stairs contains an elaborately moulded arch, the entrance into the great hall, but this was later blocked and converted into a fireplace. While the rest of the keep is of flint rubble with ashlar facings on pilasters and corner buttresses, the forebuilding is entirely cased in ashlar and decorated with a continuous arcade and, above it, a line of circles containing carved heads. The extent of the ornamentation is singularly prolific for a military building. The keep was divided by an internal cross-wall and had only one floor over the basement.

More humble but eloquent of grim border warfare is Clun's broken keep in the Welsh Marches, just a league on the English side of Offa's Dyke, rising starkly above what was once the moat. This is the Garde Douloureuse described by Scott in *The Betrothed*, where the butler brewed "mighty ale from the best barley in Shropshire". It is one of the earliest of Norman castles, and its stone keep appeared some time in the twelfth century. Curiously it does not stand on the original small motte. Its foundations start at the level of the ditch and it covers the whole east end of the eminence, three of its five storeys overtopping the level of the summit, but the other two rising from the ditch and being actually below the curtain wall.

The appearance of the twelfth-century keep at Bamburgh in Northumberland is curious. Here the castle is long and narrow with its north-east side facing the sea. On such a site a fortress of the motte and bailey type was unnecessary from the beginning, and instead three wards were built. The inner or east ward contained the halls, kitchens, vaults and living quarters and the detached chapel of which only the foundations remain. It would then appear that the keep was added to a completed castle, by Henry III in 1163. The castle was in the van of the fighting against the Scots and of the Wars of the Roses, and it was during the latter that Bamburgh gained the uneasy distinction of being the first castle upon whose walls was triumphantly demonstrated the supremacy of artillery.

Distant Durham's double crown of cathedral and castle was described by Sir Walter Scott as "half church of God, half castle 'gainst the Scot". It was on William the Conqueror's return from an expedition against Malcolm of Scotland in 1072 that he

ordered a castle to be built at Durham above the Wear. From
that time the history of monastery and castle were closely linked
together. It has been said that here the lion lay down with the
lamb, for the bishopric was erected into a palatinate and the
palatine bishop had every temporal power that did not infringe
upon the sovereignty of the king. He was *"rex atque sacerdos"*, the
ruler of a district which was regarded as a buffer state between
England and Scotland. This episcopal power was also shown in the
castle, and to Bishop Pudsey (1153–95) is due some of the finest
later Romanesque architecture in England. The keep was rebuilt
in its present octagonal form in the fourteenth century (though it
is similar to the earlier shell keeps, but the range of buildings in
three storeys along the north curtain remains. At the east end of
this range is a chapel, or rather the undercroft of a chapel, which
recalls the Chapel of St. John in the Tower of London, though
the piers supporting the groined vaulting have capitals carved
with animals and plants. A magnificent doorway, the arch deeply
massed with pattern carving in four orders, gives access to the
hall on the first floor. Above this, on the second storey and
approached by a spiral stairway, is another hall of late twelfth-
century date formerly known as the Constable's Hall, where the
walls are constructed in a continuous arcade with windows in
every other archway, with detached shafts in couples set between
the windows.

In such important castles the buildings within the bailey included
a large hall for the common life of the garrison. In these instances
the hall was virtually the keep of the castle. Such was the great
oblong hall built by William Fitz Obern at Chepstow about
1170, standing on a narrow tongue of rock between the river
Wye and a deep ravine. This powerful structure has a basement
and two upper storeys, measuring 89 feet by 30 feet, and though
the upper stages were remodelled in the thirteenth century the
walling is original and retains the original windows in the basement and internal wall arcading on the south and west sides of the
first floor.

These early Norman halls are magnificent. At Richmond in
Yorkshire there is a long rectangular hall in one corner of the
bailey, standing against the curtain, which is contemporary with
the earliest part of the curtain wall, *c.* 1070–80 and probably the
earliest in England. It is known as Scotland's Hall, after the lords

of Bedale, powerful feudatories of the Honour of Richmond. The hall proper was entered by an exterior stair through a round-headed archway flanked by pillars, and the lighting is confined to ranges of coupled round-headed windows at the sides and by a triplet of narrow windows at the west end. The so-called Robin Hood's Tower has a little tunnel-vaulted oratory with mural arcades, 10 feet by 12 feet, that was built during the time of the Conqueror. The keep, perhaps uniquely, is built on top of the gatehouse, the most accessible part of a castle. A later barbican was built here so that the original gatehouse is now the ground floor of the keep, a somewhat complex arrangement. This keep was built between 1150 and 1180, over 100 feet in height and complete to the two-storeyed top turrets and the battlements. It is of the same rectangular type as Castle Hedingham and Rochester and has a hall on both upper floors. An unusual feature is an octagonal pillar on the ground floor carrying four rib-vaults of early fourteenth-century date.

At Oakham in Rutland the hall consists of a nave and two aisles, all of stone and having arcades richly decorated with leaf and dog-tooth ornament. The hall of Leicester Castle was built about 1150, some thirty years earlier than Oakham, and while it is similar in plan with nave and two aisles the pillars and struts between the nave and aisles are of oak. Many great halls were altered or rebuilt, like those of Winchester and Kenilworth. At the ruined episcopal palace of Wolvesey, Winchester, excavation has recently revealed an early twelfth-century hall which, with the exception of Westminster Hall, is the largest of its date in the country.

Rectangular keeps were obviously convenient for the disposition of the rooms inside them, but they had disadvantages. Angles and corners were vulnerable to the attacking sappers and the battering ram, and the defenders could not see or shoot round corners. In the Levant keeps and towers were round and multi-angular, and we had learned the lesson when we returned from the Third Crusade at the end of the twelfth century. Meanwhile, however, there were experiments with what might be called transitional keeps, and among these new keeps, sometimes called juliets, are Conisborough, Yorkshire; Orford, Suffolk; and Longtown, Herefordshire. The keep of Conisborough, one of the principal scenes of Scott's *Ivanhoe*, is one of the finest in the

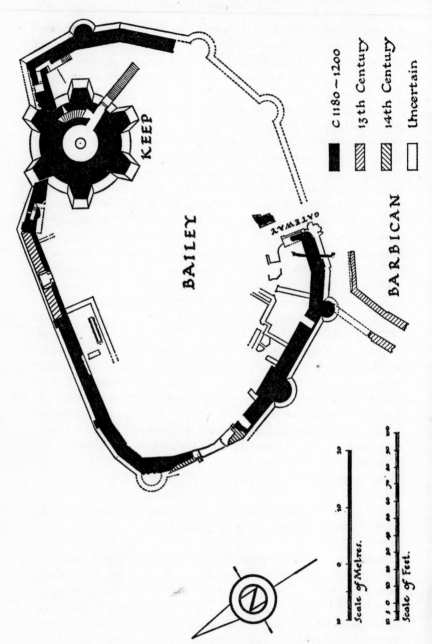

KEEP

BAILEY

GATEWAY

BARBICAN

C 1180–1200

13th Century

14th Century

Uncertain

Scale of Metres.

Scale of Feet.

Conisborough Castle (*courtesy of the Department of the Environment*)

country. Built *c.* 1180–90, it is a tall cylindrical tower with very thick walls supported by six massive buttresses which rise to the full height of the building. It is of four storeys, only the two uppermost being lighted with a single two-light window. The vaulted ground storey, which contains a well, is reached only through a large hole in the centre of the vault. The entrance is on the first floor, reached by a flight of steps and, originally, a drawbridge from the courtyard. Mural stairways lead up to the upper floors and the battlements. Each of the two uppermost floors has a large fireplace and a stone lavatory basin, and a vaulted chapel with a small sacristy opens out on the east side of the third floor. There were two fighting lines, one from a gallery which runs round the roof at the level of the gutters, and the other from the battlements. Three small vaulted chambers and a domical-roofed oven formed in the buttresses opened on to the gallery. The oven, as at Orford, was probably for the use of the garrison. (There are remarkable and enormous round ovens with low vaults at Kidwelly Castle in Pembrokeshire, and at Durham the castle kitchen is still used to cook the meals for the university students.)

Castle-building was always considered a royal prerogative, and though circumstances sometimes compelled the king to wink at its infringement a subject could fortify his house only under special licence. A large number of unlicensed castles—*castra adulterina*—were erected during the troubled reign of Stephen by the lesser nobility and used by them for purposes closely akin to brigandage. When Henry II came to power he ordered the destruction of these and of some castles of the greater nobility, a measure which gave undue prominence to the great old castles, many of which the king strengthened. At the close of his reign there were more than 1,000 castles in England and Wales. The further development of the castle takes us beyond the Norman era and into that of the Plantagenets.

The earliest Norman churches were often the private chapels of the manorial lords so that church and castle often stand in close juxtaposition. In places like Manorbier in Pembroke, beloved of Giraldus Cambrensis, all the appendages of a Norman manorial estate have survived—castle, church, dovecote, mill and pond. By the time of the Norman Conquest two types of churches had been developed, the 'Celtic' type with nave and chancel and the

Byzantine type with turriform nave. With the twelfth century the parish church settled down to its final rectangular form, with the chancel either square-headed or apsidal. Early and primitive is the austere two-celled square-headed chapel of Heath in wild Corvedale in Shropshire, perhaps built by English (i.e. Saxon) craftsmen slowly learning Norman ways. It is of rough rubble walling with angle pilasters and provision for belfry openings in the apex of the west gable. In strong contrast the church of Kilpeck in Herefordshire is three-celled, with nave, choir and apsidal chancel, a sophisticated essay exploiting the entire gamut of ornament.

Towards the western end of the nave two doors were usually set facing each other. In processions such as that held on Palm Sunday the congregation left the nave by the north door, processed through the churchyard and round the east end of the church and re-entered the nave by the south door. Where the sanctuary was square-headed a tower was sometimes raised above the choir space, as at Iffley, Oxfordshire; Studland, Dorset; and Stewkley, Buckinghamshire. In three-celled churches having an eastern apse the axial tower rarely occurs, preference being for a tower at the west end of the nave as at Birkin, Yorkshire; and East Ham, Essex. Churches in the border country of the Welsh Marches have strongly fortified towers. At Clun the tower has a pyramidal cap pierced by a line of louvred openings. Not until the late-medieval bell-towers were being added to the west ends of churches, however, did the west door come to be accepted (many north doors were then blocked up).

The apse was gradually ousted, and the most striking introduction into the form of the twelfth-century parish church was the arcade of semi-circular arches carried on piers or pillars, thus increasing the width of the nave. At first many church arcades were carried on square Anglian piers, but from early in the twelfth century, under the influence of the Cluniac monks of Burgundy, the circular pillar made its appearance. This was a true Romanesque feature, for the French abbeys had derived it from the classical buildings of Roman Gaul and ultimately from the architecture of Ancient Rome. The Normans copied the Roman round arch, the Roman barrel vault, the Roman column and capital construction.

The half-way position which Romanesque holds between

Roman and Gothic is illustrated by the treatment of the arch. It is of many orders and is elaborately ornamented, but the ornaments are enrichments rather than mouldings. Norman mouldings are few and simple, consisting of a hollow chamfer under the hood-mould and a bowtel, round or pointed, on the edge of the outer order with a shallow hollow on the face, while the inner order is often plain. Characteristic ornaments are the cable, diaper and diamond, billet and the ubiquitous zigzag or chevron. Most of them derived from carpentry. Followers of those arch symbolists the medieval Durandus and the Victorian Hawker of Morwen-stow may be disillusioned to find that the chevron ornament is of wood-carving origin. Far from representing the ripples on the lake of Galilee, it is purely functional and was probably developed from taking two opposing swings of an axe at the edge of the timber to remove what woodsmen call a 'kerf', and then continuing all along the edge of the timber until the whole edge had become serrated.

The enrichment of tympana and door jambs, chancel arches, capitals and fonts, is an artistic expression uniquely associated with this twelfth century and ending with it. We call it 'Norman' but most of it is almost certainly the work of Anglo-Saxon masons expressing themselves in the vernacular with bucolic joy and humour, naïve credulity and an uncomprehending faith. We call it Romanesque, and indeed some of it is that, but much of it too is Byzantine. The tympanum developed from the arch and lintel combination in Syria, and it was probably brought back by the Crusaders to become a tablet for pictorial representation. Doorways are voluptuous with barbaric splendour. At Kilpeck the arch orders of the south doorway drip with beak-heads from Nordic mythology, and on the outer moulding are nine medallions of birds, fish and monsters linked together by grotesque heads. The jamb shafts are carved with intertwining foliage, serpents and figures of trousered Celtic warriors in Phrygian caps, and the tympanum bears a relief carving of a vine spray. A corbel table running right round the church is similarly enriched, and the chancel arch, heavy with chevron ornament, has three figures of Apostles on each side (instead of nook shafts), tiered above each other.

At Barfreston in Kent there is a little more restraint in the church doorway, though capitals, arch and tympanum are loaded with scriptural allegories and bestiaries. Under the hood are medallions filled with the activities of a twelfth-century manor, the minstrel with his viol, the cellarer drawing ale from a cask, an armourer polishing his lord's shield, hawking, the forester, the reeve, the miller, and so on. The tympanum portrays Christ in Majesty with attendant angels and seraphim. In the grim church of Elkstone high on the Gloucestershire wolds the tympanum has a Christ in Majesty in a vesica with symbols of the Evangelists, and there are beak-heads on the arch, while high on the tower is a band of aerial musicians.

At Tickencote in Rutland the church is mainly a Georgian rebuilding in neo-Norman, but the original chancel remains and it has a superbly enriched chancel arch in six orders. This may be compared with the porch of Malmesbury Abbey in Wiltshire, one of the finest achievements of late Norman architecture in Europe. The entrance doorway has eight recessed orders of arches exuberantly carved in Byzantine manner and depicting scriptural scenes, the Virtues and Vices and much else, while within the porch are lunettes containing almost life-sized seated figures of the Apostles, conventional and somewhat stiff. The personification of Virtues and Vices was introduced into medieval art chiefly through the *Psychomachia* of Prudentius (the Christian Latin poet who died in 410), in which the Virtues, as warrior virgins, overthrow the Vices in single combats before uniting to build a New Jerusalem. The oldest carved *Psychomachia* in England is here on this south door of Malmesbury Abbey. They appear again in more humorous vein carved on the fonts of Stanton Fitzwarren, Wiltshire; and Southrop, Gloucestershire. Here warrior figures of Virtues trampling upon conquered Vices are framed in the arcades above which, at Southrop, are carved small domed and castellated buildings. This is the kind of imagery, dramatic sermons in stone, which led to the morality plays.

The medallions and figure sculpture of Malmesbury are to be found, slightly later in date and more refined, in the north and south doorways of the Lady Chapel at Glastonbury Abbey. It was probably the intention to carve on the south doorway an Old Testament, or at least a Genesis series, but it remained unfinished, with only the Creation of Eve and the Fall actually carved.

Finally it may be noted that small parish churches with ornate west fronts are rare. Examples are Stewkley, Buckinghamshire, with a trinity of arches filled with chevrons, and Iffley, Oxfordshire, and Castle Rising, Norfolk, both of which have a Franco-Norman wheel window and other ornament. The last was no doubt the work of the noble lord whose aesthetic sense was allowed full play in his castle keep.

Monastic ruins apart, few Norman churches that are no longer in normal use are to be encountered, though here and there one has been converted to domestic use. At Broad Campden in Gloucestershire an early twelfth-century chapel that belonged to Tewkesbury Abbey was early this century converted into a private house by C. R. Ashbee, the craftsman-disciple of Ruskin and William Morris. There are substantial remains of the walling, and the chancel arch and the north and south doorways, one round-headed with plain imposts and a complete lack of ornament, have survived. At Dosthill, near Tamworth, Warwickshire, there is a small primitive two-celled rectangular church, now disused and the chancel arch blocked.

At Netherton under Housman's Bredon Hill in Worcestershire is a ruined church which as early as the fourteenth century was recorded as being disused. In 1783 it was converted into a barn but the accretions were later removed. Its only remarkable feature is the tympanum over the south door, depicting a winged saw-fish, a symbol of worldliness finally drawn beneath the waters to hell. At Liscombe near Milton Abbas in Dorset is a complete two-celled church, nave and chancel divided by a good Transitional or late Norman arch with massive round columns, in use as bakehouse and storehouse. It is mentioned in the charter of Milton Abbey as an annexe by King Athelstan.

There is one major building in East Anglia, that graveyard of churches, and that is the church of Orford in Suffolk, where the ruined chancel has columnar piers encircled with a spiral band of bowtel moulding in high relief, an interesting variation on the pier-design of Durham Cathedral. The ruined church in the ward of Ludlow Castle in Shropshire was a private chapel, and it is mentioned here as the only Norman round church in ruins in this country. It retains its chancel arch, though it opens now into an empty space and it exhibits some good ornament. The building of round church naves, miniature reproductions of the Church of the Holy Sepulchre in Jerusalem, is attributed to the returning

Crusaders, and only four survive, including Ludlow. The others are the Temple Church in London and those of Northampton and Cambridge.

One of the most remarkable sites is that of Old Sarum, where a conical hill rises sharply from the valley of the Avon. The hill was probably the site of a Celtic settlement, became a Roman town and then continued as a place of some consequence beyond the Norman Conquest. The fortifications consisted of two concentric circles of defensive earthworks, the outer ring or bailey surrounded by a Norman curtain wall. This outer area was once crowded with streets and houses, and Pepys described a chapel over the east gate. In the inner bailey, enclosed by a wall and gatehouse, are the keep, chapel, hall (thirteenth-century) and a building containing ovens, though the remains are fragmentary. As late as 1092 Bishop Osmund, a cousin of the Conqueror, completed a cathedral within the strong line of outer defences, where he established the new ritual *ad usum Sarum* (the Sarum Rite). In 1220 Pope Honorius III gave his consent for the building of a new cathedral in the fertile meadows where now stands the town of Salisbury. Gradually Old Sarum was abandoned, and in 1331 the old cathedral was pulled down.

The site of the Norman cathedral was concealed until excavation revealed its ground-plan. This, as originally built for Bishop Osmund, consisted of a nave with aisles, transepts, each with an eastern apse, a central tower and a short choir with narrow aisles and an apsidal termination. The ground-plan shows that in the first half of the twelfth century the church was extended eastwards with a square end containing three eastern chapels, the transepts were greatly enlarged, with aisles to both east and west and a porch to the south transept, and western towers were added to the original nave. A pulpitum or stone screen with central passageway divided the nave from the choir. North of the choir were the cloisters, and on the west side against the north transept is a twostoreyed building which may have been the vault of the chapterhouse. With the sole exception of this building nothing remains above the foundations.

Towards the end of the twelfth century changes in style became apparent as the English Byzantine style (long conveniently labelled as 'Norman') merged with the embryo Gothic. A good illustration of what was happening may be seen in the church of

St. Mary de Haura (that is, of the Haven) at New Shoreham on the Sussex coast, which, however, losts its nave in the seventeenth century, the chancel of *c.* 1175–1200 now serving as the parish church. Here the south chancel arcade has typically Norman massive compound piers, but the piers of the north arcade are alternately cylindrical and octagonal, with capitals that are no longer the old-style cushions carved with grotesques and strap-work—instead they are carved with foliage and leaf. More significantly all the arches are pointed, as are the windows of the triforium and clerestory. The windows and wall arcading in the aisles are round-headed, and the originally central tower of the church has round-headed windows in the lower stage and pointed ones in the upper. The church is also vaulted throughout. This, then, is what is traditionally known as Transitional. It was soon to open out, in the thirteenth century, into the full flower of that English version of Ile de France Gothic known as Early English.

10

The Monasteries

In the first years of Norman rule a comprehensive scheme of reorganization and reform within the English Church was introduced. The existing monastic estates were swept into the feudal system, and the monasteries were staffed with superiors from the great abbeys of Normandy. Thus the observance and culture, the architecture, liturgy and ritual of Bec, Fécamp, Jumièges and Caen were planted here. Cathedral-monasteries already existed here—they were established by Dunstan and were peculiar to this country alone—but now the system was extended, largely under the direction of Williams' great primate Lanfranc, Archbishop of Canterbury and a former monk of Bec. By the end of the twelfth century there were nine cathedral-monasteries, among them Canterbury, Worcester, Durham, Rochester and Norwich. The ruler of the monastery was the abbot (from *abba* or father) and under him was his deputy the prior, but where the monastery was also the cathedral of the diocese the bishop was nominally abbot and the actual ruler of the house was the prior, hence the designation cathedral-priories. Existing monasteries were rebuilt on a magnificent scale, and from the moment that Battle abbey appeared to mark the victory at Hastings there was a long series of new foundations. The welfare of the soul after death prompted many a baron to found a religious house, and if it was not his passport to heaven it was at least an act of piety that would be recorded in his favour.

Many of these monasteries became seats of an intense literary culture and schools of calligraphy, illumination, painting and wood-carving. The monks were self-supporting, with farmlands and granges and numerous secular offices, even holding, in the earlier period, manors and knights' lands from which men of war were supplied. They set up almonries and even, on occasions,

(*right* The keep of Rochester Castle. (*below*) The keep of Kenilworth Castle

Caernarvon Castle

Bodiam Castle, Sussex, from the south-east

infirmaries for the poor, and hostelries for all classes, and they had to provide for large numbers of pilgrims, especially where there were popular shrines. They were often schoolteachers, and they were reasonable landlords. Despite such necessary provisions for the running of what virtually became landed corporations, and despite the many external accomplishments, the life which St. Benedict had prescribed was intended solely to develop supernatural motives and supernatural virtues. Liturgical prayer, spiritual reading and manual labour were the chief instruments necessary to attain this.

Monastic life all over Europe now conformed to a single pattern and had the same regularity and rhythm. The day, based on the Roman reckoning, began at about two o'clock in the morning and ended at six in winter and eight in summer. The focal points were the six canonical hours and the night office ("Seven times a day do I praise thee, O Lord," sang the Psalmist). The monks slept in their habits and made their toilets not on rising for the night office but when they had changed into their day shoes before Terce. Shaving and bathing took place on fixed days about five times a year. The bloodletting or *minutio* which began in the interest of health became a regular relaxation (since it brought the privileges of the infirmary) which the monks underwent four or five times a year. Meals were confined to the *duo pulmentaria* (two portions) of St. Benedict—*prandium*, the chief meal, at midday and *cena* or supper, known as *collatio*, at about 5.30, though times of meals as of the offices changed with the seasons. Prior to the chapter mass the old and infirm were given extra sustenance in the form of *mixtum*, bread soaked in wine.

The business of the monastery was done in the chapter-house, where there was also a daily Chapter which usually consisted of the *pretiosa*, martyrology, necrology, sermon and *clamationes* or complaints. The officials of a large monastery were numerous, but common to all were such offices as the cellarer, infirmarian, sacristan, treasurer, librarian, chamberlain and hosteller. The cellarer had to provide wine, bread, salt, honey and incense, numerous specified pittances and all seasonings, and he had to furnish the refectory with plates and napkins. The infirmarian had to keep the entire convent in infirmary time, and he obtained and prepared all meat. The sacristan provided oil, wax and candles, kept the lamps trimmed and burning, repaired bells and ropes,

8

had the custody of altar ornaments and relics, kept the church clean and even in some places provided pittances during Lent. The treasurer was in charge of the binding of choir books and the repair of vestments and choir capes, and he had the custody of the plate and the treasury key, while he sometimes served a common pittance on feast days.

Church and domestic buildings were grouped about a cloister, a well of light and fresh air with arcaded walks for exercise, and the prototype must have been one of the angular sheltering wall structures of the deserts, such a monastery perhaps as that of Qalaat Seman in Syria. Adjoining the church, in the eastern range, were the chapter-house and parlour, in the southern range were the refectory and kitchens, and on the upper storey of the western range was the dormitory, with the calefactory or warming-house, the common room as it were, beneath it. This was, more or less, the traditional plan, with deviations due either to the terrain or to special characteristics of later Orders. Like the castle, the form of the monastery grew out of its function, but its plan was early standardized and, basically, it never changed.

Since the destruction of the monasteries at the Reformation few Benedictine houses remain on such a scale as to convey an adequate picture of the religious and domestic arrangements. The complete layout, in essentials at least, can in fact be identified only in some of the cathedral-monasteries, where it was expedient to retain many of the buildings. Such are Durham, Canterbury, Gloucester, Chester and Westminster Abbey (the last three being elevated to cathedral status after the Suppression). Let us look at Durham as a typical Benedictine abbey of the late Norman period. The church was built in 1093-6 by the Norman Bishop William of St. Carileph, formerly abbot of St. Vincent in France, the previous church on the site being demolished. It is cruciform, with western and central (later) towers and a western narthex, an aisled nave with a clerestory of round-headed two-lights and a triforium of round-headed four-lights, the whole vaulted. Everywhere are massive cylindrical and compound piers, with much ornament, chevron, lozenge, cable, billet and the rest, the whole neither grotesque nor elaborate, but solid, powerful and of an impressive homogenity, and the nearest English equivalent to such great French Romanesque basilicas as St. Benoit-sur-Loire and Vezelay.

The transepts, following Benedictine custom, are aisled on their eastern sides to provide chapels (altogether there were thirty altars in the church). The choir, which contained the monks' stalls, usually occupied the crossing of the transepts beneath the central tower, but here, as at Canterbury, it is east of the crossing, so that the pulpitum or stone screen dividing nave from choir lay between the eastern tower-piers, the rood-screen between the western piers. The laity were admitted only to the nave and there is still a line of blue marble across the church floor from north to south, eastward of which no woman was allowed to pass—Durham seems to have been a stronghold of misogynism. Built against the west end of the church is the celebrated but curious Galilee chapel, for it is virtually not a Galilee at all and has no western entrance because of its position on the edge of a precipitous cliff. Shortly before 1200 Hugh de Pudsey, who built the great hall of the castle, began to build a Lady Chapel in the normal position at the east end of the church, but because the foundations proved to be insecure he was compelled to abandon it and, instead, build it at the west end. It consists of five aisles of four arcades each, the round arches cut with chevron-work, supported by shafts of Purbeck marble and sandstone. The whole has a decided affinity with a Moorish mosque, and its crowning glory is the tomb of the gentle Bede covered with a plain slab.

What was eventually built at the east end, in 1242, was the unique elongated transept spreading across on a north and south axis. It was, however, not quite unique, for it was copied from that at the Cistercian abbey of Fountains, then on the verge of completion. Until this time the eastern arm had terminated in three apses, with the shrine of St. Cuthbert in the central apse behind the high altar. The new wide-spreading transept afforded space for nine chapels and served as an ambulatory and processional path round St. Cuthbert's shrine, which was moved a little eastward and elevated on a high platform. This, of course, is not characteristic of Benedictine churches, which were usually square-headed, though local requirements, often determined by feretories or shrines, led to variations. Westminster has an eastern chevet of chapels with a Lady Chapel projecting from the centre, and Tewkesbury still has five polygonal chapels though its projecting Lady Chapel has gone. Such developments largely belong to the thirteenth century.

A later work at Durham is the screen or reredos to the high altar, known as the Neville Screen from its having been commissioned by John, Lord Neville to mark the victory over the Scots at Neville's Cross. It was made in 1379, in London, and is attributed to the great architect Henry Yevele, and it is of elaborate Perpendicular style with spires of open-work, canopies and gablets and side doorways, though the statuary is missing. This rich tabernacle-work is reflected in Bishop Hatfield's chantry chapel of much the same date.

From the church two doorways lead into the cloisters (*claustrum*) and the central garth enclosed by four ranges of domestic buildings. Often the cloisters were open shafted arcades, but often too, especially in later buildings, they were closed in with windows, as here. They were rebuilt from 1390 and are of Perpendicular style. Taking the north walk alongside the church we see that this cloister was allocated to study, for it is recessed into thirty carrels (*carols* or enclosed spaces) or three to each window. Originally each one was wainscoted and entered by a door, and each was ceiled at window transom level. The finest series of carrels is that in the cloisters of Gloucester Cathedral. Against the church wall of this walk there would have been book cupboards (*ammaria*).

Taking the east range there is, next to the church, a vaulted passage which was used as the parlour (*locutorium*), where the rule of silence was relaxed and the monks made conversation. Next to this is the chapter-house (*domus capitularis*) with large windows flanking the entrance, all in Norman moulded arched heads. Here every day after prime the convent assembled for the confession and correction of faults, discussion of monastery business and the reading of a chapter (*capitulum*) of the rule. The prior and his chief officers sat at a table at the east end and the convent sat on stone benches round the walls. The bodies of dead monks rested here and offices were sung for them before they took their last journey through the parlour to the graveyard, but in earlier years bishops and priors were buried here. The building was normally oblong, unaisled and vaulted, but here it is apsidal, with wall arcading. It was originally one of the finest Norman chapter-houses in the kingdom, some 77 feet long and paved with the slabs and brasses of many bishops and priors, but at the close of the eighteenth century it was barbarously mutilated to make a comfortable room for Georgian clerics, though it has since been restored to a reasonable condition. Fine Norman chapter-houses remain at Bristol, a splendid chamber of two bays richly decorated with wall arcading, Much Wenlock and Worcester, where it is circular and a central pillar carries the vault (Worcester's chapter-house stands at the beginning of a uniquely English development, the polygonal chapter-house, which culminates in the magnificent examples at Lincoln, Salisbury, Westminster, Wells and York). Adjoining the chapter-house here at Durham, at the end of the east walk, is another slype or vaulted entry passage into the outer court.

The south range is largely taken up by the frater or dining-hall (*refectorium*), raised upon an undercroft or cellar and parallel with the cloister. Projecting from this cloister into the garth was originally a great octagonal washing-place (*lavatorium*), now lost. This was a chapel-like conduit, the interior built of marble, with spouts of brass from which the water flowed, the whole surmounted by a dovecote. There was a similar one at Much Wenlock and a hexagonal one in the middle of the garth at Sherborne; both have vanished. There is a circular one at Mellifont in Ireland, and a laver house still stands in the infirmary cloister at Canterbury, but such fountains are more common on the Continent (Valmagne in France, Maulbronn in Germany, Poblet in Spain, Batalha in Portugal). More normal in England was the washing trough recessed in the cloister wall, as at Gloucester, Worcester and Norwich. The frater is a large aisle-less hall with a timber roof. Near the high table, on the wall opposite the cloister, was the pulpit from which some edifying homily was read by one of the brethren during meals. This was usually of stone, perhaps corbelled out of a window recess and entered by a stair as at Chester. A stair leads up through the frater doorway to the west end of the hall, which was screened off to form a passage to the kitchen at the back.

The kitchen (*coquina*) is an engaged building on a square plan, with fireplaces in the angles, the arches of which support an octagonal superstructure and vaulted roof, the smoke being conveyed through the flues to a central louvre. Designed in 1366 by John Lewyn, who designed the cloisters and the great hall of the castle, it is still in perfect condition. The vaulting is quite remarkable, and it has been remarked that it reproduces almost exactly (though doubtless unconsciously) the forms of Persian brick vaults of some centuries earlier. The only comparable kitchen still standing in England is that at Glastonbury. This is of early fifteenth-century date and thus of Perpendicular architecture, rectangular, with an octagonal roof surmounted by a pretty louvre or lantern with mullioned windows. There were others at Christ Church, Canterbury and Ely, and a fragment of an octagonal kitchen remains at Furness. The most celebrated of all such monastic kitchens is that of the abbey of Fontrevault in France (where lie two Plantagenet kings of England), the sole survivor of a group of some half-dozen such kitchens in the Loire district.

The west claustral range is wholly given over to the dorter or dormitory (*dormitorium*) with the warming-house and other offices beneath it. Originally this was in the normal position in the eastern range, but it was transferred here in 1398. The dorter occupies the entire upper floor and overlaps the end of the south range. It is reached by a stair in the cloister, close to the church, which served for both day and night use (there was often a night stair directly leading from the dorter into the church, used for the night office). The dorter is lighted by traceried windows and retains its oak-timbered roof. It was partitioned into forty little wooden cells, though there is now, of course, no sign of these. The south end was allocated to the novices. Connected with it to westward was the rere-dorter or lavatories (*domus necessarium*). The aisled and vaulted undercroft of the dorter was the common-room or warming-house (*calefactorium*), the only place where a fireplace was allowed other than the kitchen. *The Rites of Durham* tells us that once a year it was the scene of a conventual feast. "Within this house did the master thereof keep his O Sapientia once a year, namely between Martinmas and Christmas, a solemn banquet that the prior and convent did use at that time of the year only, when their banquet was of figs and raisins, cakes and ale; and thereof no superfluity or excess, but a scholastical and moderate congratulation amongst themselves." The northern-most bay of the undercroft, however, was walled off to contain the treasury and muniment room. Near the south end of the range is a passage which led through the range to the infirmary on the west between the monastery and the river, while the bays beyond the passage contained the cellar and buttery and communicated with the kitchen and cellarer's office at the west end of the south range.

When the dorter was transferred from the east range, part of

that range was altered for different purposes, mainly for the building of the prior's lodging with hall, solar and guest chambers.
Much of this is embodied in the present deanery and cannot
readily be identified. Well-preserved examples of a prior's
lodging can be seen at Much Wenlock, with its thirty or more
Perpendicular windows lighting each floor, at Ely, Castle Acre
and Westminster Abbey, where the fourteenth-century apartments are grouped about a courtyard. Beyond this, on the east
side of the curia or inner court, stood the gatehouse, which at
Durham is still intact. Splendid monastic gatehouses survive at
Bury St. Edmunds, St. Albans, Worksop and elsewhere. The
guest-house (*hospitium*) also stood near the gatehouse, and normally consisted of an aisled hall, central fireplaces and separate
chambers or lodgings. The monastic infirmary (*infirmatorium*) on
the west would have comprised the large rectangular hall for the
beds, chapel, misericord or flesh-frater, kitchen and rere-dorter.
Remains of such Benedictine infirmaries can be seen at Worcester,
Gloucester, Canterbury and Peterborough.

Benedictine monastic churches still in use, wholly or in part,
are fairly numerous. In addition to the cathedral-priory churches
and those refounded as cathedrals by Henry VIII (and St. Albans,
raised to cathedral rank in 1877), there are complete churches now
serving parochial purposes at Great Malvern, Romsey, Sherborne
and Tewkesbury. Among Benedictine churches which have survived in part and have been adapted as parish churches are
Dunster, Hurley, Leominster, Malmesbury, Milton Abbas,
Pershore and Tutbury. At Pershore there remains only the
fourteenth-century presbytery, but this is the very essence of
English Gothic in its first impulse, austere and pure, the graceful
balance of shafts and vaulting having an effective unity of design
from floor to roof.

Few Benedictine churches that lie in ruins have much to show,
but there are some notable exceptions. Lindisfarne still has its
short choir, north transept, north nave arcade and aisle and walling
of the nave, all Norman. Whitby has the shell of the aisled choir,
the north transept and walling of the nave, all thirteenth to
fourteenth-century. Of the great church of Glastonbury there are
only the two eastern piers at the crossing and some fragments of
the choir and aisles. The main features here, however, are the
ornate Lady Chapel, its doorways loaded with Romanesque or

Byzantine ornament, and the Early English Galilee (the abbey kitchen has already been noticed). At St. Mary's, York, there is part of the west front, the north wall of the nave and fragments of the north transept, but these are richly ornamented and fenestrated in Decorated style; also surviving here are the gatehouse and *hospitium*. Tynemouth priory on its sea-girt cliff where the monks froze in damp and wind has fairly substantial remains with its enriched stone rood-screen *in situ*, a feature also to be seen at Croyland of St. Guthlac and the triangular bridge. Of Evesham's great abbey church which had 164 gilded pillars nothing remains beyond a stately detached bell-tower, with Perpendicular panelling and crockets and an air of panache. Perhaps the best example of conventual buildings in a ruined state is that of Finchale priory in Durham, that haunt of St. Godric and other hermits beside the Wear, with remains of the east and south claustral ranges and of the ample prior's lodging.

Following hard on the heels of the Norman Benedictines were the monks of the Cluniac Order, based on their great abbey of Cluny, which had the largest Romanesque church in Europe. Though they introduced a more sophisticated architecture into England they added nothing of permanence or significance to English monastic life. Little but the excavated ground plan remains of their chief English house at Lewes. At Castle Acre, however, the substantial remains include an intact gatehouse and a church façade overlaid with wall arcading, and at Much Wenlock there are some splendid survivals (including the prior's lodging mentioned above) partly embodied in a private house.

The first call to a life more eremitical and austere than the Benedictine appeared in Italy with the institutes of Camaldoli and Vallombrosa. These Orders had little influence west of the Alps and none at all in England, but the movement towards a stricter simpler faith with varying interpretations of the Rule of St. Benedict was felt and developed in France. The Carthusians, founded in 1084 by St. Bruno, held a unique place, a *ne plus ultra*, in medieval—and later—monastic life. Of their nine English houses, six were founded as late as the fourteenth century and the last in 1414, and they will be dealt with in another chapter. The orders of Tiron, Savigny and Citeaux came into existence about the same time. Tiron and Savigny sent colonies to England before Citeaux (the abbeys of Buildwas, Byland and Furness were originally Savigniac), but since their characteristics were similar to those of Citeaux, and since, moreover, their houses were shortly absorbed by the greater Cistercian Order, they may summarily be dismissed.

It was on Palm Sunday in 1098 that a group of Benedictines led by St. Robert left Molesmes to make a foundation in the swamps and thickets of Burgundy. This attempt to follow a more literal observance of the Rule was not immediately associated with the birth of a new order, but further dissensions at Molesmes, to which St. Robert was recalled, created a wider rift, and an isolated experiment soon developed into the new and powerful Cistercian Order. The initiation was largely due to St. Robert's successors at Citeaux, St. Alberic and the English St. Stephen Harding. Soon the *Carta Caritatis* and other documents were compiled to uphold the principles of the new foundation. The man virtually responsible for its survival was St. Bernard of Clairvaux, who at the head of thirty companions arrived at Citeaux in 1112.

Bernard abhorred the Order of Cluny and its champions Peter the Venerable and Abelard (not a monk, though he died under the wing of Cluny), and he delivered a fierce tirade against Cluniac luxury. He referred scornfully to candelabra like "veritable trees of bronze", and concerning Cluniac sculpture he asked, "Of what use are these ridiculous monsters, these ferocious lions, centaurs, tigers and soldiers, in places where monks devote themselves to study?" This summed up his ideas on architecture and decoration, and the logical extension was the prohibition of stained glass, painting and richly carved capitals. This austerity was now extended even to the choir. Altar cloths were to be of linen, crucifixes of wood, and all ornaments of base metals. Certain vestments were completely abolished. Church services were simplified, not only to avoid ostentation but possibly also in order to place more emphasis on manual labour, which included a great deal of manuscript illumination but which later came to be interpreted as agricultural work. A habit of undyed wool, which later became as white, was adopted in contradistinction to the 'black' Benedictine and as a symbol of a new life. The monks slept in their habits on hard pallettes, rose at one or two o'clock in the morning, and lived for the greater part of the year on one meal a day, renouncing the pleasures of flesh, meat, fish, eggs, milk and white bread. They observed an almost perpetual silence and spent many hours in prayer. They hoed and planted and reaped and garnered in the fields, in harvest time keeping their rakes and pitchforks by their bedside instead of returning them to the common store. Finally, the most revolutionary changes were in the constitutional framework and the introduction of *conversi* or lay-brothers, who by performing the greater share of menial work safeguarded the seclusion of the monks.

The first flush of Cistercian austerity in all its primal simplicity can be seen in the Burgundian Romanesque churches of Senanque, Le Thoronet, Silvacane and Fontenay, with such features as arcades of unmoulded pointed arches, clerestories, square-headed east ends, pointed barrel vaults and a complete lack of ornament. These are reflected in the earliest English foundations, and indeed the entire introduction and early evolution of the Gothic style in England, even to the dissemination of vaulting systems, is closely linked up with the Cistercians. Thus while there is no such thing as Benedictine architecture one may legitimately speak of a Cistercian architecture. Incidentally, it may be held that, in general, Anglo-Norman monasteries were the work of imported craftsmen, that the early Cistercian abbeys were built by Burgundian masons, and that native masons came into their own during the Gothic centuries.

Cistercian monks made their first appearance in England at Waverley in Surrey in 1128, but their first major and significant abbeys appeared in the North in 1131, with Rievaulx directly colonized from Clairvaux under the patronage of Walter L'Espec of Helmsley Castle, and Fountains a year later. This Yorkshire country with its abundant water supply and grazing land for vast flocks of sheep was to receive many more foundations of the white monks, and because of their remoteness their ruins have survived in a much more complete state of preservation than those of other orders. Let us look at Rievaulx as being typical in its essentials of a Cistercian monastery, though it was one of the largest abbeys in the country, with 140 monks and 500 lay brothers in 1186 (but only twenty-one monks when it was suppressed).

Rievaulx's dramatic cliffs and gullies of stone lie on the banks of the little Rye river in Ryedale, though the water supply was

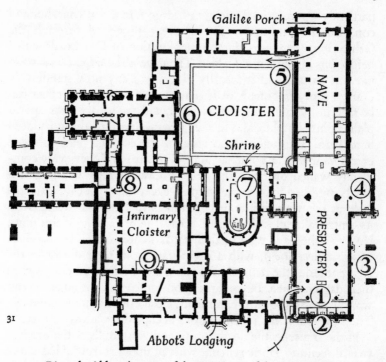

Rievaulx Abbey (*courtesy of the Department of the Environment*)
Numbers refer to: 1 High Altar, 2 east window, 3 flying buttress, 4 north
transept, 5 cloister, 6 refectory door, 7 first abbot's shrine, 8 main drain, and
9 infirmary cloister doorway

not taken from the river but from springs on the hillside. The
water was brought to a conduit house near the west end of the
church and thence distributed in pipes to the different buildings.
It also flowed in a stone-built channel under the frater to the
rere-dorter, and thence to the river. Due to the terrain, the
monastic church lies nearly due north and south instead of east
and west, but for convenience we shall describe the buildings as
if they had the normal orientation. Apart from the choir and
presbytery, the church and all the essential buildings were completed by *c.* 1166, and it will be seen that, due to several factors,
not least of which was the large body of lay brothers, the arrangements of church and domestic buildings differ in some respects
from those of the Benedictines.

The church is entered through the Galilee, a low western

narthex or porch characteristic of large Cistercian churches and common in Burgundy. The convent processed through the Galilee into the church in commemoration of Our Lord's entry before His disciples into Galilee. The nave is the largest Cistercian nave in Britain and is actually older than any now standing in France. Only fragments of it remain, but the original effect can be seen in the transepts. It was aisled, and the square piers carried plain pointed arches, the first in Britain and directly introduced here from Burgundy. The aisles were covered with pointed barrel vaults, as at Fontenay and Fountains, and they were completely walled off from the nave, a Cistercian peculiarity, each bay being filled in from pier to pier, except the first bay, immediately at the west end, and the ninth bay. The rood-screen with its central altar closed the nave across the beginning of this ninth bay, and the nave west of this was the choir of the lay brothers (*chorus conversorum*), with a night-stair from their dorter in the adjacent aisle; the *conversi* used the west processional doorway as their day entrance. Beyond the rood-screen and the adjacent bay was the crossing over the transepts, closed by the stone pulpitum. The retro-choir for infirm monks occupied the crossing area.

In the transepts the north, south and west walls of the original twelfth-century fabric remain, with an upper storey added in the thirteenth century, and in the south transept is a doorway leading to the dormitory for use at the night office. The eastern walls of the transepts, each with an aisle and two chapels, belong to the thirteenth-century rebuilding, as does the whole of the long ritual eastern arm of the church from the pulpitum. The primal austerity of the Cistercians lasted barely a century. The first church extended only two bays east of the tower, but about 1230 it was enlarged by the addition of the splendid aisled choir and presbytery of seven bays, still standing but lacking the stone ribbed vaults. The remains of the pulpitum with its central entrance still stand under the eastern arch of the lost tower. Beyond it is the monastic choir, and beyond that the presbytery and the high altar, the whole originally enclosed by stone screens or plain walling to the full height of the church, the Cistercian custom. The square east end contains the remains of five altars aligned in a straight line.

All these additions are in Early English Gothic. The columns or piers are compound, with sixteen shafts. An elaborate gallery intervenes between arcade and clerestory, with, mostly, two-pointed openings for each bay under a super arch, with quatre-foils in the spandrels. The new windows are lancets, and the ter-minating east wall has two tiers of them. Ornament is largely confined to nailhead.

A doorway just below the south transept leads into the cloisters. The cloister walks had open arcades of round-headed arches on twin shafts. These have completely vanished, but from fragments found on the site one corner has been reconstructed, the capitals having waterleaf and leaf crockets of the late twelfth century. Taking the east claustral range, the first feature to be noticed is the book cupboard in a square-headed recess in the wall of the south transept. At the sound end of the transept is a narrow tunnel-vaulted chamber, of which the western end held the monastic library and the eastern end a vestry, over which was the original sacristy, entered from the east chapels of the transept. Next comes the chapter-house, though there are little more than foundations. This, however, differs in plan from the normal Cistercian chapter-house, which was rectangular and divided into three spans by columns and arches. Here it is oblong and apsidal and is, or was, aisled all round except for a vestibule inside the entrance. There is evidence of several alterations, and it is clear that the east end was originally intended to be square. In the fifteenth century it was reduced in size, the aisle running round the apse was pulled down and the arcade of the apse walled in and buttressed. The walls show shafts with scalloped capitals, indicating that the aisle and ambulatory were vaulted, though the central area must have had a wooden ceiling. (Cistercian vaulted chapter-houses can be seen at Kirkstall, Buildwas, Valle Crucis and elsewhere.)

There are several grave slabs of medieval abbots, but the most unusual feature is the thirteenth-century shrine of St. William, first abbot of Rievaulx, who died in 1148. A monk of Clairvaux, he was at one time secretary to St. Bernard, and he led St. Bernard's mission into Yorkshire and subsequently founded the monastery. No memorial remains of his more celebrated succes-sor, St. Ailred, abbot from 1147 to 1166. Perhaps the most attrac-tive of all English Cistercians, his life was written by his friend Walter Daniel.

Next to the chapter-house is the passage-like parlour with transverse arches and rib-vaulting. Next to this was the daystair to the dormitory, of which a few of the lower steps remain.

Beneath the stair is the barrel-vaulted treasury. Then comes a narrow passage leading through the range to the infirmary buildings to the east, and adjoining it and entered from it is the warming house, a spacious undercroft with an arcade down the middle and two fireplaces. When the later warming house was built this was probably used as a day room for the novices. Above the whole of this east range was the monks' dorter, of which only part of the walls remain, and at the rear of its southern end was the reredorter, forming part of the south range of the infirmary cloister. At the southern end of this east range and on a lower level was a building which was allocated to the novices' quarters, with an undercroft having an arcade of square pillars down its middle. There are indications that the dorter once extended over the entire range, an enormous length, which would have made the end novices' building three-storeyed.

Now the south claustral range, almost wholly rebuilt early in the thirteenth century. First, the new warming house with a blocked-up aisle and a large fireplace. Here a fire was lit on 1st November, All Saints' Day, and kept burning until Easter. The day stair to the dorter adjoins it on the east, superseding the original day stair in the east range. Then the handsome large refectory. This is placed at right-angles to the cloister, the common Cistercian position as opposed to the Benedictine custom of placing it parallel. It was lighted by tall double-chamfered windows set in wall arcades and had originally a high-pitched roof which was lowered in the fifteenth century. On the west side are the remains of the pulpit and of the flight of steps in the wall to reach it. Beneath the pulpit can be seen a newel stair leading to the vaulted undercroft below. On either side of the refectory entrance is the recessed lavatorium for hand-washing before meals, set in a wall arcade of which most of the arches remain though their shafts are missing. The kitchen adjoins on the west, but apart from the south fireplace and the site of the central hearth, as well as parts of the serving hatches, very little remains. The Cistercian kitchen was so disposed as to serve both the adjoining monks' frater and the frater of the lay brothers on the other side, that is, at the southern end of the west claustral range.

The west range (*domus conversorum*) was wholly allocated to the *conversi* or lay brethren. It is of late twelfth-century date, and being reduced to the lower storey contains few features of interest.

It was not vaulted. The door into the church, by which the lay brothers entered remains at its northern end and must have opened to a wooden stair leading to their dormitory on the first floor. The range is so small that one cannot understand how the 500 brothers were accommodated. The disappearance of the *conversi* from Cistercian houses in the fourteenth century—due to several factors, chief among them being the prevalence of the great plague known as the Black Death which struck in 1349—brought about everywhere the dismantling or remodelling of the west range. Here it was used mainly for storehouses (at Hailes and Ford it was converted into the abbot's lodging).

The loss of the *conversi* also had its repercussions in the church, where the lay brother's choir and its screen walling were removed, and chapels with wooden screens were fitted up in the eastern bays of the aisles. These chapels retain much of their tiled pavements and steps and their floor drains, and the altars are unusually perfect (two of them, when discovered during the clearing of the nave in 1919, still contained the relics which had been sealed in their masonry at their consecration).

There remains the complex of infirmary buildings beyond the east range, accessible by the passage in the south-east corner of the cloisters. The infirmary, little different from the Benedictine model, had its own cloister. The walks are missing but, again, a small section of the original open-shafted arcade has been reconstructed. The south range contains the rere-dorter already referred to, and here a windowless wall stands to its full height. In the east range is the infirmary itself with an aisle of round piers having scalloped capitals and large round-headed windows. It extended well to the north, towards the east end of the church. The plan here is not clear, for early in the sixteenth century when abbots waxed worldly and lived in state the infirmary was converted into the abbot's lodging (the same thing happened at Furness), when it was remodelled as a two-storeyed building with a screened hall and buttery at the south end and a solar and chambers on the north. The Norman windows were enlarged with mullions, and an elaborate entrance with a carving of the Annunciation was created, approached by a flight of steps from the infirmary cloister.

There is hardly anything remaining of the abbey gatehouse, but the *capella ad portas* (chapel at the gate) for the use of persons not allowed within the great gateway, has become the parish church, mainly thirteenth-century, with a Victorian chancel and small steeple. This was fairly characteristic of Cistercian houses, and excellent examples can be seen at Merevale, Warwickshire, and Tiltey, Essex, both enlarged as parish churches, and Kirkstead, Lincolnshire, now disused but in perfect condition.

The foregoing is perhaps a somewhat laborious account, but it does give some idea of the scale and complexity of a great Cistercian monastery. We may single out individual features in other Cistercian abbeys. At Fountains or 'Fontes', where the domestic buildings are in an even finer state of preservation than at Rievaulx (due, perhaps, to the landscaping of the park by the genteel William Aislaby), even to the perfect standing tower of Abbot Marmaduke Huby, we might notice the western range since it is a perfect example of the *domus conversorum*. The sub-vault or undercroft is 300 feet long and of twenty-two bays, divided by columns into two alleys with vaulting springing from the piers. The two bays next the church were probably the earlier outer parlour. The cellar occupied the next four bays and the buttery the next two. Then comes the entrance passage of two bays. The remainder was taken up by the lay brothers' refectory, The day-stair to the dorter is on the west face of the range. The whole of the upper storey is occupied by the dorter, with the night-stair descending into the church. The range projects over the stream, with an engaged range containing the latrines to the west.

Another great Yorkshire abbey, Kirkstall on the edge of Leeds, has much to show, including a chapter-house with a six-arched façade, two doorways and two windows either side, an almost perfect church nave—early, unaltered and aisleless—and a kitchen where the fireplaces for monks and *conversi* stand back to back. Well preserved too is Tintern Abbey with its great cross-church beside the Wye river, the occasion if not exactly the subject of Wordsworth's "Lines composed above Tintern Abbey." The church is of late thirteenth-century Decorated work, and the great windows of west front and north transept have retained almost the whole of their tracery. There are here some peculiarities in the conventual arrangements. The calefactory has for its fireplace a central hearth surrounded by open arches and connected by smaller arches with the end walls.

The most perfectly preserved and roofed claustral ranges of a

An aerial view of Beaumaris Castle

(*above*) The roof of the Prior's Kitchen, Durham Cathedral. (*below*) The Abbot's Kitchen, Glastonbury Abbey, Somerset

Cistercian abbey of modest size are to be found at Cleeve on the edge of the Quantocks in Somerset, "compact and functional as a last year's bird's nest", as Sylvia Townsend Warner has remarked. It was founded in 1198 by William de Romare, nephew of the Earl of Lincoln, who in the time of Richard I gave his lands at Cleeve to the abbot and convent of Revesby, Lincolnshire, in trust to found a Cistercian monastery. The church and the cloister walks have vanished but the three domestic ranges are intact. The east range has the sacristy with a rose window at the far end, then the library passage, then the chapter-house, vaulted, with a two-light window flanking the arched entrance, then the day-stair to the dorter, then the slype with wall recesses, and finally the parlour. Above is the dorter projecting beyond the south range and lighted by single lancets, with seats in the embrasures, and at the north end is the doorway for the night-stair (missing) into the church.

The south range is almost wholly occupied by the splendid refectory and its undercroft. The refectory departs from Cistercian custom in being placed at right-angles to the cloister, having been rebuilt in this position in the fifteenth century when the absence of lay brothers led to a more convenient remodelling. The same thing happened at Whalley, Lancashire, in 1425, but there are indications that at Fountains, Kirkstall and Tintern the frater was originally set out on this east-to-west axis, as it certainly was at Waverley, the first English house of the order. The floor of the original Cleeve frater, parallel with the cloister, may be seen at the rear. The new refectory, over the original thirteenth-century undercroft, is lighted by handsome Perpendicular windows, and the carved timber roof is intact. On the east wall is a painted rood where the abbots table would have been, and there are other mural paintings on the west. Near the stair to the refectory is the recess for the washing trough. The calefactory or warming house is at the east end of the range, in the lower storey.

On the west is the *domus conversorum*, with the lay brothers' dorter above and their refectory below, but there are more fifteenth-century alterations here when the range was adapted to other purposes. Only a fragment of the outer gatehouse remains, but the inner gatehouse is almost perfect, a thirteenth- to fourteenth-century work with later additions.

We have seen that later Cistercian churches were rebuilt with

9

aisled presbyteries and ranges of eastern chapels for the greater
celebration of the liturgy and the facilitating of processions. Special
Cistercian models were provided by the rebuildings of Clairvaux
(1174) and Citeaux (1193). At Clairvaux an apse took the place
of the rectangular presbytery, the eastern walls of the chapels
next the presbytery were removed, and these chapels were continued round the apse as a processional path, out of which opened
a series of chapels, one from each bay and screened off by walls.
The plan of Citeaux was simply a rectangular version of that of
Clairvaux. Of the Clairvaux plan the only known English
example is, or was, the church of Beaulieu in Hampshire, which
was almost an exact copy. Beaulieu was founded in 1204 by
King John in expiation of his persecution of the Cistercians, and
today its refectory, perfectly preserved even to its beautiful stone
reader's pulpit, is the parish church.

The Citeaux plan in a modified form was more general. It is
well seen at Abbey Dore in Hereford, where the ambulatory has
a processional path and an eastern arm containing five chapels,
originally divided from each other by perpeyn walls. This choir
with its transepts (the nave is lost) is Early English Gothic at its
best with an admirable purity and economy of line. It is now the
parish church. The Citeaux plan was also followed in the earlier
church at Hailes, Gloucestershire, before the eastern arm was
extended to include the chapel and shrine of the Holy Blood.
The abbey was founded by Richard son of King John, the founder
of Beaulieu, and it was colonized from Beaulieu, so that the
Beaulieu church was virtually reproduced. After a fire in 1271,
however, the choir arm was rebuilt with the typical French
chevet that had developed from the apse-and-ambulatory construction, and here it had a five-sided apse and ambulatory with
five polygonal chapels. Croxden Abbey, Staffordshire, also had a
church with a *chevet*, a copy of that at Aunay, the mother house
in France. Another was at Vale Royal, Cheshire, founded by
Edward II in 1277 and rebuilt in 1359 at the instance of the Black
Prince, when the *chevet* had no less than seven radiating polygonal
chapels. Unfortunately little but foundations remain of all these
eastern arrangements, but the type can be studied in such Benedictine churches as Westminster, Canterbury and Tewkesbury.
Incidentally, symbolists saw in the *chevet* a representation of the
Crown of Thorns.

Of new growths during the early monastic years the most notable were the communities of canons or regular clergy. Bodies of canons regular lived a quasi-monastic life based on a rule modelled on an instruction of St. Augustine of Hippo. They had neither the limitations nor the rigours of the purely monastic orders. For all their vows they were in close touch with the outside world and were virtually administrators of parishes. They retained the rights of private property and did not have to resort to a common library or store. They were thus highly successful both on the Continent and in England. Augustian arrangements can best be studied in the cathedrals of Bristol, Carlisle and Christ Church, Oxford. Important churches of the order surviving almost in their entirety are Brinkburn, Dorchester (Oxfordshire); Cartmel and Christchurch (Hampshire); while substantial portions of the church survive at Bolton (Yorkshire), Dunstable, Lanercost, Llanthony, St. Bartholomew's, Smithfield (with a pure Norman choir, Lady chapel and transepts) and Hexham (where the night-stair from the dorter is perfect). The ruins of Haughmond and Lilleshall, both in Shropshire, have much to show and indicate that the claustral buildings were, like the churches, largely influenced by Benedictine planning. At Haughmond, where the church has completely vanished, the east claustral range is almost intact, and there is a complete infirmary hall, kitchen and abbot's lodging. The fortified gatehouse of Thornton (Lincolnshire), perfectly intact, is remarkable for its barbican and portcullises. The Augustinian nunnery of Lacock (Wiltshire) is unique in that all the claustral ranges are perfectly preserved even to their roofs, though these are embodied in a private house.

In many ways the most attractive body of canons, since it comprised between the Augustinians and the strictly monastic orders, was that known as Prémonstratensians or Norbertines. This was founded *c.* 1120 by St. Norbert, a native of the Rhineland and a friend of St. Bernard, at Prémontré near Laon. These canons wore white habits, and while they largely followed the Augustinian rule their constitutions showed a tendency to follow Cistercian models. Their architecture too was influenced by the Cistercians, and indeed for a short time they authorized the latter to make visitations on their houses, an arrangement which soon terminated because of differences of opinion. The order was slow to reach England, where it ultimately had thirty-one houses,

mostly colonized from Newstead and Welbeck, but it came to
have over 600 houses in Europe. Planning of church and conventual buildings more or less followed those of Cistercian houses.

The only Prémonstratensian church now in use (as a parish
church) is Blanchland, Northumberland, though this consists only
of the choir and north transept. There are substantial remains at
Bayham, Sussex; Beeleigh, Essex; Coverham and Egglestone,
both Yorkshire; and Leiston, Suffolk; but the most important
buildings are those of Easby near Richmond in the North Riding
of Yorkshire, founded by the Constable of Richmond Castle *c.*
1155. The gatehouse is intact, with round-headed outer and
inner portals and internal rib-vaults. Within the abbey precinct,
in the outer court, is the parish church of Easby, a strange juxtaposition perhaps partly explained by the fact that the vicar of
Easby was always a canon of the abbey. The abbey itself is also
strangely planned, partly because of the uneven lie of the land.
The church nave is entirely missing, but other survivals show
that the twelfth-century church resembled Fountains, with a
square-headed chancel and three eastern chapels in each transept.
The claustral buildings, largely thirteenth-century, are fairly
intact. The east range has sacristy, chapter-house, which was
vaulted and has windows bearing dog-tooth ornament, and parlour, but the dorter was not over it despite the mysterious stairway, and, in fact, an upper storey of obscure purpose was not
built until the fifteenth century. The south range is almost wholly
occupied by the refectory, lighted by a row of large windows
with much tracery, and its vaulted undercroft divided in two by
short octagonal piers. Foundations remain of the kitchen projecting from the south-west end. Because of the position of the
Swale river and the necessity for drainage from the latrines, the
dorter is over the west range, a rarity that we have seen, however,
at Durham. Below the dorter is an undercroft divided into
calefactory and cellarer's guest-hall, vaulted, and with octagonal
piers down the middle. The entire plan is complicated by the
varying ground levels. There is an ornate arched entrance, with
Norman beakhead decoration, to the dorter stair. Near it is an
Early English blank arch with trefoiled and dog-tooth decoration
that was probably part of the washing trough. A projecting west
block contains guest-halls and very well preserved garderobes or
lavatories, and there are numerous doorways and stairways

ingeniously inter-communicating with all these western elements. The entire complicated ensemble is completed by an infirmary block with hall, misericord (where monks could eat meat), kitchen, chapel and infirmarian's lodging, uniquely grouped with the abbot's lodging, to the north of the church and reached by a long passage from the north transept.

The Order of Fontrevault, which was established in 1110, had only four English priories, of which the most important was Nuneaton. These houses were bi-sexual communities served by nuns and priests who followed the Benedictine rule (all were merged with the Benedictines in the fifteenth century). The only tangible remains are those of the Nuneaton priory, which are extremely meagre. Fragments of the church with mighty crossing piers stand out from a Victorian neo-Norman restoration (as the parish church), and there are traces of the east claustral range. More rewarding are the Gilbertines, the sole order of English origin and one that never reached the Continent. Founded by St. Gilbert at Sempringham in Lincolnshire in 1131, this also provided for double houses of nuns and canons. It was an order with some intriguing facets. Like the Cistercians it held great sheep farms, and it had a ritual which seems to have been largely borrowed from the cathedral church of Lincoln. There were twenty-seven houses in England, mainly located in Lincolnshire and the east. Only the site is known of the mother house at Sempringham, where even the village has disappeared, and the only tangible remains are at Old Malton, Yorkshire, now the parish church; Watton, Yorkshire, where the entire ground plan was revealed by excavation and then covered up again; and Chicksand, Bedfordshire.

Two military orders, the Knights Templar and the Knights Hospitaller, should be noticed. Warrior monks who formed the standing army of the Crusades, they essentially departed from the principle of monastic enclosure, founded priories all over western Europe and possessed strong castles in Syria. The Templars were founded by Hugues de Payens and nine knights in 1118 for the protection of pilgrims en route to the Holy Land, and their headquarters stood in the Dome of the Rock on the site of the Templum Domini—hence their name. The institution was an outcrop of the feudal system and was not popular in England (see Sir Walter Scott's *Ivanhoe*). Their rule was based upon the

Cistercian *Carta Caritatis*. They took the usual vows, were
allowed to kiss no woman, to hunt no animal other than the
lion, and to possess nothing but their armour and swords, with
which they wore a white girdle and a white linen mantle with an
eight-pointed red cross on the left shoulder. They amassed great
wealth, were constantly at loggerheads with their rivals the
Knights Hospitaller and were abruptly and violently disbanded
in 1312. They were accused of a form of idolatry identical with
that of the Gnostic sect known as Ophites or worshippers of the
serpent, and despite the scepticism of such scholars as Dean Milman
(in his *History of Latin Christianity*) carved serpents are uncomfort-
ably present in some of their churches.

Their churches differed in one important respect from those
of other orders in having a circular nave, sometimes called a
'round', attached to the choir, a form adopted in imitation of the
Temple in Jerusalem. It is extraordinary that in nearly every one
of the order's score of houses in England this 'round' has been
demolished, though in places the foundations may be seen. The
finest surviving example is the Temple Church in London, which
was consecrated in 1185 by Heraclius, the Patriarch of Jerusalem,
in the presence of Henry II. Here the 'round' has an encircling
aisle with an arcade of six clustered piers of Purbeck marble that
carry the clerestory wall, and the west entrance is enclosed by a
porch of 1195, open on three sides, the whole an excellent example
of Transitional architecture. Early in the thirteenth century the
choir was pulled down and an Early English rectangular choir
was built, with north and south aisles to the height of the choir
and quadripartite vaulting springing from the capitals of the
clustered piers.

At the Templars' preceptory of Temple Balsall in Warwickshire the chapel, now the parish church, has no 'round' but is a
wide aisleless rectangle on an elaborate scale, of late thirteenth-
century date with Decorated enrichments and a vaulted south
porch. There is a large 'wheel' window in the western gable and
whole groups of 'wheels' in the heads of other windows, there
are corbelled heads of Templars, and the painted glass has portraits of Knights Templar and Knights Hospitaller, for, greatest
humiliation of all, all the preceptories were later handed over to
the Hospitallers. The chapel is a major ecclesiological excitement
that recalls Balliol chapel, Oxford, but how much of it is the work

of the Victorian Sir Gilbert Scott, who restored it as the chapel of the nearby hospital or almshouse? West of the church is a row of cottages which was probably part of the preceptory, for they conceal an aisled hall of thirteenth- to fourteenth-century date, of three bays, with a cross-wing of the fifteenth century having tie-beams and wind-braces.

The chief commandery of the Knights Hospitaller was the priory of St. John at Clerkenwell in London, founded about 1150, to which were attached some fifty small commanderies up and down the country. Its church consisted of a round nave with a west porch, a short unaisled apsidal choir and a crypt. The nave has vanished but the western portion of the crypt with late Norman quadripartite vaulting survives, and the original choir was replaced by a late twelfth-century rectangular triple-aisled chancel. There are no remains of domestic buildings, but south of the church is the great gatehouse of the precinct built in 1504. Of the commandery at Little Maplestead, Essex, there remains the fourteenth-century round nave of the church, and at Quenington in the Cotswolds there is the Norman gateway and a contemporary dovecote with its original potence.

11

The Medieval Village

Via - viaticum - voyage, or the way and its business; villa - villaticum - village, the vill and all its doings. In referring to the 'medieval' village we are no doubt offending the modern school of specialists in local history, but we do so since the Middle Ages were the formative period in the life of most English villages (and indeed, towns), and because we are here looking at villages in that context and noting some of the characteristic features which have survived. We are not immediately concerned with Calendars of Close Rolls, Charter Rolls and all the documents and records shelved high in the county archives, and we are not seeking out the implications of ridge and furrow, boundaries, walls and hedges, hollow-ways and the like. Nor shall we pursue the consequences of land enclosures in Tudor and early Stuart times, which brought up the break-up of medieval manorial economy and created the farmer, the copy-holder and the yeoman.

We are, in fact, still in quest of ancient stones, architectural survivals, which may be regarded as being primarily associated with villages and rural parishes. That it must be a bird's-eye view may be inferred from the fact that there are today some 11,000 parishes in England. The earliest village settlements date perhaps from the early Saxon period, but the founding of villages was still going on in the tenth and eleventh centuries and occasionally even later. It is rarely that any original buildings survive beyond church and manor house, the latter often indicated only by its moated site, though there are frequently traces of early buildings altered by mutilation or rebuilding. While a few medieval parsonages have survived, the rectory or vicarage is likely to be Georgian or Victorian with a suggestion of Trollopian affluence. Rare too is the kind of mill described by Chaucer, though later mills familiar from the paintings of Turner, Constable and David

Cox are not too uncommon. Enemy action in the last war and subsequent development have done away with medieval shops which had survived in Coventry, Shrewsbury, York and Chester, but there survives, or did until recently, such a shop in the village of North Elmham in Norfolk. In the medieval shop goods were made as well as sold, and the owners and apprentices lived in the upper storey. The building was almost invariably of wood. The shop window was fitted with two folding shutters. The lower shutter was hinged at the bottom and could be let down to form a table or counter projecting into the street for merchandise. The top shutter was hung by its upper edge and was raised to form a penthouse roof to shelter the stall, "With your hat penthouse like o'er the shop of your eyes," says Moth in *Love's Labours Lost*.

Farmsteads, perhaps the oldest form of human settlement, are often the oldest buildings in any parish, though identification is often difficult since a farm may have been rebuilt at two or three periods. The tell-tale clues are roof structure, stonework, chimneys, windows, doorcases and mouldings, and, of course, the shape of the structure. On remote uplands in the north, in Wales and on Dartmoor there are primitive and often abandoned dwelling houses which may date from the fourteenth and even the thirteenth centuries. On the lowlands where building materials are less durable it is rare to find much secular building earlier than the fifteenth century. More often farmhouses of regional type reflect the yeoman's activity in the sixteenth and seventeenth centuries, but in the remote upland areas cottages and farmhouses may well preserve living and working arrangements characteristic of an age much earlier than the actual building.

The oldest type of dwelling is the cruck-built house (to be seen on the Bayeux Tapestry) consisting of a pair of curved timbers set up in inverted V form, the timbers crossing at the apex of the triangle thus formed, so forming a fork in which the ridge-piece is fitted. The rafters and purlins are placed on the crucks, which therefore bear the entire weight of the roof, the walls themselves having no constructional relationship to the roof. The roof reached right down to the ground like the stone roofs of the ancient Irish oratories, but this type of timber building was also well distributed in Scandinavia. When Britain was extensively forested it was comparatively easy to find an oak-tree naturally bent in such a form that it was easily adapted to form a fork.

Although the Romans do not seem to have used this technique the couples of bent trees were anciently known by the Latin name of *furcae* or forks. Vitruvius, writing before the conquest of Britain, refers to this type of dwelling as primitive and obsolete. "First men erected forks," he said, "and weaving bushes between them covered the walls with mud," Among the well-known early types of cruck-house are those at Clifton, Oxfordshire, and Didbrook, Gloucestershire, but the later type is fairly common in the West Midlands, Yorkshire and Wales. The cruck may be regarded as a Gothic arch, and its place in the development of medieval English architecture, notably in the elaboration of high Gothic wooden roofs, is not yet fully assessed.

Even older in origin is the long-house, for its arrangement may derive from the Iron Age houses at Chysauster in Cornwall, each of which consisted of two apartments, a living-room and a byre for cattle. The long-house is a single long low oblong building which houses both the family and its cattle under one roof, and while there are regional variations the living-room or kitchen almost invariably adjoins the cow-house, with direct access and no more division than a partitioned 'feeding-walk' or cross-walk. There is usually a central hearth. This arrangement persists among pastoral peoples in wild and mountainous regions all over Europe, and it is still to be encountered in the highland zone of Wales,[1] Devon and Cornwall, Yorkshire, Northumberland, Cumberland and Scotland. Galen, describing the Greek peasant's house as it existed in Asia Minor in the second century A.D. speaks of "a single big room with the hearth in the middle and the cattle stalls on the right and left". Houses of a similar character are known in Yorkshire, where, however, the 'house and shippon' is more common.

Public health requirements are gradually eliminating the old long-house and many have been substantially altered, but many can be identified. There is a good example at Alwinton, the last village up the Coquet river in Northumberland, and others can be seen at Kildale and Hutton-le-Hole, both in the North Riding. Indeed the North Riding of Yorkshire, notably the areas of Ryedale and Cleveland, is rich in both cruck-houses and long-houses, which often have the additional feature, unique in

[1] See Iorwerth C. Peate, *The Welsh House* (Liverpool, 1944) on both the cruck-house and long-house.

England, of a 'witch-post'. Carved with symbols and human figures somewhat in the manner of a totem-pole, the 'witch-post' is a local and traditional safeguard against witchcraft and evil spirits, though it does serve a functional purpose since it usually stands beside the hearth or ingle-nook and supports the smoke hood. Elements of the long-house may be detected in later purely domestic buildings. The cross-walk, for example, was ultimately replaced by the screened passage-way sealing off the hall. Characteristic of Lakeland villages is the farmhouse of about 1600 or a little later in which fitted cupboards, often richly carved, form a screen with a central doorway dividing the entrance passage from the living-room. The partition or screen is traditionally called a 'heck' and the passage is known as the 'hallan'. Some are now derelict but excellent examples survive.

Among the most important and visually satisfying features of vernacular village architecture are the old tithe barns which, as in France, bear witness to the acumen of the monasteries, which farmed so much of the country. Interwoven with pastoral landscapes as in a Samuel Palmer painting, these granaries and storehouses of the earth's fruits seem pregnant with scriptural significance. For reasons not immediately apparent they are almost entirely confined to the south-west of England. The fourteenth-century barn at Bredon in Worcestershire's Avon country, 130 feet by 40 feet, is divided into nave and aisles by massive posts which support the roof principals. There are two great cart porches like transepts, and a solar room for the bailiff is approached by an external flight of steps. Even larger and almost a century earlier is the barn of Great Coxwell in Berkshire, where the monks of Beaulieu garnered and slept at harvest. This fine patriarchal building, stone-buttressed and stone-roofed, is also naved and aisled like a cathedral of timber. It has moulded doorways and two gabled projecting cart porches, and it can shelter a score of waggons. At Stanway in Gloucestershire the fourteenth-century barn stands in a superb grouping of Tudor manor and Jacobean gatehouse, medieval church and formal garden, all of golden stone. There is another at Bradford-on-Avon, already remarkable for its church of St. Aldhelm, and this has double transepts as well as projecting porches so that it too resembles a church, though internally it recalls the great single-halled dwellings of the pre-Norman and early Middle Ages, its great posts, tie-beams, windbraces and trusses showing all the principles of construction employed in later and more elaborate craftsmanship. Then there is Abbotsbury in Dorset, where the monks kept the swannery and sold quills for pens, and here the great barn has a hexagonal staircase-tower adjoining the great doorway.

There are plenty of other such barns. In Gloucestershire they still stand proudly at Ashleworth, Frocester and Calcot. In Somerset at Englishcombe, Pilton, Doulting and Preston Pluncknett. There is Enstone in Oxfordshire, Middle Littleton in Worcestershire, Tisbury in Wiltshire, St. Leonard's in Hampshire and Haseley on the Isle of Wight. Not all are now in normal use, but all belonged to monastic granges or manorial estates. There are several perfectly intact granges adapted as private houses, but Leigh Grange at Churchstow in Devon is a rare and excellent example of a derelict fifteenth-century monastic grange, and many other sites, notably Cowton Grange near Richmond, which belonged to Fountains Abbey, have recently been scientifically excavated and recorded.

The monastic grange was little more than a collection of farm buildings which served as a depot for exploitation of land at some considerable distance from the abbey, though it usually had a small oratory and common dining-room and sleeping accommodation. Initially it functioned as a demesne farm supervised by lay brethren and worked by hired labourers and artisans. Simon the cellarer had his hands full, but under the cellarer was another monastic official, the granger, who was responsible for recruiting local labour and for the harvesting of the crops. It seems that from an early date the grange became increasingly staffed and worked by a dependent peasantry, particularly among the Cistercians of Yorkshire, where economic troubles dictated a speedy transformation in the character and management of the granges. Ultimately the Cistercians acquired entire peasant families and established them on land beside the granges, and by the fourteenth century these estates were leased to laymen. A recent writer on the subject disputes the accepted isolationism of the Cistercians, at least as it concerned their estates, and argues that re-settlement rather than depopulation was frequently their purpose.[1]

Characteristic of the manor in the Middle Ages, when the pigeon was a gastronomic delicacy, was the *columbarium* or

[1] Colin Platte, *The Monastic Granges in Medieval England* (London, 1969).

pigeon-house or dovecote, the right to which was enjoyed only by the lord of the manor and the rector (a similar *droit de colombier* pertained in France). Many of these survive, of all shapes and sizes, their inner walls honeycombed with nesting recesses for hundreds of birds, with a lantern-like opening at the apex of the roof for the birds' entrance and exit. Originally there would be, inside, a potence or central revolving post with two horizontal arms projecting from top and bottom, against which a ladder could be set to provide easy access to the nests.

In Cotswold villages they are invariably of stone and usually square and gabled, with high-pitched stone roofs and little cupolas for the passage of the birds, as at Naunton and Withington. Warwickshire villages have some grand early specimens. At Kinwarton is one dating from 1360, of stone, round with conical roof and an ogee-head doorway. It has a circumference of 75 feet and contains 600 nesting holes, reached from a ladder attached to a central rotating beam. At Hilborough (Shakespeare's "haunted Hilborough") is a round stone giant 100 feet round, probably as old as Kinwarton, with 900 nesting holes. There is an octagonal brick and sandstone example at Wasperton, and a rectangular one at Wilmcote. In the rich fruit country of Worcestershire (which boasts about 100 specimens) they are usually timber-framed and related to the timber-framed church towers of the area. Most are rectangular and gabled, as at Oddingley, Dormston, Himbleton, Grafton, Hanbury, Huddington, Offenham and Uphampton. Great Comberton at the foot of Bredon Hill has a massive round dovecote of stone and a smaller one of brick, square and gabled. There are some intriguing regional variations. At Willington, Bedfordshire, is a remarkable wide and tall rectangular dovecote with steep crow-stepped gables at two ends, the high roof broken midway into two pitches by a full-length louvre, with nests for 1,500 birds. The building, probably early sixteenth-century, belonged with the Gothic stables opposite to a large mansion built by Cardinal Wolsey's Master of the Horse. At Castleton, Oxfordshire, the seventeenth-century square and gabled stone structure is supported on arches. At Brympton d'Evercy, Somerset, there is a wooden dovecote on a tall stone pillar. A handsome octagonal dovecote at Whitehall near Shrewsbury and that at Trotton in Sussex show that the same essentials of design extended from the Tudor to the Jacobean period.

Wells, 'holy' and others, are not so rife as formerly, and where they still function they are apt to be Victorian, but there are groups of early vintage in the West Country. The holy wells of Cornwall are survivals from the days of Celtic Christianity, though, where they are not derelict, they were usually rebuilt in the fourteenth and fifteenth centuries. In Dupath near Callington there is a little square granite building containing a sunk basin or bath for immersions with the water flowing through it, the whole enclosed beneath a gabled roof with barrel vault and crowning bell-cote. At Madron the fourteenth-century well of St. Madron, also known as the Baptistery, lies in ruins, but its oratory still has its altar *in situ* as well as the sunk basin of water serving as font or baptistery and remains of stone seats round the internal walls. At St. Cleer is another granite well-house, square and gabled with high-pitched roof and pointed barrel vault, with an open arcade of two arches on each of three sides, with niches for statues and openings for the water on the inside face of the rear wall. The well beside the churchyard at St. Clether is the largest in the duchy and is curiously designed, for the water flows from the gabled well proper and through the chapel with its primitive altar. The holy well of St. Keyne, though celebrated in Southey's famous ballad, is of little architectural interest, having fallen into complete ruin before being rebuilt early this century by the Old Cornwall Society. The well of St. Cyricus in Luxulyan village, set in a valley of fern-smothered boulders, and the restored well of St. Julian in Maker are also of interest. In the street of St. Mawes the well and stone 'chair' of the patron saint are of extremely dubious provenance.

Stone-hooded and canopied springs and fountains are homely mannerisms of Cotswold villages like Stanton and the Slaughters, and northward, still in stone country, there are Derbyshire villages like Tissington where the wells are garlanded with floral pictures at Whitsuntide. Often the stone work is Victorian but just as often the wells themselves are ancient, as they are in the two wells in Saxon Lastingham on the North Yorkshire Moors, one dedicated to St. Cedd and the other to his brother Chad. Here Victorian structures embody medieval stones brought from nearby Rosedale Abbey, though the Latin inscription is itself suspect. And northward again at Holystone in Northumberland is the ancient Lady Well which may be associated with St. Ninian. Nor must we overlook the three wells, still flowing, in the little dead port of Winchelsea in Sussex, all that remain of six built in Edward I's new town.

Anchorites and hermits were often associated with these wells as with churches. An anchorite's cell (*domus inclusi*) was not infrequently attached to a church. Many a so-called *domus inclusi* has proved on examination to be merely the chamber of the resident priest, but many authentic examples are known.[1] At Hartlip church, Kent, the cell is a small square building at the western end of the north aisle. An excellent example is that at Chester-le-Street, Durham, where a two-storeyed anchorage with two chambers on each floor is attached the north-western end of the church. Another perfect house-like cell is that at Llaneilian on Anglesey, connected to the church by a slype or passage in the eighteenth century. Anchorites—and anchoresses—were enclosed by the bishop of the diocese, and they had to be supported by funds, diocesan or municipal, while their mode of life was regulated by such rules and documents as the *Ancren Rwle*. In these respects they differed from hermits, who, however, had also to be approved by the bishop, were clothed in a habit and made some kind of profession, as did a monk, though they were self-supporting (begging was not excluded) and free to come and go.

Many medieval English hermits became celebrated, among them St. Godric of Finchale and St. Robert of Knaresborough. The Knaresborough hermitage survives in the limestone cliffs of the ravine cut by the Nidd river. A small oratory 10 feet by 9 feet is hollowed out of the rock, with a window which seems to be of the fourteenth century, with an adjoining cell. St. Robert was traditionally said to have been buried in a cave lower down the river, and the discovery of a medieval burial here inspired Lord Lytton's novel *Eugene Aram*, in which the cave figures. A hermitage with three rough arches is hewn out of the rock at Dale in Derbyshire. There is another on the edge of Bridgnorth, and another, probably fourteenth-century, in the grounds of the hospital at Pontefract.

The most celebrated hermitage is certainly that at Warkworth in Northumberland, carved out of the rocky bank of the Coquet river on the edge of the village. It was briefly described in

[1] R. M. Clay in *Hermits and Anchorites of England* (London, 1904) lists 303 such cells, though comparatively few survive.

Spenser's *Faerie Queene*, and the story of the hermit Bertram was related at length nearly two centuries later in Bishop Percy's *Reliques of Ancient English Poetry* in the ballad "The Hermit of Warkworth". A stone staircase now leads to the vestibule and chapel with its tiny sacristy. The chapel is about 20 feet by 7 feet, and fourteenth-century columns, groins and arches are hewn out of the rock. The altar mensa retains its five consecration crosses, and above it is a walled recess which originally contained a pyx. There is a carved recumbent figure in the sill of a window and another figure, niched, both defaced. The chapel communicates with a smaller inner oratory, which has a mutilated altar and a small closet from which a doorway leads to an open gallery. Adjoining the chapel are remains of the cell or hermitage proper, which had a kitchen below and a bedchamber above. Later the Percy family maintained a chantry priest to reside here, a practice continued until the tenure of the last hermit-chaplain was ended by the dissolution of religious houses under Henry VIII.

An incalculable number of crosses in village streets and church-yards, at cross-roads and parish boundaries, were destroyed at the Reformation and later periods of mob iconoclasm. Yet many survive, often headless or otherwise mutilated. Many were restored by the Victorians, and it was fashionable among the Georgians to surmount headless crosses with sundials. Up and down the country the village cross is still a prominent feature. There are remains of some 300 crosses of pre-Conquest date, mostly in Cornwall and the north, some of which we have already noticed. More intact are the crosses of the fourteenth and fifteenth centuries. A typical example is that at Bishops Lydeard, Somerset, its plinth set on three octagonal steps and adorned with sculptured reliefs of our Lord, the Apostles and the Resurrection. In the same county, at Somerton, the cross is a market cross, octagonal, with eight rounded arches forming a continuous open arcade, with stone seats between the arches for the merchants; there are battlements adorned with gargoyles, and the whole is covered by an octagonal stone roof held by spreading beams and rafters. Cheddar has a similar market cross, its fifteenth-century preaching cross enclosed by a roofed arcaded structure in the following century. Somerset also has at least two perfect canopied enriched crosses in the churchyards of Spaxton and Chewton

The Galilee Chapel of Durham Cathedral

(*above*) An aerial view of Fountains Abbey
(*below*) Looking east down the aisle of Rievaulx Abbey

Mendip, and at Horsington near Wincanton is a remarkable thirteenth-century cross on circular steps with a large tapering octagonal shaft decorated with curious carvings.

Iron Acton, Gloucestershire, has a gabled canopied cross, open on four sides, with traceried heads to the open panelling, the whole crowned by a lofty superstructure. At Castle Combe, Wiltshire, is a market cross consisting of a square stone pedestal upon two steps, ornamented with shields and roses on panels, and a high stone pier supporting a pyramidical and pinnacled roof. Also in Wiltshire are Steeple Ashton, where the cross is traditionally held to have been erected in 1066, though it was restored at various times, and Ashton Keynes, with its series of little bridges spanning the Thames, where there are remains of no less than four ancient crosses. Deeping St. James, Lincolnshire, has a curious fifteenth-century market cross with a high square base with two tiers of steps at the angles, ogee-cusped panels and crenellations, but the shaft was destroyed when the cross was converted into a lock-up in 1819.

Perhaps the most beautiful of all village crosses is the Eleanor Cross at Geddington, near the narrow medieval bridge over the stream, in Northamptonshire. It was in 1291 that Queen Eleanor, the wife of Edward I, died at Hardby in Nottinghamshire, and within three or four years twelve monumental crosses were erected on the sites where the coffin had rested on the journey from Hardby to Westminster Abbey. Of these only three survive —at Geddington, Northampton and Waltham (Charing Cross in the forecourt of the railway station is a Victorian replica of one that originally stood on or near the site). The Eleanor Crosses were more or less identical in form and ornament, designed by John of Battle and Richard Crundale, who also worked on the queen's tomb. The Geddington cross is hexagonal and of three stages raised on plinth and steps, with elegant diapering running up the shaft. Beneath the gabled canopies of the third stage are four statues of the queen, and there is a great deal of sculptured crockets and finials and ogee-heads, and the whole is surmounted by a towering enriched and slightly tapering superstructure. The draperied figures of the queen were sculptured by William de Ireland and were probably copied from the gilt effigy on the tomb in Westminster Abbey. More significant, perhaps, is the appearance here of the ogee curve, which had only now arrived

10

in England and which was to become a characteristic of the later mature Gothic of this country.

Regional vernacular building is, or was, largely dependent for its materials on the geological nature of the terrain. Thus the limestone belt running from Lincolnshire into Dorset is conspicuous for the stone-built villages which reach their apotheosis on the golden oolite of the Cotswolds, and the same architectural mannerisms are to be found in the Somerset villages of Ham stone. In Somerset, however, we find stone, brick and cob or rammed earth as we move westward. In Devon there is much cob, with granite on Dartmoor, and in Cornwall granite and sandstone. Flint is common in the south-east and in East Anglia, but in Norfolk there is also brick, which was rediscovered there at an early date. Sussex and Surrey have, in addition to flint, timber-framing with brick and vertical tile-hung upper storeys, while horizontal weatherboarding is a feature of the Weald of Kent as it is of Essex. In Essex, Suffolk and Cambridge plaster facing on timber is much used, often with pargetting or patterned plasterwork. The timber-framing tradition, either with plaster or brick, often colour washed, extends from Warwickshire and Worcestershire through Hereford into Shropshire and Cheshire. Finally, there are ranges of sandstone and black gritstone running through the dark Saracenic country of Biddulph Moor and the Bridestones, the Derbyshire Peak, the stark Brontë country, the Yorkshire dales (and the limestone again) and the fells of Cumberland and Westmoreland, until once again the granite is encountered in the Cheviots, with their circular dry-walled sheep 'stells'.

As an example of a perfect hill village of the limestone we may consider the Gloucestershire village of Stanton, its single tiny narrow street withdrawn into a wooded recess of the Cotswold hills. The place-name Stanton—the enclosure where stone was quarried—has come down to us very much in its Anglo-Saxon form. The manor was given to the abbey of Winchcombe by Kenulph, King of Mercia, in whose hands it remained until the Dissolution of the Monasteries in 1539, when it was conferred upon Katherine Parr as a portion of her marriage dowry by Henry VIII. The parish church is largely Norman and Decorated, with an awesome medieval stone mask of a sun god and a churchyard flooded with Baroque tombstones. The village cross of late medieval simple traditional type was rebuilt, above the steps and plinth, in the seventeenth century. Most of the houses are of the very early years of the seventeenth century, many of them having dated labels, but the manor house was built by Thomas Warren in 1577, and its arcaded windows with arched heads illustrate the persistence in this area of the Gothic tradition. Generally, however, the architectural details of the village are of the Renaissance—the mullioned windows, the moulded labels and dripstones, the stone-coped gables with kneelers and finials, the steeply-pitched roofs with graduated stone tiles, the doorways with depressed arched heads. The Court is mainly Jacobean, and to judge from old prints it was probably the work of the same craftsman who designed the parsonage of 1625, demolished during the Regency period to make way for a ponderous building of about 1820. There are several barns, timber-framed upon buttressed stone walls.

In the middle of the fifteenth century, village and church were in a dilapidated condition, and, despite the yeoman affluence which created the wave of rebuilding nearly two centuries later, the village was near derelict in 1906 when a wealthy northern mill architect, Sir Philip Stott, bought the estate. He restored the Court on traditional lines, externally at least, for it was found impossible to recreate the original screened hall, he restored most of the farmhouses and cottages, converted the old malthouse buildings with their dovecote into the present Manor Farm, and introduced street lighting with lanterns on wrought-iron brackets, a water supply and much else over the course of thirty years. Strangely enough, William Warren's manor house stood derelict until 1951, when a talented local mason restored it, making good the ornate plaster ceiling, uncovering frescoes on window splays and discovering a variety of objects, including an elaborate metal woolstapler's punch embodying the original Warren's initial W. Despite the commuters who have now discovered it and some measure of development, Stanton remains an authentic village of the limestone and a vision of yeoman England.

As an example of what is practically a wholly medieval village let us turn to Lacock in Wiltshire, in the midst of the Avon water meadows, set so well out on the Oxford clay between the chalk and limestone scarps that these materials are on the threshold of the village. It is a paradox that the wealth of different fabrics—stone, brick, timber and plaster—blends into such a felicitous unity. Its 'big house', Lacock Abbey, has already been referred to for the large-scale survival of its pre-Reformation monastic buildings, though these are sealed in a Renaissance envelope. The south front is oddly at variance with the vertical medieval buttresses, but Sanderson Miller's Strawberry Hill Gothic additions of 200 years later illustrates a throw-back in public taste. The parish church, cruciform and steepled, is a treasure-house of ecclesiology. Yet it is the village itself with its parallelogram of ancient streets illustrating the development of English domestic architecture over some five centuries that gives the greater satisfaction.

The earliest house to survive in Lacock is part of the interior of No. 21 Church Street embodying Early English work, a cottage merely, though a dubious tradition associates it with King John. Another cottage in the same street has a striking gable of huge oak timber baulks, and yet another has a fourteenth-century doorway with stone jambs and moulded hood. A fourteenth-century tithe barn stands at the end of East Street. No other village is so rich in houses of the fourteenth and fifteenth centuries, by-products of the great wool trade, though Lacock also owes much of its character to the timber-framed buildings of the sixteenth and seventeenth centuries with stone foundations and, often, projecting upper storeys. 'The Angel' is a notable Tudor specimen with fern-leaf symbols in the spandrels of the arched doorway. Even the doorway to the blacksmith's forge is of the fifteenth century. In the nearby George Inn is the well-preserved wheel of a seventeenth-century turn-spit *in situ*. The Georgian brick façade of the 'Red Lion' conceals earlier fabric, and before it stands the wayside cross removed in the eighteenth century from its original position west of the church.

Up and down the country are lost or deserted villages, due to enclosures, the conversion of arable land to pasture, plague (especially during the period 1450–1550), fire, erosion and even the clearance of an estate by the squire in order to improve and enlarge his park. There are known to be some 2,000 deserted village sites in the country, most of them concentrated in the Midlands and Eastern England.[1] Such sites are most easily identified by aerial photography, but on the ground the tell-tale clues include hollows, depressions and tumps, ridges and furrows left

[1] See Maurice Beresford, *Lost Villages of England* (London, 1954); W. G. Hoskins, *Fieldwork in Local History* (London, 1967); W. E. Tate, *The English Village Community and the Enclosure Movements* (London, 1967).

by arable strip farming, ruined churches and churches standing alone, especially when near moated sites. It is hoped that excavation in progress on some of these sites will reveal evidence of medieval peasant cottage architecture, a subject of which we have comparatively little knowledge. At Hangleton, Sussex, four thirteenth- to fourteenth-century houses have been investigated. At Wythemail, Northamptonshire, plans of houses and outbuildings with a paved yard occupied from the twelfth to the fourteenth century have been recovered. At Hound Tor in the middle of Dartmoor a spectacular collection of ruined granite farmhouses and buildings is being recovered—about twelve buildings with their crofts, early medieval in plan and apparently of the 'long-house' type.

At Wolfhamcote, Warwickshire, all that remains above ground is the thirteenth-century church, still intact and even furnished, but now abandoned. At Knaptoft, Leicestershire, which had twenty households including the priest in the closing years of the eleventh century—a considerable village by medieval standards—the church is in ruins, the site of the medieval manor house can barely be traced, and even the squire's Elizabethan hall is now mouldering. Charweltin, Oxfordshire, with church and parsonage alone in the fields and tumps and hollows nearby is an obvious example. So are Quarrendon, Buckinghamshire, with its ruined church, and Stretton Baskerville and Cestersover, both in Warwickshire. In the North Riding of Yorkshire there is Whorlton on its eery moor, with a ruined church and the earthworks of castle and fishponds, and just over the East Riding border is Wharram Percy. The village of Griff near Helmsley was obliterated by the Cistercians of Rievaulx Abbey, who set up their grange here, but we have already noted the argument made by a recent writer against the accusation of depopulation levelled against the Cistercians.

What happened to Newtown, the most ancient borough on the Isle of Wight, which down to 1832 returned two members to Parliament? Today a tiny early eighteenth-century town hall stands alone in a deserted meadow (marked as 'Bread Street' on ancient maps), and only one other building has survived in the immediate neighbourhood. And what mystery lies behind the Shropshire signpost which states *To Ruyton 11 Towns*, for Ruyton itself is a mere hamlet?

12

The Medieval Castle

The Crusaders were astonished to find at Constantinople a triple wall 3 miles in length with 100 flanking towers, the outer walls lower than the inner, so that the defenders could simultaneously present three lines of fire. At the sieges of Acre and Antioch the Crusaders had to capture the flanking towers, which were fortresses in themselves, before they could hope to carry the walls commanded by them. Consequently the Crusaders themselves built such castles, like Kerak in the desert beyond Jordan and the mighty fortress of the Krak des Chevaliers in the mountains of Tripoli. These scientific forms of fortification were gradually adopted throughout Europe, where one of the earliest and most formidable castles was built by Richard I during the wars with France. Perched on a precipitous cliff above the river Seine, it was completed in 1198. It has three baileys or wards, the inner bailey lying on the edge of the cliff. The outer and middle curtain walls are strengthened by cylindrical mural towers, and the vast donjon or round keep partly overhangs the precipice. It is roughly of the same type and date as Pembroke, but it had ingenious devices that had not yet reached England. The King of France haughtily remarked to Richard, "I will take Chateau Gaillard if it be made of iron." To which the English monarch retorted, "And I will hold it, were it made of butter." It was not made of butter, but it nearly slipped through English fingers in a prolonged and terrible siege in 1203. Other castles in France were just as formidable, and the great round keep of Coucy was the largest, strongest and most magnificent of all medieval towers, occupying more than three times the area and more than twice the height of the keep at Pembroke.

In British castles of the early years of the thirteenth century the keep still retained its position as the main centre of defence, but the outer fortifications were strengthened. Along the straight curtain walls were built projecting towers with loopholes that looked right along the foot of the wall. A small square castle would require no more than four, one at each corner, as at Porchester. A larger castle would require not only angle towers but also intermediate ones, as at Skenfrith, Scarborough and Richborough. Often these towers were built with deep battered plinths, or with prows like spurs, as at Chepstow, Goodrich and Caerphilly, thus giving greater stability and additional protection against sapping operations. New castles had an outer and an inner bailey, and sometimes even a third or middle bailey. The keep and bailey at Pembroke were built at the end of the twelfth century, but early in the following century the castle was extended by a large outer bailey. At Corfe Castle in Dorset it is clear that the great ditch dividing the outer bailey from the west bailey and the inner ward is a secondary construction dating only from the mid or late thirteenth century, displacing part of the castle's original eleventh-century layout.

Invariably, of course, the wall walks on the curtain and on the towers themselves had crenellated parapets or battlements with embrasures, and from the thirteenth century the embrasures were often covered by wooden shutters, placed on the outside and hung from the top, to afford protection from enemy missiles. Temporary wooden galleries known as hoards or brattices were often attached to the outside of parapets during sieges. There were holes in the floors of these galleries through which iron bolts, stones, hot pitch and even molten metal could be dropped on beseigers who had actually reached the wall foot. These wooden hoards were gradually replaced by permanent stone machicolated parapets, especially at such vulnerable points as gateways. At Conway, 1283–7, the walls containing the east and west gateways were surmounted by such machicolations from end to end, but it was not until the fourteenth century that machicolated parapets were in general use.

From the beginning of the thirteenth century more emphasis was placed on the gatehouse, an obvious measure since this had always been the weak point of a castle. The typical gatehouse was now a projecting building of some depth containing a barbican or long narrow passage, which limited and narrowed down the attackers' approach. The actual gate lay recessed between two circular or drum towers. A portcullis, a heavy screen of oak and iron, could be dropped in front of the gateway from a chamber above it, which contained the windlasses or pulleys or ropes to drop and draw up the portcullis. There would be more portcullises on the inner side, so that if the attackers managed to enter the barbican the portcullises would be dropped to trap them like sheep in a pen. The great Carthagenian general Hannibal was defeated by such a device, virtually an early portcullis, as long ago as 208 B.C.

The gatehouse reached its highest and fullest development in the second half of the thirteenth century, when it became the stronghold of the castle, the keep having declined into a purely domestic building—where it existed, for the new castles were designed without keeps. Fine examples of a typical gatehouse with drum towers can be seen at Kidwelly, Chepstow, Harlech, Corfe, Carisbrooke and elsewhere. Elaborate barbicans remain at Pembroke, Kidwelly, Arundel, Warwick, Alnwick and most of the royal castles of North Wales, notably Caernarvon where there were no less than eight portcullises.

While castles with wide deep moats were protected against sapping those surrounded by marshes or muddy watercourses were similarly protected, and in some places streams were dammed up in order to make artificial lakes. This was done at Leeds in Kent and Caerphilly in Glamorgan. In its prime Kenilworth was the greatest of all the lake fortresses, though it took shape gradually. In King John's time there was already a 'pool', and in 1231 we find Henry III ordering "a fair and beautiful pleasure boat" to be moored near the door of his private chamber. He was probably responsible for the great dam that pent up the waters of brooks and created the lake of 111 acres which was in existence in 1266. The effect of this was to make three of the four sides of the castle inaccessible. Except for the main entrance on the northeast, the only approach was along the crest of the dam, which was guarded by a gatehouse in the outer ward and a barbican tower at the south end of the dam, as well as a formidable outwork at the point where the causeway reached dry land. The high-lying inner ward, standing in the south-western corner of a much larger outer ward, was still dominated by the Clintons' great Norman keep, with the domestic buildings grouped in front of it, and the outer ward had five important towers on the curtain wall falling to the water.

After perfecting such a fortress Henry III made the fatal mistake of presenting Kenilworth to his son-in-law Simon de Montfort, the great Earl of Leicester, who became the king's biggest enemy. De Montfort was slain on the battlefield of Evesham in 1265, but his son, the younger Simon, held the castle during a siege which lasted from June of 1266 until late December of that year, a siege ended only by starvation and disease. Kenilworth became a royal castle again, only to be given to the king's youngest son, Edmund 'Crouchback', the founder of the Lancaster branch of the House of Plantagenet. This proud race held the castle until it was returned to the Crown in 1399, when the heir of Lancaster came to the throne as Henry IV. In the interim John of Gaunt raised the buildings, including the fine banqueting hall of 1392, which compares with Westminster Hall, and which retains its oriel window, panelled fireplaces and fine springing arches, which supplanted the Norman fabric.

Thirteenth-century Shirburn had none of the complexities of Kenilworth and is a miniature, four-square, with round angle towers, lacking outworks and even a gatehouse. It has, moreover, been fitted with seventeenth-century windows and refaced with contemporary plaster, so that it is now merely a country house in a lake. Leeds is a different proposition. Once the home of Queen Eleanor, possessed by William of Wykeham and visited by Froissart, it stands on two islands in a 15-acre sheet of water, the islands connected by a double drawbridge. There are thus virtually two blocks of buildings which with the gatehouse and barbican formed four distinct forts, each capable of separate defence. There were inner and outer baileys. Only the foundations remain of the inner curtain wall but there are remains of the bastions and mural towers on the outer curtain. The nucleus of the castle was later converted into the existing desirable residence.

Caerphilly was a Marcher castle, an outpost of the lords of Glamorgan to protect Cardiff and the coastal plain from the forays of unbeaten Welshmen in the Brecon hills. It was begun in 1271. As at Kenilworth, a large square island in the middle of a broad expanse of water was produced by the damming up of two streams. The outer contour of the island was provided with a complete encircling wall, rounded at the corners with four semi-circular bastions. This formed the outer ward, which had an entrance on each of the east and west fronts protected by a strong

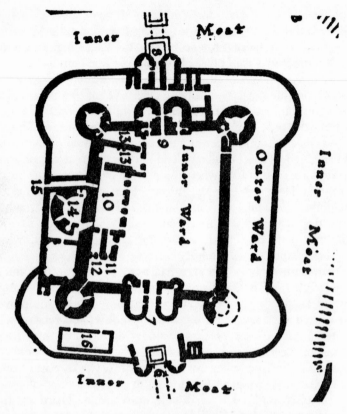

Caerphilly Castle (*courtesy of the Department of the Environment*)
Numbers refer to: 6 east gate to outer ward, 7 east gate to inner ward, 8 west
gate to outer ward, 9 west gate to inner ward, 10 great hall, 11 buttery, etc.,
12 chapel, 13 state rooms, 14 kitchen tower, 15 water gate and covered passage,
and 16 storehouse

gatehouse. Rising high above the rather low outer ward was the
immensely strong but smaller inner ward with a high curtain
wall and even higher circular towers at each corner, with two
gatehouses on the east and west corresponding to the smaller
gatehouses of the outer ward. This inner ward was piled high
with buildings, including a fine banqueting hall in the Decorated
style, still one of the best preserved buildings. There was, of
course, no keep. On the further side of the lake, covering the
east front of the castle, was an elaborate and impregnable screen

wall with mural towers and a large central gatehouse having an effective barbican. This eastern Grand Front was a complete line of defence and there was a moat in front of it. On the west side of the outer defences was a wall known as a 'hornwork', not seriously fortified since it was almost inaccessible across the water. Caerphilly was the largest castle in Wales and, at that time, the most complex and scientifically designed castle in the kingdom, but it ultimately decayed and the waters drained away. Lord Tennyson on seeing it exclaimed, "It is not a castle; it is a town in ruins." In recent years the lake has been partly reconstructed, so that today one has some idea of its pristine condition.

During the last twenty years of the thirteenth century Edward I made his final bid to subdue the Welsh with a series of castles which represented the high watermark in medieval fortification. His new castles were termed 'concentric' since each ward was wholly contained within that outside it. In other words there were two or three rings of walls one inside the other. Each defensive wall was strongly fortified by towers placed astride it, and the inner walls were raised in height. Since each of these wall towers was as strong as the old keep and could be separately defended, it followed that a keep proper was unnecessary. Further protective measures were the additions of more gateways and posterns.

Now these principles were largely observed at Caerphilly, and indeed it has commonly been held that Caerphilly was the first of the 'concentric' castles. It is now being suggested, however. that the concentric works there are later than 1271 when the castle was begun. The new castles, all in North Wales, were the direct products of English war-time experience in the Middle East and amid the *bastides* of Gascony. The king employed a brilliant team of military architects led by Master James of St. George. Little is known of him except that he was probably a Frank born in Palestine and that he was *magister operacionum regis in Wallia*—master of the royal works in Wales. At one period he was drawing a salary of 3s. a day in the currency of that time, and later a yearly retaining fee of 100 marks. We know that he worked on the castles of Rhuddlan, Conway, Harlech and Beaumaris, and it is considered that the architect of Harlech must have been responsible for Caerphilly. Other prominent architects in the team were Master Richard Lenginour, who, as his name suggests, was an engineer, and Walter of Hereford, who was also prominent in important church-building.

The first of the new royal castles was the rebuilding of Rhuddlan, begun in 1277. It was an imposing example of a concentric castle of simple design, though only fragments remain. In the same year Flint was begun, and it was planned with a small rectangular town as a single composition like a French *bastide*. It is a rectangular fortress with round angle towers, and its strong point is the great cylindrical keep-like tower (mentioned in Shakespeare's *Richard II*) which stands isolated outside the south-eastern quadrilateral enceinte of curtain and towers, approached from the inner bailey by a drawbridge over the moat. Only the lower portion of this powerful structure remains. Its counterpart is the Tour de Constance at Aigues Mortes in Languedoc. After yet another Welsh uprising Denbigh Castle was strengthened, and here the most important feature was the powerful triangular gatehouse (now in ruins) with three polygonal towers ranged round a central hall, an ingenious plan which with its portcullises, machicolations and meutrières must have given the assailants a thin time of it. The outer arch of the gateway is surmounted by a sculptured figure which, as at Caernarvon, is thought to be that of King Edward. Flint and Denbigh, however, are not of the new concentric type, of which the first example is Harlech.

Harlech, begun in 1285, stands boldly upon a high rock, with a piece of land separating it from the sea. It is a quadrilateral castle of orthodox concentric type, for its two lines of defences lie one within the other forming inner and outer baileys. The outer bailey extended down the precipitous rocky slopes of the hill to the sea. On the west side was the water-gate, defended by a pit and a drawbridge. Thence a steep path, the way from the marsh, led upward, commanded at all points from the walls of the enclosure, to an upper gate in the wall defended in the same manner. A survey in the reign of Henry III described how this cleverly protected "Waye from the Marshe", with a drawbridge at the lower level, "to issew forthe horsemen or footemen, is forced upon the side of the rocke, having a strong wall towards the sea, being in length to another drawbridge c yerdes". The gatehouse with flanking towers on the east front of the inner bailey was the stronghold of Harlech, for it had a barbican with three gates and three portcullises. There was only one gatehouse, not two as at Beaumaris and elsewhere, but it lay astride the wall so that it could be held against the inner as well as the outer bailey. It still retains its three floors, containing the private dwelling rooms of the Constable, two private chapels and guardrooms.

Harlech put up some desperate resistance in the time of Owen Glendower, but it was equally hard pressed as a Lancastrian stronghold during the Wars of the Roses. Jasper Tudor, Earl of Pembroke and half-brother of Henry VII, made it his headquarters, but when things got too hot for him he fled to France. The castellan or keeper of the castle, Sir David ap Jevan ap Einion. beat off several Yorkist attacks. He is reputed to have boasted that "he had once in his youth maintained a castle in France so long that every old woman in Wales had heard of it, and in his old age he had held a castle in Wales so long that every old woman in France had heard of it". He was, however, finally starved into submission, in 1468, by Edward's Welsh champion, Sir Richard Herbert. The well-known song of the "March of the Men of Harlech" is said to recall some forgotten episode of this long siege.

Two of the greatest of the new castles were Conway and Caernarvon, and though they are not strictly concentric castles, since in each case the two wards are adjacent on a narrow site, all the other principles of concentric type are implied. Conway closed the approach to Snowdonia by land and river. It was roughly oblong in plan and was divided by a cross-wall into two baileys, the outer bailey containing the great hall and garrison offices, the inner bailey the royal apartments. There were no gatehouses, and the gateways were defended only by the adjacent mural towers. There were eight of these strong cylindrical towers. The approach from the walled town led through an outer gate up a steep ascent, over a drawbridge thrown across the ditch separating town from castle, and then through a barbican and inner gate. With all its enfiladed towers intact Conway looks the ideal medieval castle.

Caernarvon was the most important of the Edwardian castles, and from 1284 to 1536 it was the administrative centre of Wales. The castle was built over three main periods, or in three stages. Begun to designs by Walter of Hereford in 1285, it was not completed until 1322. In shape it is like an hour-glass with the two wards almost merging in the middle, and it has a polygonal tower at each angle. The Eagle Tower is one of the largest single towers built in the Middle Ages, and it has many of the qualities of a keep. The lofty curtain walls and towers have two tiers of mural passages containing loopholes, so that, including those on the battlements, there would be three tiers of armed men. There are two gatehouses, of which the King's Gate provided direct entrance from the town to the inner bailey. Nine towers stand astride the walls, so that each passage could be closed off, an advantage over the continuous wall walk at Conway. Altogether the castle would be bristling with archers standing at different levels. On one side it is washed by the waters of the estuary, and

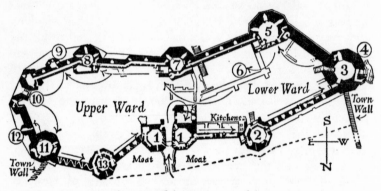

Caernarvon (*courtesy of the Department of the Environment*)
Numbers refer to: 1 King's Gate, 2 Well Tower, 3 Eagle Tower, 4 remains of stone eagle, 5 Queen's Tower, 6 site of hall, 7 Chamberlain Tower, 8 Black Tower, 9 Cistern Tower, 10 Queen's Gate, 11 North-east Tower, 12 Watch Tower, and 13 Granary Tower

the waters were diverted to form a moat on the other side, though this is now filled in and paved over. Caernarvon ranks among the finest examples of medieval military art, and its curtain walls, towers and gates stand intact, though the great hall was destroyed.

To safeguard Anglesey, Edward built Beaumaris at the opposite end of the Menai Straits. This is the latest of the great castles of the Edwardian Conquest, and it is the finest example in Britain of a concentrically planned fortress, a perfectly symmetrical composition that survives almost intact. It stands on the sea shore, roughly rectangular in form, with two lines of fortifications forming the inner and outer baileys, and it is surrounded by a moat except at a point on the south where the sea enters to form a small dock. The inner curtain walls are defended by six towers and two

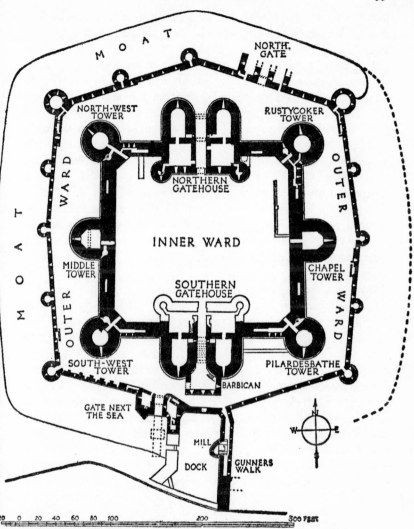

Beaumaris Castle (*courtesy of the Department of the Environment*)

large gatehouses, set opposite each other as at Caerphilly. These gatehouses are very substantial, containing large halls and other rooms. Each was defended by three portcullises, and, as at Harlech, each could be held against both inner and outer baileys. Originally the inner bailey as completed about 1290 formed the entire castle, but by about 1320 the outer curtain wall of nine panels with twelve towers and two gateways had been added. A notable feature is the chapel with stone arcading and a groined vault, in a good state of preservation.

Edward's practice was to attach to each castle a borough planted with an English colony as part of his scheme of support for its administration, and nowhere in Britain can we see in better preservation the full layout of a medieval walled town and castle than at Caernarvon and Conway. At Caernarvon the walls were for the defence of the free borough established in 1284 and were built immediately before the three south-west towers of the castle. After the revolt of the Welsh in 1294 these walls were replaced at a cost of £1,000, a fortune in those days. Almost the entire circuit remains to the level of the wall walk, with ten half-drum towers and four main gates. From the promenade and the sea the vision is perfect, and here is another Avila or M'dina, a Carcassonne or an Aigues Mortes.

At Conway too a bracelet of walls girdles the homes of the people, not quite perfect now for there are gaps, but there are still twenty-one broken half-drum towers and three gates climbing and bestraddling the streets. There is far less at Denbigh. What remains is contemporary with the foundation of the borough in 1282, but the eastern salient is an addition of the early fourteenth century. Most of the enceinte is still traceable and the Burgess Gate is intact. It was Edward too who planned New Winchelsea in Sussex after the old town had been swallowed up by the sea in 1250, of which Holinshed gives a vivid account. The new town was designed in squares and rectangles, 'quarters' as they were called, with parallel streets, and their houses still have cellars with fine carved corbels. The walls have fallen, but three gates remain, through which the French came when they attacked the town in 1380.

The most perfect of the larger walled towns are, of course, York and Chester. York's walls, intact with a circuit and wall walk of close on 2 miles, were built of Tadcaster stone in the thirteenth century, and the great bars or gates were built in the following century. Micklegate, the royal entrance from the south, is the most elaborate. Bootham Bar kept out intruders from the north, including the wolves and robbers of the Forest Galtres. This and Monk Bar have retained their portcullises, but Walmgate Bar is the only gate to have preserved its barbican.

Gloucester Cathedral: the monk's lavatorium in the cloisters

The west front of Castle Acre Priory, Norfolk

There is also the Fishergate tower with a postern added in 1501.

Chester's walls almost follow the plan of Roman Deva. Of red sandstone, they vary in height from 12 to 40 feet, with a continuous wall walk and a circuit of much the same length as York. Here too are four gates and enfilading wall towers. Restored though the walls of York and Chester may be, they have merits not present in the much-lauded French walled towns of Carcassonne, Aigues Mortes and Avignon, where Viollet-le-Duc, the nineteenth-century arch-restorer, dealt with the problem of dilapidated historic buildings in terms of total rehabilitation. As he put it, "To restore a building is not to preserve it, to repair or rebuild it; it is to reinstate it in a condition of completeness which could never have existed at any given time. . . ." Such pedantry often resulted in the setting up of a fictitious unity. Finally one should not overlook Berwick-on-Tweed, with its four gates, an unusual example of a town walled as late as the sixteenth century.

While many medieval fortified bridges still exist in Europe (one need only recall those of Tournai, Toledo and Cahors), extremely few remain in England. Most important bridges, including London Bridge and those of Bristol, Chester, Durham, Newcastle and York, had defensive gates or towers, but they have all disappeared. The only intact example is the bridge, with three ribbed arches, over the Monnow at Monmouth, built in 1272 and spanned by a fortified gatehouse of about four years later. Warkworth bridge over the Coquet in Northumberland, a fourteenth-century structure, narrow and of only two low arched spans, still has a broken defence tower astride one end of it, rectangular and squat with a low arched passageway.

Few scientifically designed purely military castles were built after the reign of Edward I for the simple reason that they were no longer necessary, except perhaps in the area of the border with Scotland. The power of feudalism had been broken, or was about to be broken, and there was little point in building expensive defences when explosive artillery was becoming increasingly effective, as Sir Ralph Grey found out at Bamburgh in 1464, when the stones of the most formidable fortress in the north "flew like flinders into the sea". Moreover it had been discovered, long before the Wars of the Roses, that a system of passive defence behind stone walls (or even behind the sand-bagged trenches of 1914–18) may protract a war but does not decide it.

II

Where new castles were built residential comfort and aesthetic considerations loomed large. Battlements still appeared, but walls were thinner and windows larger. By the closing years of the fourteenth century the almost standard plan was reduced to four ranges of largely domestic buildings grouped around an inner courtyard, though angle towers still appeared. The two most perfect examples are Bolton in the North Riding and Bodiam in Sussex. Bolton castle received its licence in 1379 but may have been begun slightly earlier, and it was designed by John Lewyn, the brilliant architect who did so much in Durham. It was intended to guard Wensleydale, and it thus combined military expediency with residential comfort. Dominating the village of Castle Bolton, it is almost intact though largely gutted internally. There was here no attempt at a gatehouse, and the entrance is merely a major archway leading into the courtyard. The notable features are the great hall in the north range, the chapel on the second floor of the south range which reaches up through the third floor, and the numerous tunnel vaults.

Bodiam, completed *c*. 1390, has a more martial appearance, despite such cossetting as its thirty-seven fireplaces. It has a rectangular plan with a drum tower at each corner and a square tower in the middle of each of three sides. The centre of the north side is occupied by a gatehouse with flanking square towers notable in that they embody the first loopholes for firearms. The gatehouse has machicolations and a barbican with three portcullises. The castle rises sheer out of a moat studded with water-lilies, and it has drama and visual delight. The domestic buildings, ranged round the court as at Castle Bolton, are ruinous.

It seems, after all, that castles had not quite yet turned away from their original purpose, and about the same time as Bodiam, perhaps a little after 1390, a remarkable keep was built at Warkworth in the north. A substantial castle had existed there for some two centuries, but now the Percys added a keep that was a castle or mansion in itself, probably designed by John Lewyn. It was described in the sixteenth century as "A marvellus donjeon of eight towres all joined in one howse togethers". It contains a great hall, various minor halls and a chapel, and it was restored by the Victorian castle-builder Anthony Salvin, which accounts for the loss of patina and the perfect stonework. In 1380 at the Northumberland coastal fortress of Dunstanburgh, crouched on a sea-washed ledge of rock amid the sand dunes, John of Gaunt blocked the gatehouse and turned it into a keep encircled by a stone wall, and then rebuilt the gatehouse on the west side. And as late as 1405 a powerful gatehouse was built at Lancaster Castle.

So it would seem that new castles were not purely domestic until the fifteenth century, the age of Hurstmonceux, Tattershall and Raglan. Hurstmonceux in Sussex was built in 1440 by Sir Roger de Fynes, who had served in France and was influenced by French fashions in both design and materials, so that he built his castle of Flemish brick, and, despite the heavily fortified gatehouse, it is a castellated quadrangular mansion with a grand staircase. Tattershall in Lincolnshire began as a fortified stone manor house with a curtain wall and mural towers in 1231, but it was rebuilt in 1443 by the third Baron Cromwell, Treasurer of England under Henry VI. It was a brick version of the hall house and tower house design, but now the six-storeyed tower stands alone, a compelling monument in the flat Fen landscape and one of the earliest and finest examples of East Anglian brickwork. Again, despite the battlements and machicolations, the tower was a commodious country house with generous traceried windows, sculptured fireplaces and delicate brick vaults with carved bosses, but today it is an empty shell. Raglan in Monmouth started about 1465, under the ambitious Sir William Herbert, head of the Yorkist party in Wales, to be the last of the great military castles but ended by being a splendid Tudor palace. It is moated and it has a gatehouse and a great hexagonal keep, but instead of military baileys there are pleasant courts and even a bowling green, while the splendid apartments, now shattered and roofless, are genteel with Tudor windows and heraldic carving.

The castle had had its day, and most of those that were not abandoned by their owners were to be 'slighted' in the Civil War of the seventeenth century, to be left to moulder into ruin. There was, however, early in the sixteenth century an isolated development for which Henry VIII was responsible. Fearing a French invasion, he erected from 1538 onwards a chain of small castles or forts along the coast from Kent to Cornwall, designed for artillery and equipped with the latest type of guns. All were ingenious variations on the theme of grouping semi-circular units or bastions. Their designers and engineers (or *devisors* as they were called) were mostly foreigners, among them Stefan von Haschen-

perg from Moravia, who had a talent for constructing *culs-de-sac*
in which the enemy could be grilled with boiling lead, though
the ornamental details were chiefly the work of John Molton,
architect of the St. James's Palace gatehouse and parts of Hampton
Court. It seems that John Leland, the antiquary and chaplain to
the king, also had a hand in the work. Each is built as a compact
block which could be defended all round by guns mounted on
platforms rising in tiers one behind the other. For this reason
they are all roughly circular, with a low round tower or keep in
the middle. The whole is covered by a flat roof, and an internal
gallery pierced with loopholes runs all round the outer wall. The
best-preserved examples are those of Walmer and Deal in Kent,
Camber in Sussex, and St. Mawes and Pendennis in Cornwall.
Walmer, long the residence of the Lords Warden of the Cinque
Ports, is a quatrefoil in shape, with four lobes or semi-circular
bastions. Deal, much larger, has six such bastions and, like Walmer,
is surrounded by a moat and approached by a drawbridge.
Camber, now isolated in the marshes, is rather like Walmer. At
St. Mawes trefoil-leaved semi-circular gun emplacements, open
to the sky, are ranged round the low central keep, and at Pendennis a wide gun emplacement rings a circular tower except
where it is broken by a gatehouse. Later Pendennis was enclosed
by a curtain wall, forming a large bailey. All these forts had
accommodation for a garrison, but they were never actually put
to the test any more than were Mr. Pitt's later Martello towers.

In the extreme north of the country, where Border warfare
was endemic, fortified buildings of one kind or another continued
to be built into the sixteenth and even the seventeenth century.
Here are tower houses which fall into two distinct groups. The
larger type often has wings. At Thirlwall in Northumberland the
meagre ruins indicate that it was an *L*-shaped building of four
storeys with walls thick enough to accommodate mural chambers.
The remains of such a tower at Biddlestone form the ground floor
of a modern Catholic chapel. At Elsdon, still in Northumberland,
the fourteenth-century one-time rectory survives in something
approaching its original condition. In the North Riding there are
intact tower houses at Crayke, South Cowton and Aske Hall, the
last embodied in a later mansion.

In the Border counties, both in England and Scotland, strong-
houses called pele-towers were built in large numbers during the

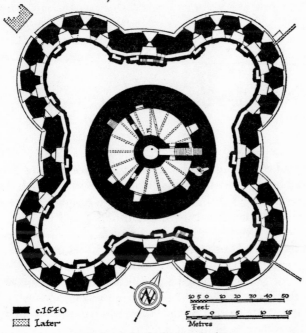

■ c.1540
▒ Later

Walmer Castle, basement plan
(*courtesy of the Department of the Environment*)

fifteenth and sixteenth centuries—there are some 200 in Northumberland alone. The term 'pele' seems to derive from the Latin *palus*, a stake. Normally the building consisted merely of a tower and barmkyn or courtyard, a refuge for the local inhabitants and their cattle during the constant raids from both sides of the Border. It was some 35 feet by 23 feet and stood two or three storeys high beneath a pitched roof, and it was usually of rubble, with dressed masonry in doorways and windows. Many are still fairly intact, often used as barns or farm outbuildings, as at Gatehouse and Raw. A few have been converted to dwellings. Others stand derelict and ruinous, as at Boughthill, Iron House, Highshaw and Low Cleughs. Internal stone staircases are rare, but may be seen at Crag and Dueshill. There are outside stone stairways at Black Middings and Gatehouse. At Highshaw and Branshaw the ground floor was vaulted, and there is a trap in the vault, presumably reached by a wooden ladder. All these pele-towers are in Northumberland.

13

Cathedrals and Parish Churches

By the end of the thirteenth century the mason-craft of England was established, and from that point the era of High Gothic reaches across the first half of the sixteenth century. It comprises those periods popularly known as Decorated and Perpendicular, though these overlap, and a more satisfactory division can be seen in the Black Death which brought architecture to a standstill for a generation. The spirit of mystic lyricism, as exemplified in the ideals of St. Bernard and St. Francis, which found its expression in the Early English style, gave way to the whimsy, luxury and mannered elegance of the fourteenth century, which produced the ornate ogee arch and the delicate tracery of the Decorated style. Windows were complex patterns of foliations and lobes, ornament consisted of foliage sculptured with close attention to nature, especially of ball-flower, of crockets, cinquefoiled canopies and tabernacle work, and there was panache in finials, pinnacles and gablets. Then the flowing lines of the Decorated merged into the panelled ordinance of the Perpendicular, the final phase of medieval architecture, which featured the four-centred arch, tiers of vertical mullions in generous windows, high walls and soaring clerestories, battlements, flamboyant towers and the apotheosis of the porch. Rectilinear panels spread beyond the confines of windows and were largely used for wall decoration. Columns usually consisted of small half-shafts alternating with wide shallow hollows, and capitals, appearing only on the half-shafts, lost their importance and were small and more often moulded than carved, though such Decorated forms of ornament as the ogee and the crocketed pinnacle persisted. This was also the age of the fan-vault, elaborate 'angel roofs' and painted screens.

We have thus reached the ultimate in medieval ecclesiastical architecture, but we cannot within the compass of these pages examine the riches that remain over the length and breadth of the country, for our avowed aim here is to notice, in general, only such buildings as are ruinous or otherwise abandoned. This severely narrows our range, for England is in the happy position, though not uniquely so in Western Europe, of having all its cathedrals, minsters and major parish churches intact. This was not always so, and whatever outrages Victorian architects (and Georgians before them) committed on some of our broken pre-Reformation fanes these great churches were at least preserved and rehabilitated. Yet, in fact, two former cathedrals lie in ruins. One, abandoned long ago, stands upon the strand of an island to the west, its rocky perch washed by the Irish Sea. The other, in the heart of the Shakespeare Country and the industrial Midlands, was blasted by Nazi bombs in 1940.

The cathedral of St. German on the Isle of Man is part of our English fabric, for centuries the episcopal seat of the ancient diocese of Sodor and Man. Whether there is any truth in the tradition that Germanus was here first consecrated bishop of the Sodorenses or Southern Isles, by St. Patrick in 447, it is certain that there was an early church on the site, and that a Norman building preceded the existing structure. The present church, with Peel Castle, lies within an enceinte wall of different periods, with bastions at the angles and a late fourteenth-century gateway-tower. It is a cruciform building comprising nave and south aisles transepts and central tower and a choir with crypt, all of local grey stone with red sandstone quoining. The church is a shell, almost fully intact but open to the sky. The tower and transept, are of *c.* 1300, but the transept windows are of three different periods and there is a Decorated doorway. The choir is of *c.* 1240 and has transitional lancet windows. It was built by Bishop Symon, who had been abbot of Iona, and indeed there is much in this church that recalls that distant fane. Beneath the choir, entered by a mural staircase, is an unorthodox crypt with a barrel vault and thirteen groins springing from pilasters on the solid rock, lighted only by a single small aperture. Until 1780 this crypt was used as the ecclesiastical prison. There is a romantic fiction that Eleanor Cobham, the haughty wife of Humphrey, Duke of Gloucester—Shakespeare's "presumptuous dame, ill-nurtured Eleanor"—here dragged out fourteen years of imprisonment for witchcraft.

Standing close to the ruins of St. Patrick's church, of Manx rectangular plan with some herring-bone masonry in the walls, is a round tower probably coeval with St. Patrick's, that is, probably, tenth-century. This is one of only four Celtic round towers to be found outside Ireland. There were probably domestic buildings north of the cathedral transepts in Symon's time, but those now standing are of sixteenth-century date. Though known as the Bishop's Palace, these buildings were certainly never seriously used as such, but they were so mutilated during the building of the battery below the castle early last century that their form and arrangement are obscure. St. German's is a highly evocative place and there have been many calls to restore it, but this would virtually mean rebuilding; moreover the site is difficult of access, with a bridge across the harbour at low water and a ferry at high water.

Up to 1940 Coventry was a medieval town where the fishponds of the great abbey founded by Leofric and Godiva lay beneath the pavements. St. Michael's, raised to cathedral status in 1918, was one of the major English parish churches until its wartime destruction, and its wraith now stands in striking juxtaposition with the new cathedral designed by Sir Basil Spence. It is a roofless empty shell, the outer walls standing to their full height, buttressed and battlemented with Perpendicular fenestration, but the piers merely marked in the ground. The scale and character of St. Michael's were largely due to the Coventry gilds. The importance of these gilds is evident from the royal patronage bestowed upon them from time to time. Henry VII and his queen were enrolled as honorary members of the famous Trinity gild formed by the union of three of the foremost fraternities in the city in the time of Edward III. The religious and trade gilds were virtually chantry founders, and from the fifteenth century they were building their own chapels in the parish churches. Here, the nave was widened in 1432, and early in the sixteenth century short outer aisles were grafted on to the church to provide chapels for craft gilds associated with the cloth industry—dyers, cappers, mercers, girdlers and drapers, chapels unimaginable now for those who never saw them.

The oldest surviving part of the building is the south porch, late thirteenth-century, with a trefoil-cusped arch and moulded capitals. Beneath the north aisle is a small rib-vaulted crypt of *c.* 1300. Everything else is Perpendicular architecture, though it ranges from 1371 into the early sixteenth century. The chancel, its high walls embattled and pinnacled and its three-light windows with panel tracery almost intact, has a polygonal apse, a rarity in England at such a late date in the early fifteenth century; ranged round it is a series of Victorian low vestries. The glory of St. Michael's, however, is its tower, begun in 1371 and completed somewhere in the 1430s, and still standing bravely. It was built to stand west of the thirteenth-century nave, but the later widening of the nave on the north and the addition of the outer aisles, making a total width of 120 feet (wider than York cathedral), left it in an anomalous and aesthetically unsatisfactory position. It is a handsome composition, with windows in ogee-sided crocketed gables, bell-openings flanked by statues, a battlemented octagonal storey and then the soaring spire supported by slim buttresses. "Neither the directness of Giotto's famous campanile nor the complexities of Ulm can be ranked above the steeple of Coventry, which deserves mention as one of the wonders of the world."[1]

There are, of course, ruins of ancillary buildings yet grouped about some of our cathedrals. Monastic cathedral buildings have already been noticed, and it is the secular cathdrals which now engage our attention. In a few instances the episcopal palace has long been abandoned, adding an intriguing touch to a cathedral close. At Southwell, a cathedral remarkable for the foliated capitals, wonders of naturalistic sculpture, in the chapter house, there is but a fragment of the palace begun in 1360 and completed in 1430, though the north and south outer walls still stand, with a five-light window in the east wall of the chapel. Lincoln and Wells are more rewarding, but first we must journey once more westward into Wales, to that far corner of Pembroke where the village of St. David's is a cathedral city in the heart of a windswept tree-less peninsula.

The history of St. David's goes back to the sixth century, when the saint himself founded a monastic settlement near here. The cathedral lies in a hollow of the Vallis Rosina or valley of the roses, on the edge of the wild marsh called the Dowrog and backed by the gaunt crag of Carn Llidi. To reach it one passes the miniature market place and ancient cross to descend the

[1] John Harvey, *Gothic England* (London, 1947).

Popples, the steep lane paved with pebbles leading down to
Porth y Twr, the Tower Gate. The gateway, of *c.* 1300, is the
sole survivor of four gates originally piercing the enceinte wall.
It is flanked by an Early English octagonal tower, which seems
never to have been completed, and a circular one contemporary
with the portcullised doorway. Within this partly ruined enceinte
wall lie cathedral church, episcopal palace, college and houses
appropriated to the precentor, treasurer, chancellor, the four
archdeacons of the diocese and other dignitaries. Much of all this
is in ruins, and it has been referred to as a living Pompeii.

Before exploring this rare and fossilized medieval colony one
may fleetingly notice the great church itself—the magnificent
stone choir-screen, canopied and crocketed, niched and effigied;
the unique nave roof of almost Eastern opulence, its elaborately
fretted wooden arches springing from peculiar Transitional and
Early English piers; the Celtic *olla podrida* of stone below St.
David's altar and, opposite, all that remains of the saint's shrine
with his alleged casket.

The broken palace is largely the work of that fourteenth-century
Bishop Henry de Gower who brought a hint of Italian Romanesque into this grey country and whose open-arcaded parapets,
seen here to perfection, are also to be encountered at Lamphey
palace and Swansea Castle. The buildings, occupying three sides
of a vast quadrangle, of checkered stonework, purple, cream and
white, were begun about 1280 and completed *c.* 1370. They are
approached through a vaulted gateway in a two-storeyed gatehouse. East of this, against the courtyard wall, is a building with
arcaded parapet and doorways, now blocked, which led to the
bishop's solar. Despite the absence of a piscina this was probably
a private chapel. The main block in the east range is occupied by
the bishop's hall and solar, late thirteenth-century, where the
principal chambers are, rather usually, carried on a series of barrel
vaults set transversely across the building. The hall itself, entered
by a porch covering an external stair, is a large room with
evidence of the usual screened passage and is well lighted by
generous lancet windows. The solar has similar windows, but
their inner recesses have delicate shafts carrying foliated capitals.
There are also a fireplace and a passage in the thickness of the
wall which originally led to the garderobes, demolished when
the bishop's private chapel was built. Originally both hall and

solar had an open roof, as may be seen from the magnificent series of corbels carved as human heads from which sprang the main roof trusses. There are three vaulted undercrofts beneath the hall and two beneath the solar, and each of the two series has a separate entrance from the courtyard and is lighted by narrow windows with trefoiled heads.

A wing of *c.* 1500 projects to the rear of the solar. It is two-storeyed, the ground floor covered by a barrel vault, and it probably linked up with vanished garderobes. The kitchen of *c.* 1350 adjoins the hall at the end of the range. It is a rectangular building and was carried on two barrel vaults. The kitchen proper was on the first floor and was entered by two doorways opening out of the passage leading from the porch of the bishop's hall to the east end of the great hall.

The great hall, completed in 1347, occupied the south side of the courtyard. It is a large building, some 120 feet by 30 feet. The ground floor is covered by six transverse barrel vaults and is lighted by small ogee windows. There is an elaborately decorated entrance porch with external steps from the courtyard, with an enriched ogee archway. Lighting was provided by traceried two-light windows with transoms and some smaller plainer windows. The great east gable is pierced by a rose window of trefoiled lights. The building, like the others, is roofless and crowned with arcaded parapets. A western chamber adjoins the hall proper, and in the north angle a doorway leads to the chapel which lies north-west of the hall.

The late thirteenth-century chapel, which has two entrances from the courtyard, is small, with a vaulted undercroft, and is lighted by two-light traceried windows. The east wall has a later Decorated window of three lights, flanked externally by canopied niches similar to those on the porch of the great hall. This, like the richly ornamented piscina, is an addition by Bishop Gower. The west gable has a small round window, below which is the pentise roof of a narrow annexe extending across the width of the chapel. A bellcote surmounted by a small octagonal spire rises from the north-west angle. The north wall is remarkable for its columns embedded in the wall, rising from corbels in the form of human heads and surmounted by simple capitals from which spring the arch rings, occasionally decorated with an eight-petalled flower, a favourite motif in Gower's work. Unlike the

rest of the buildings, the arcaded parapet is topped with battlements.

There remains the western range, the oldest of the palace
buildings, thirteenth-century and possibly even earlier. The long
gabled building has no original features, but a vaulted undercroft
was later inserted. Finally, there are the remains of St. Mary's
College on the north of the cathedral, with which it is linked.
This was founded by another great building bishop, Adam de
Houghton, in 1377, for a master, seven fellows or chaplains and
two choristers, the whole under the control of the precentor. The
ruins are in an early Perpendicular style and there is a graceful
tower, and the building is another intriguing element in the
archaic and romantic composition that is St. Davids.

On the other side of England is Lincoln with its trinity of
serene cathedral towers and its Angel Choir, which marks the
beginning and the peak of the Early English style in all the kingdom. Here, the ruined episcopal palace lies, unseen and un-
suspected, behind the precinct wall, approached through a
sixteenth-century arch. It is a fascinating and highly complex
composition of the thirteenth and fifteenth centuries. The great
hall, begun by St. Hugh early in the thirteenth century and completed by Hugh of Wells, who died in 1234, is one of the most
impressive halls of its date, over 100 feet in length and having,
originally, arcades on piers of Purbeck marble. The twin windows
were shafted on both sides, the inner shafts also being of Purbeck
marble so that the general effect must have resembled St. Hugh's
Angel Choir. The stylish porch has pointed arches with stiff-leaf
capitals and dog-tooth enrichment. Three doorways from the
entrance bay lead to kitchen and offices. Because of the fall in the
ground the solar was above the buttery. The kitchen is a separate
building with enormous fireplaces under double-chamfered
arches rising direct from the ground. East of the main hall and
parallel with it is a range containing the lesser hall and dining-
room above a tunnel-vaulted undercroft. On the north are
buildings of mid fifteenth-century date, including a three-
storeyed gate-tower, which link up with the other two ranges.

The most beautiful of all ruined palaces is undoubtedly that of
Wells in the Mendips, the City of Many Streams, the Wellys or
Ad Fontes of our forefathers. Wells is the essential cathedral city
(the very place for reading Huysmans or Trollope or Parson

Woodforde), its medieval episcopal ensemble miraculously surviving intact and without peer in Europe. All the component
parts are here—cathedral and close with its four gateways, moated
bishop's palace, deanery, Vicars Close, originally the College of
Singing Clerks, with its fifty small houses, hall and chapel forming the most perfect Gothic thoroughfare in England, the parish
church of St. Cuthbert (one of those splendid Perpendicular fanes
known in Somerset as 'quarter cathedrals'), the ingeniously
contrived water conduit, and yet much more.

The palace-castle of the bishops is set in the middle of a broad
swan-haunted moat. The core of the present residential part of
the palace was built by Bishop Joceline early in the reign of
Henry III, to which belong the two lower storeys (the upper
storey is comparatively modern). It was Bishop Robert Burnell
who left his successors a fortress where he had taken over a fine
manor house. In 1285 he coaxed the abundant waters of St.
Andrew's spring, which wells up from the ground, into a quadrangular moat, and within it he built an enceinte wall with towers
at each corner and a bastion or two here and there. On the face
which looks towards the cathedral the curtain is broken by a
substantial gate-house with portcullis and flanking octagonal
towers, a permanent causeway now replacing the original
drawbridge.

Within this enclosure Burnell built his banqueting hall, chapel
and domestic buildings, which for all their battlements are purely
civil in character, with large handsome windows having tracery
of the early Decorated period. This building bishop who was
long Chancellor to Edward I was a wealthy and ambitious prelate,
and in the fond hope that his cherished nephew would sire a
baronial line he bought up over a score of manors in Shropshire,
and there, at Acton Burnell, he built a fortified manor house
with a banqueting hall much akin to that at Wells, also now in
ruins. The vandal Bishop Barlow, who was responsible for the
sacking of the palace at St. David's, disposed of the Wells palace
in the cataclysmic middle years of the sixteenth century to My
Lord Protector Somerset, and a minion of My Lord Protector
Northumberland, who got his share of the plunder, carted off the
panelling, the carved ceiling beams, the roof lead and much else.
All but the chapel mouldered into ruin, including what was once
one of the finest banqueting halls in England, now rising from a

lovely garden enclosed by the mellowed curtain walls, one of
them espaliered with old fruit trees.

Until the Second World War Norwich retained thirty-four of
her sixty-one ancient churches, and about half of these are no
longer in normal use. At the time of Agincourt there were
forty-one churches in York, and today there are twenty-five, six
of which have outlived their original purpose. The remarkable
fact, however, is that of over 9,000 parish churches of medieval
foundation, plus those monastic and collegiate churches appropriated for parochial use at the Reformation, extremely few lie
in ruins. Most counties have one or two, and we have already
hinted at some of them in lost and deserted villages. Let us look
at a few of the more significant ones.

When Edward II built his new town at Winchelsea an ambitious
cruciform church seems to have been planned but never completed. What remains is an Early Decorated chancel with north
and south aisles, now used as the parish church, though parts of
the transept walls are *in situ*. Whether the nave and aisles were
ever built is doubtful. It may be that after the Black Death funds
were lacking, or it may be that the complete church was built
but partially destroyed in one of the French raids along this coast.
The surviving remnant is one of the earliest examples of a pure
Decorated building before the mannerism of the fourteenth century overtook the style, as may be seen in the traceried windows
of the aisles and the gabled and crocketed piscinae and sedilia,
with their cinquefoiled arches, foliated corbels and clustered
shafts. Later Decorated exuberance is, however, displayed in the
Alard tombs with their steeply-gabled canopies, crocketed with
panache and rising to finials, the rich tabernacle-work on the
front niches of the tomb-chest and the diapering on the back
of the tomb of Gervase Alard, an Admiral of the Cinque Ports.
In fact this church was built by the team of masons who
worked on the Eleanor Crosses and who laid the foundations of
a new national style, and the shape of things to come is here
apparent.

A rarely encountered feature of Winchelsea is the consecration
cross incised on the exterior of the building. When medieval
churches were consecrated twelve crosses were painted or otherwise indicated on the interior and twelve carved on the exterior,
to be annointed with holy water or oil by the bishop. While

quite a number of churches have preserved their internal crosses (Crosthwaite in Cumberland and Trocking in Hertfordshire have each retained a complete set), external ones have mostly weathered away.

The partly ruined church of Howden in Yorkshire is another monument of the Decorated or Geometrical period. It was made collegiate and served by a resident dean and secular canons in 1267 by Archbishop Giffard of York. When the later Bishop Skirlaw of Durham built the chapter-house he utilized the space to the east of the vestibule for his chantry chapel. When the college was dissolved in 1547 the parishioners wanted only the nave. The choir was walled up in 1609 and after being abandoned collapsed in 1696, so that this and the chapter-house now lie in ruins. The nave, still in use, has a noble west front rising to a central gable and flanked by the lower aisles. The great west window is vertically mullioned into four lights with a richly traceried head of rectilinear design, sculptured above with a crocketed canopy. The central buttresses have tabernacle work and figures of saints, and there are four lantern-like turrets with more crockets and finials. Within the church is a considerable amount of weathered figure sculpture which once adorned the exterior of the church, saints, bishops and an Annunciation angel, which shows the fourteenth-century York school of carvers at its best.

At Whorlton-in-Cleveland on the lonely moors of Yorkshire's North Riding the ruined church chaperones, at a distance, the ruined castle. The arcades are Norman, the south arcade having round piers with scalloped capitals and square abaci supporting round arches. The north arcade is later Norman, with the same arches but slimmer piers, moulded capitals and octagonal abaci. This is of two bays, as a Perpendicular tower with two-light bell-openings has been set in the third bay. The chancel arch is depressed and has heavy scalloped capitals and chip-carved stars on the hood-mould. In the chancel is an early fifteenth-century tomb recess, clearly brought from elsewhere, having a round arch with trefoil cusping, with panelling inside the canopy. In the recess is a fine oak effigy of early fourteenth-century date.

Still in Yorkshire, there is another ruined church at Hepstonstall, near Halifax, an intriguing village lying fossilized on its steep hill, which until only a decade or so ago retained its streets with stone setts. The village is a Victorian mill-smoked and blackened period piece, though it has, surprisingly, handsome architecture of all periods. The first church here is said to have been built about 1340 and to have been rebuilt in the closing years of the fifteenth century. The existing ruins, comprising twin naves with aisles, two chancels, south porch and west tower, are certainly of Perpendicular date and style, though the lower part of the tower may be thirteenth-century. Some repairs had been made upon it in the seventeenth century, but it was so decayed by the 1850s that it was dismantled. Both churchyard and village have the distracting moody quality of the Brontë country, which indeed is near at hand.

In Worcestershire the very different and serene hill village of Abberley has a small church of golden stone, all crumbling except for a fragment of the chancel, which is repaired and contains aumbry and piscina, a splayed Norman window and some good ledger stones. Addison came often to the hall here, reputed to be the original seat of Sir Roger de Coverley, so that both Addison and his host must have worshipped here long before the Victorian church was built. At Sapey Prichard in the Teme valley there is another derelict Norman church, almost the twin of Abberley, tucked away in a flowering wood beside a stream. At Upton-on-Severn in the same county nothing is left of the medieval parish church except a large Gothic tower of red sandstone, surmounted with a Georgian conceit in the form of a wooden cupola and sea-blue copper dome.

The Suffolk coast, with its marshes, hidden creeks and sea birds, is the graveyard of many a prosperous fishing community and thus of many a church. At Covehithe, in an area strewn with cornelians and agates, the church, largely fourteenth-century, was purged and dismantled as long ago as 1643. The sturdy tower was too useful to seamen to be taken down, but the walls of nave, aisles and chancel are crumbling away. The east end with a great window frame is intact. Within the nave of the immense skeleton is a little thatched church built in the time of Charles I.

This pattern is paralleled at Walberswick, where the south aisle of the otherwise completely ruined building has been newly adapted as a parish church. The joy of this ruin is the parapet of the tower, built in 1426, a rich confectionery of decorative ornament in stone and flint, to be matched in this area in such towers as that of Woodbridge and in the south porch of Mendlesham, all,

(*above*) Raglan Castle
(*below*) The ruined gatehouse of Titchfield Abbey, Hampshire

Kirby Hall

possibly, by the same masons, Richard Russel and Adam Powle of Dunwich. The south porch, with its upper chamber in which the priests' vestments were stored, is also intact. This is one of the few great provincial churches to be built in the first quarter of the fifteenth century, though that century marked a good deal of church work in East Anglia.

At Orford, still in Suffolk, the nave of the church is intact and is notable for its Perpendicular font, the bowl resting on demi-figures of angels with outspread wings and divided by buttresses into oblong panels containing the Evangelist symbols and sacred figures such as the Trinity, while the base is supported by lions alternating with Suffolk wild men or 'Wodehouses'. The Norman chancel, however, built at the same time as the nearby castle with its great eighteen-sided polygonal keep, is in ruins. Here the column piers are encircled with a spiral band of bowtell moulding in high relief, an interesting variation of the Durham pier-design, as we have already remarked.

In Norfolk the decline of the medieval port of Cley, which once sent ships to Iceland, is again reflected in the parish church, where the transepts are in ruins. The remainder of the church is intact, and the nave is notable for the alternation of traceried roundels and small pointed two-light trefoil-headed windows in the clerestory, a local mannerism in the fifteenth century. It has been suggested that, as at Winchelsea, the Black Death or some other disaster prevented the completion of the transepts. Certainly there is a hint of this in the incoherence of the north transept, but the south transept was clearly more advanced by that fatal summer of 1349, for the window tracery is pure Decorated, and there are pinnacles and crockets on the gable.

In the north-west corner of the parish churchyard at Salthouse are the ruins of a medieval chapel with piscina and altar. Why this detached chapel was here is not clear. The fifteenth-century tower of Blakeney church is matched by a very slender but lofty tower at the north-eastern end of the church, the latter having a lantern turret that was used as a beacon and seamark. Dr. W. G. Hoskins suggests that these two towers were placed in line in order to give a navigational 'fix', and that the chapel in Salthouse churchyard may have been lined up with the tower of Salt-house church in a similar way. We are still in Norfolk. In the village of Hillborough in wild Breckland are the remains of one of the 'Slipper' chapels on the pilgrims' way to the great shrine of Walsingham. In the churchyard of Reeping were the three churches of Hackford, Whitwell and Reepham, but Hackford was burned down in 1543 and only a broken arch remains. The church of East Somerton is in ruins, and at Eccles on the coast a mound of stones revealed on the beach at low tide is all that remains of St. Mary's church.

Medieval bridges were often placed under the protection of a saint by the building and dedication of a chapel or oratory. Both Old London Bridge and the High Bridge of Lincoln were under the protection of St. Thomas of Canterbury. Bow Bridge had its chapel of St. Catherine. St. William held the old Ouse Bridge at York. There were others at Rochester, Bedford, Durham, Chester, Bristol and elsewhere. Most of them were ultimately demolished after having declined into prisons or second-hand shops. Yet four of them survive in almost pristine condition, restored but no longer in normal use.

The best example of a bridge chapel is that of St. Mary at Wakefield in Yorkshire. It was endowed by Edward III in 1358, and forty years later Edmund Langley, Duke of York, founded chantries in it. The bridge is coeval; it spans the Calder river and it has nine arches with chamfered ribs. "On the east side of this bridge," wrote Leland, "is a right goodly chapel of Our Lady and two cantuarie priests founded on it." Despite the severe restoration by Sir Gilbert Scott in 1847, which involved reproducing the chapel front (since the original was carted away to act as a folly in the park of Kettlethorpe Hall), the building remains a tolerable specimen of Decorated Gothic. The Victorian façade, already badly weathered, copies the original five-arched bays with canopied ornament. Each of the side walls contains three large windows with curvilinear tracery in square hood-moulds, and the parapet has a blind arcade, each panel having a traceried head. The turret and slender staircase tower are intact. A feature of the interior is the Easter Sepulchre, which has a figure of Christ rising from the tomb, flanked by kneeling angels, while three soldiers below are gazing up in awe. The Sepulchre was the setting of a medieval ceremony, a kind of liturgical drama symbolizing the Entombment and the Resurrection. Generally it was a portable piece of furniture, but often it was a permanent sculptured feature, to be seen in its most elaborate form at Heckington in Lincolnshire and Hawton, Nottinghamshire.

Rotherham Bridge, now over dry land, still has Leland's "chapel of stone wel wrought". Of 1483, it is pinnacled and embattled and has richly traceried windows and a tunnel-vaulted crypt. It later became the town jail—the bridge is called Jail Bridge—but is now restored to its original condition. Three of the bridge arches belong to the original structure. At St. Ives in Huntingdon St. Leger presides, rather unaccountably, over the bridge, over the middle pier of which is his chapel of 1426, hexagonal and quite plain, with simple two-light windows. The bridge has four pointed ribbed arches and two rebuilt round ones. At Bradford-on-Avon in Wiltshire the fourteenth-century nine-arched bridge has a small oratory which replaces an earlier chapel. Dedicated to St. Nicolas, patron saint of seafarers, it is a small square structure corbelled out from the end pier of the bridge, and it has a seventeenth-century domed roof surmounted by a weathervane bearing the saint's gudgeon emblem. It resembles a village lock-up, which indeed it long was. At Derby the chapel of St. Mary has outlived its bridge.

14

Monastic Developments

We have already seen that the first important and significant monastic reforms were developed in France in the eleventh century, at Citeaux and the Grande Chartreuse. The impact of the Cistercians on English life and art has been described, but our review of the Carthusians was postponed until now since this was the only order that continued to make foundations right into the fifteenth century. The Carthusians, the Poor Brothers of God, were founded by St. Bruno, a canon of Cologne and a teacher at Rheims and Paris, who appears to have entered the Benedictine abbey of Molesmes. From there in 1084 he retired with a handful of similarly minded men to a lonely site in the mountains of Dauphiné, wishing for nothing less than to contemplate eternity in a return to the spirit of the Thebaid desert. St. Bruno was to die at La Torre in the mountains of Calabria, but the hermits of Dauphiné followed the precepts of their leader even at that distance, and their hermitage became the Grande Chartreuse.

The original tendency to be purely eremitical was soon coloured by a compromise combining Benedict's Rule with the ideas of the Desert Fathers. The Carthusians, however, remained solitaries, or as near to being solitaries as monks ever came. They initiated their own bye-laws or what might be regarded as supplements to the original Rule. Thus about 1127 Dom Guigo, fifth prior of the Grande Chartreuse, compiled the *Consuetudines* or *Customs*, a remarkable document, as too is his *Meditationes*, an account of his own spiritual life which is almost unique in medieval literature.

The Carthusians retained the traditional elements of liturgical prayer, *lecto divina* (holy reading) and manual work, but just as the Benedictines stressed study and the Cistercians manual labour, so the Carthusian emphasis was placed squarely on the contemplative life. Thus the brethren met in church only for the night-office and vespers, the rest of the canonical hours and devotions being recited privately in the cell. Meals were also eaten in the solitude of the cell and passed through a *guichet* or hatch by a lay brother—save on Sundays and feast-days when meals were served in the common refectory. Diet was rigorous and flesh meat wholly excluded. Discipline included the wearing of a hair shirt, held in position by *lumbaria*, bands resembling loin-cloths around the waist. Reading and work was also done in the cell or its little garden. Later, to soften the rigours of such a life and in the interests of physical and mental health, there was the weekly *spatiamentum* or fraternal gathering and walk outside the monastic enclosure. At the beginning there was no 'Carthusian rite', but the Mass was the shortest of the Latin Masses (and remains so today, barely altered since the eleventh century). Nor was there an organ, since instrumental music, along with monstrances and copes, was prohibited.

The distinctive architectural features of the *chartreuse* or charterhouse were the ranges of cells or individual small two-storeyed houses opening out from three sides of the great cloister, with another cloister for the lay brothers' quarters, while the church was divided in two by a screen separating the choirs of monks and lay brethren, resembling the *iconostasis* of the Byzantine and Eastern Churches, though there is no evidence to support the theory that there was a connection. The Carthusian monastery thus resembled the *laura* of the desert hermits.

There were but nine Carthusian monasteries in England. The first was established at Witham in Somerset in 1181, the second at Hinton in the same county in 1227. The remaining seven were founded between 1343 and 1414. The Witham foundation made a precarious beginning, and it took St. Hugh himself, journeying from the Grande Chartreuse, to set it on its feet, presiding over the house until 1186 when he became Bishop of Lincoln. It was for the monks of Witham that an anonymous monk of the Grande Chartreuse wrote *A Book of the Fourfold Discipline of the Cell*, which is as valid for Carthusians today as it was then. Nothing remains of the Witham house but the *frary* or lay brothers' church, a small attractive twelfth-century building with a vault, which has a curious effect on the splayed windows, an apsidal east end and some notable buttresses. It now serves as the parish church. Traces of the *frary* have also been found at Hinton, and

Stone Lined Channel

SPRING
HOUSE

GARDEN

GARDEN

GARDEN

GARDEN

CELL Nº 5

CELL Nº 4

CELL Nº 3

CELL Nº 2

GARDEN

CELL Nº 6

GARDEN

CELL Nº 7

CELL Nº 8

SITE
OF
CONDUIT

GARDEN

CELL Nº 9

CLOISTER   GARTH

GARDEN

CELL Nº10

GARDEN

CELL Nº11

GARDEN

CELL Nº12

GARDEN

CELL Nº13

GARDEN

CELL Nº14

GARDEN

CELL Nº15

GAR

HATCH   CLOISTER

LOBBY

STAIRS

FIRE-PLACE

WATER TAP

PENTICE

LIVING ROOM

STUDY

BEDROOM &
ORATORY

GARDEN

PENTICE TO
GARDEROBE

10 5 0   10   20

SCALE OF FEET

GROUND FLOOR ARRANGEMENT
OF A TYPICAL CELL

5   0   10   2

SCALE OF METRES

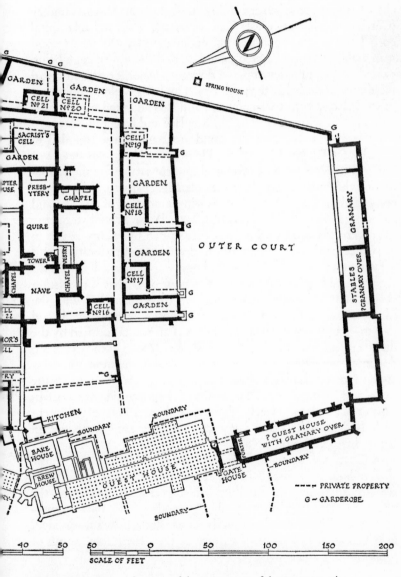

Mount Grace Priory (*courtesy of the Department of the Environment*)

it is clear that in the early houses of the order the *conversi* or lay brethren had oratory, cells and offices wholly separate from those of the monks. What survives at Hinton, however, is the chapter-house, a beautiful fifteenth-century building which was formerly attached to the church. It is of three storeys, the lowest a vaulted chapel of three bays, with a trefoil-headed piscina and an aumbry (Carthusian chapter-houses had an altar), a remarkable spiral corbel and a group of three lancets in the east wall, the second storey also having a vaulted chamber, and the upper stage being gabled, at one time serving as a dovecote. Another two-storeyed building was probably the refectory. This has a vaulted undercroft of three bays, with two columns, and it is adjoined on the west by a kitchen with serving hatch, fireplace and lancet windows.

Little now remains of the London Charterhouse founded in 1371 by Sir Walter Manny, the Flemish Knight in the service of Edward III who was immortalized by Froissart. After the Reformation the buildings became a nobleman's palace and were later converted into Thomas Sutton's twin foundation of hospital and school, and after the removal of Charterhouse School to Surrey they were adapted to other uses. Fire caused by enemy action in 1941 presented an opportunity for clearance and restoration, and a fascinating account of the findings was published by David Knowles and W. F. Grimes.[1] It is now clear that the existing chapel built by Sutton was in no way to be identified with the medieval monastic church, as had hitherto been believed, and that the original oratory lay west of it. This was confirmed by the discovery of the tomb of Sir Walter Manny, known from documentary evidence to have been buried in the monastic choir at the foot of the high altar. Sutton's chapel is, in fact, on the site of the chapter-house. The limits of the south side of the main cloister have been clearly defined and buildings of different periods identified, so that a new and authentic reconstruction, on paper, has become possible.

In Coventry a private house covers much of the site of the charter-house of which Richard II was titular founder, but there remains an important building which seems to have been the refectory with the prior's lodging south of it. This is two-storeyed, with the refectory on the upper floor, now sub-divided, in which are the remains of a fresco of the Crucifixion. South of

[1] *Charterhouse* (London, 1954).

this, reached from below by a stone spiral staircase, is the prior's study, with a large chimneypiece corbelling forward towards the lintel. There are substantial parts of the original open timber roof of the refectory, some Gothic window tracery and some sixteenth-century emblazoned panelling. Nicholas Hereford, Wycliff's chief henchman in the vernacular translation of the Bible, recanted and died a monk here.

The one charter-house in England in a good state of preservation is Mount Grace, lying immediately below the moors in Yorkshire's North Riding. Founded by the Duke of Surrey in 1398, who was later murdered and buried in the monastic church, it was the last but one of the English Carthusian houses. Its second prior, Nicholas Love (1410–21), was the author of *The Mirror of the Blessed Life of Jesus Christ*. The precinct is entered by a gatehouse with a gateway of two bays, formerly rib-vaulted. Adjoining it on either side are ranges that contained the guesthouses (one partly used as a granary), now partially converted into a private dwelling, and running at right-angles to these, along the southern perimeter of the outer court, are ranges that comprised stabling and barn. The church, almost intact, is entered from the outer court. It is of modest dimensions and has a west doorway with a large window over it. The original church of *c.* 1400 was even smaller, but in the fifteenth century the choir was extended eastward to flank the small square chapter-house on the north, a tower was built between nave and choir, and a chapel or quasi-transept was built on either side of the nave. The archway to the northern chapel is four-centred, and the window of the southern chapel also has a four-centred arch. The nave served as the choir of the *conversi*. The tower, almost perfectly preserved, is oblong and stands on two cross-walls as in friars' churches. The bell-openings are transomed, and the details of the arches with their triple shafts, filleted and with continuous deep hollows between them, are decidedly Decorated in style even at this late date. Beyond this is the monks' choir, now devoid of architectural features, with a chapel on the south.

It must be admitted that the plan of the church is not typical of Carthusian churches. Nor do the buildings adjoining it on the south side of the cloister correspond to normal Carthusian usage. These indeed are not easily identifiable. The chapter-house, with the customary altar against the east wall, is immediately north of the choir. The sacrist's cell adjoins this on the east. To the north-west of the church are the prior's lodging, with an oriel window overlooking the cloister, and the refectory, with an entry between them into the cloister. The great cloister at least conforms to the Carthusian plan everywhere. Off each of the east, north and west walks are the remains of five cells. Each cell was a self-contained dwelling, about 27 feet square and of two storeys, the ground floor being divided, originally, by partitions into a lobby, a living-room, a bedroom and a study. At one end of the lobby was a wooden staircase to the upper floor, which served as a workshop, and at the other a door to the garden. The walls stand high enough to retain their doorways and the (originally hatched) square openings through which food was passed into the cell. From the rear of each cell a pentise led to the garderobe built against the outer wall of the garden. The best preserved of these lavatories adjoins the cell reconstructed about 1900, when the last excavations were carried out. Water was supplied for all purposes by lead pipes from a conduit in the middle of the cloister court.

The area round the church in the outer court was further complicated after 1427, when Henry V granted the convent a number of suppressed alien priories, necessitating the building of five more cells. Finally, there is a group of buildings, brewhouse, bakehouse and kitchen, at the north-western corner of the outer court.

The most striking phenomenon of the thirteenth century was the emergence of a new form of religious life which brought a new type of humanism. This originated in the popular revival of religion inaugurated by St. Francis of Assisi and the subsequent foundation of the order of friars. "The coming of the friars," wrote Trevelyan, "was the last great wave of foreign influence that had been washing over England ever since the Norman Conquest." The changing needs of medieval society were met by the more flexible policies, organization and framework of these new religious bodies, Chaucer's "ordres four"—the Franciscans or Friars Minor, the Dominicans or Friars Preacher, the Carmelites and the Hermits of St. Augustine or Austin Friars. The first two owed their inception to the powerful heretical sects of the period, the Cathari or Albigenses and the Waldensians, for among the measures adopted by Pope Innocent III to restore unity to the Church were ecclesiastical reforms which aimed, among other things, to restore the lost art of preaching. In response to this appeal there came forward two men of marked ability and equally marked differences in character. Both founded mendicant orders of friars which later became noted for their scholastic attainments, having in each case circuits bounded by special provinces, while the members were not confined to a single house. In each case, too, there was direct contact with the people in preaching and missionary work. They settled at centres of population and commercial and intellectual life, and they ministered to sick and poor, to burgess and tradesman and leper.

Francis, a layman of Assisi in Tuscany, was the founder of the brotherhood dedicated to Lady Poverty and the purely apostolic life. It might also be said that he was the founder of that charmed bright Umbrian landscape of poetry and legend. The first Franciscan settlement was a forsaken travellers' shelter near the leper hospital at Rivo Torto, so small and mean that Francis had to chalk the name of each friar over his narrow sleeping place. Fifteen years later, in 1224, they came to Canterbury. The Spanish Dominic, a canon of Osma, was essentially a realist. His friars were a fully centralized and mobile religious order occupying a position more akin to that of the Jesuits of the later Counter-reformation, and they were to become an essentially liturgical body. They reached England three years before the Franciscans and, significantly, they went straight to Oxford. Dominican theology and philosophy rapidly attained their peak in the *Summa Theologica* of Thomas Aquinas, but after that it was outclassed by the brilliance of the English province of the Franciscans—in William of Ockham, Roger Bacon and Duns Scotus. A third mendicant order, the Carmelites, had more affinity with the Carthusians and in origin was purely contemplative and indeed eremitical. Even its foundation was obscure, but it traditionally derives descent from Elias himself on Mount Carmel, the Hebrew 'place planted with trees'. Certainly the first recorded setlement was on Mount Carmel in the twelfth century. Dislodged from Palestine by the Saracens, groups of these hermits settled in remote corners of Europe, and in the thirteenth century they reached England, where the reforms of St. Simon Stock established them as a mendicant order, officially in 1276. It can be seen from the foregoing that Sir Walter Scott slipped up badly, for his Friar Tuck, in the reign of Richard I, is clearly an anachronism.

Largely because of their urban location, the English friaries (and, including those of minor mendicant orders, there were 217 of them) have all but disappeared. No complete medieval Franciscan church has survived. At Winchelsea all that remains is the unaisled choir with three-sided apse, late thirteenth-century Decorated work. In most friary churches a central cross-aisle or passage divided the 'preaching nave' from the choir. This was the arrangement in the church of the Grey Friars in London, perhaps the largest friary church in England, of which there is now no trace. In many instances a bell-tower rose from the centre of the cross-aisle, and in each wall of the aisle were two arches opening into nave and choir respectively. At Richmond, Yorkshire, all that remains is the tower in this position. Of fifteenth-century date, it is oblong, the four arches having triple responds and polygonal capitals, and there is an attractive open-work parapet with battlements and pinnacles. At King's Lynn an octagonal lantern tower of stone supported on arches of red brick occupies the same position, and again nothing else has survived.

In Chichester a fragment of the thirteenth-century church, Early English in style, is in use as the guildhall, retaining a fine east window of five lancets and a handsome sedilia. A comparable fragment is that of Lincoln, now the county museum. What remains here is the late thirteenth-century choir and its undercroft. The choir, which has been altered, has a beautiful double piscina. The east window is of three lights, and near it in the north wall is a lancet. An oval light is over this, and over the gable is a pierced cross.

The most substantial remains of a Franciscan church are to be found in Gloucester, the friars of which seem to have been constantly badgered by the Benedictines of that town. The post-Reformation history of the friary is residential and commercial, and despite the recent and excellent de-secularization by the Ministry of Works, it has proved impossible to wholly disentangle the original from the later buildings. The west front of the church is still curiously transformed by a Georgian domestic façade, but behind this mask is an elaborate and refined late Perpendicular church, rebuilt by James, Lord Berkeley from 1519. What we now see is a double nave of seven bays and a fragment of the choir. Arches and windows are acutely pointed. The east window of six lights was clearly splendid, and the north aisle, which was possibly a Berkeley chantry, has rich stone wall panelling alternating with the windows and continuing beneath the windows, where is also a row of carved early Tudor shields.

On the whole the Dominicans have left more rewarding remains. Few of their houses were as magnificent as that described by William Langland in *Piers Plowman*, though their intellectual activities often required additional facilities. Certainly their churches were spacious and well-lighted with large handsome windows. Their church in Norwich, now in use as St. Andrew's Hall, is almost intact. Built between 1440 and 1470, it consists of an aisled nave of seven bays and an unaisled choir of seven bays, together with the dividing cross-passage that was formerly surmounted by an octagonal tower. Clerestory and porch are markedly Perpendicular in style. In Cambridge the Dominican house was cleverly adapted to the plan of the new Emmanuel College, the hall of which, despite transformation, is substantially the friary church.

The finest group of Dominican buildings is undoubtedly that in Gloucester, a thirteenth-century foundation which at the Dissolution passed to the clothier, Sir Thomas Bell, who embodied part of the church in his house. The domestic buildings became a cloth factory and then fell into decay before being put to other uses. They have recently been restored by the Ministry of Works. The church was itself contrived out of the central portion of the original cruciform church. It is mainly thirteenth-century work with a fourteenth-century north transept. The domestic buildings about the cloister garth stand south of the church. The thirteenth-century refectory in a simple refined Early English style lies on the west. The southern range in the same style contains a library more elaborate than most, especially for its date, and it must be one of the oldest, possibly *the* oldest, library buildings in England. It has carrels or study recesses in the thickness of the south wall, each with its little window and shallow-arched ceiling, and it ante-dates the famous carrels in the Benedictine abbey (now cathedral) cloisters of Gloucester by over a century.

Of the Dominican Hereford house, where Edward III was present at the dedication of the church, there remains only the west range of the claustral buildings, probably the refectory and prior's lodging of *c.* 1322. This was altered on conversion to a

Tudor house, but it retains fourteenth-century windows from a cloister alley. In the grounds is a restored fourteenth-century 'preaching cross' or 'pulpit cross', the only one in England. It is a charming octagonal structure with open traceried arcading and angle buttresses, with a spire and cross above it. Each side is opened up with a pointed arch, and inside is or was the pulpit.

Finally, the remnants of the Bristol house deserve passing notice. These are now embodied in the Friends' Meeting House, and they consist of two ranges, connected by a restored Decorated cloister. The upper hall of the north range was the dormitory (later used as the Cutlers' Hall) and is of thirteenth-century date with an open timber roof of a century later. The upper hall of the south range (later used as the Bakers' Hall) is also thirteenth-century, its original timber roof being the oldest in Bristol.

Remains of Carmelite friaries are best seen in Aylesford, Kent; Coventry and Hulne, Northumberland. The Aylesford house, founded in 1241, was closely associated with St. Simon Stock, the Prior General of the order, who reformed the eremitical Carmelites into a mendicant order and whose sanctity became a Carmelite cult. It was recovered by the Carmelites in 1949 and is now the mother house of all Carmels in the world, with many features of interest, new buildings as well as medieval. On two sides of the great courtyard are the cells of the friars, built on the Carthusian model *before* the Carmelites became mendicant. The original eremitical oratory stood in the middle of this quadrangle. The south side of the court contains the guesthouses of the later friary, fourteenth- and fifteenth-century, and a building which may have been a wing of the prior's lodging, now lost. The north range of the courtyard was rebuilt as an Elizabethan house. In the fourteenth century a second quadrangle was built, on the north side of which stood the second, or mendicant, church. The foundations of this were exposed but have now been partly covered by a new church. Other features include the medieval gate-house, chapter-house and pilgrims' hostel, with its own little quay on the Medway river.

In Coventry the Carmelite house, founded as late as 1342, was overbuilt by an Elizabethan house which later became the city workhouse. What survives here is the east cloister walk and its range. The cloister, rebuilt in 1506, is of nine bays (over 160 feet) with lierne vaults, seven of the bays containing trefoil-headed lights. The domestic range is buttressed on its western face and has square-headed three-light windows. In the middle of the range is the chapter-house, rib-vaulted, with a large cusped arch-way and two small doorways in the short entrance passage. On either side is a room with a plain rib vault. The upper storey contains the former dormitory and the *studium generale*, with a fine fourteenth-century roof, sixteenth-century four-light mullioned windows and an oriel which may be of post-Reformation date. There are fragments of the north and south ranges. Recent excavations have shown the church to have comprised a nave of nine bays and a chancel of six bays, divided by the typical mendicant cross-aisle, which doubtless carried the tower that collapsed in 1572.

At Hulne it can be seen that the church of *c.* 1240 was planned with both nave and choir unaisled, without any division, and that the night stairs led not directly into the church but into a small court adjoining it.

Of the Austin Friars the parish church of that name in London preserves the original nave intact. Here there are aisles, as there were in the lost choir, where the eastern ends of the aisles served as chapels. Of the friary at Clare in Suffolk, founded by a cousin of Henry III in 1249, there remain the ranges of the prior's lodging and infirmary, fourteenth-century, with original buttresses and some other features, largely masked by post-Reformation rebuilding when a house covered the site. Some remains of the church are embodied in a barn. In 1953 the Austin Friars recovered this house.

Meanwhile, monastic austerity (the Carthusians apart) was on the wane. The monasteries had suffered an almost mortal blow in the bubonic plague of 1349 and its recurrences of 1361 and 1368, and wealth and power had further weakened the spiritual fabric. The practice of providing entertainment was now almost as common in the cloister as in the castle. The account rolls of the Augustinian priory of Maxstoke in Warwickshire, now in ruins, refer to a "player chamber" and to "*lusores, mimi, jocatories*" and "*citharistae*"—minstrels, mummers, jugglers and others. Still to be seen in the prior's lodging there are coats of arms which formerly emblazoned a magnificent ceiling. Such luxury was reflected even more in the spectacular towers, gate-houses and fan-vaulted cloisters, which appeared in the greater monasteries, the expression and the glory of the Perpendicular. Many of the towers have fallen now, but Abbot Huby's tower at Fountains still stands, decorated with the abbot's own coat of arms and, to make amends, with quotations from the Cistercian breviary, while at Evesham the detached bell-tower built by the last abbot, Clement Lichfield, stands alone in panelled and crocketed glory with coronets sailing above the parapet.

The later gate-houses, though they may lead nowhere, are a feast. That of Ely is of *c*. 1400 and has little more than a hint of Perpendicular opulence. At St. Osyth's priory in Essex there is the gate-house of *c*. 1475, of flint and stone and patterned with vertical blind arcading, and at Colchester the gate-house of St. John's Abbey, of *c*. 1486, repeats this flushwork pattern almost exactly. Prior Goldstone's gate-house at Canterbury of *c*. 1517, has octagonal stairway turrets at the angles, and, above the archway, a row of heraldic shields, while another band with angel supporters runs beneath the windows of the upper stage. What must be the last of the great pre-Reformation gate-houses is the main gate of Christ Church, Oxford, 'Big Tom', though this is just out of the monastic province for it was part of Cardinal Wolsey's great collegiate project, left unfinished on his downfall and rounded off by no less an architect than Sir Christopher Wren.

Despite the late foundations of the Carthusians, and despite the fact that the popular Carmelites, Franciscans and Dominicans founded houses as late as 1356, 1387 and 1486 respectively, the age was one which saw the rise of colleges and hospitals rather than new monasteries. The plan of the closed quadrangle, pre-eminently to be seen in the colleges of Oxford and Cambridge, assimilated the designs of the large house, the college of chantry priests and the Carthusian monastery with its separate cells grouped about a cloister. The first quadrangular college to be built in which the analogy with the Carthusian cloister could be seen was Cobham College in Kent, and it may be significant that the architect, Henry Yvele, was in the following year called upon to design the London Charterhouse.

The medieval hospital (which, of course, existed from the earlier years of the Middle Ages) not only ministered to the sick but also provided a refuge for the aged and destitute, distributed

Bolsover Castle, Derbyshire

Lulworth Castle, Dorset

(*above*) The north front of
Seaton Delaval, Northum-
berland. (*left*) Rushton
Triangular Lodge,
Northamptonshire

alms to the poor and supported a number of chaplains who should sing masses for the soul of the founder. Three main hospital forms prevailed in Western Europe. First in point of antiquity was the lazar or leper-house, of which the best surviving English example is that of St. Nicholas at Harbledown near Canterbury, to which went Erasmus as one of Chaucer's Canterbury pilgrims. Then there was the semi-collegiate almshouse type with cells, common hall and chapel grouped about a courtyard. Many such houses survive and indeed continue to function. The most monumental of them is the hospital of St. Cross in the water meadows of the Itchen near Winchester, founded in 1133 and the oldest charitable institution in all Great Britain still doing its work.

At St. Cross the general arrangements resemble those of a college, and the church is distinct from the other buildings. The existing church is an outstanding example of the transition from Romanesque Norman to Early English. This was completed in 1225, but it was not until 1445 that, under Cardinal Beaufort's administration, the existing hospital took shape. A splendid entrance gateway opens on to a small courtyard. Across this, the Beaufort Tower leads into the great quadrangle. In front stands the church, and to the right are the great hall and kitchens. Ahead are the ancient cottages of the brethren, with tall chimneys and mullioned windows, and facing them the long sixteenth-century timber-framed ambulatory, and above that the infirmary.

The third type was the infirmary hospital, which made more provision for the sick, thus entailing the need of a new type of building resembling a church, of which the western portion constituted the hospital proper while the eastern part formed a chapel. To this type belongs the Great Hospital of St. Helen in Norwich, where the ancillary buildings are grouped about a small cloister garth. Uniquely in this country, the hospital fulfils, *mutatis mutandis*, its original function. Additional buildings have accumulated, but the original layout remains intact. It was founded on a modest scale in 1249, but it came to have a master and eight chaplains. Early in the fourteenth century the choir of the church was built, with a chestnut roof on the 252 panels of which are painted an Imperial Eagle, probably a tribute to the queen of Richard II, Anne of Bohemia, who visited the hospital. Shortly afterwards the 'infirmary hall' west of the nave was rebuilt and the great bell-tower erected at the end of its south aisle. North

13

of this a refectory was built on the west side of what was about to be a cloister garth, and a new north range provided accommodation for master and chaplains. On the south side of the church is a chantry chapel of late fifteenth-century date, with a lierne vault remarkable for forty one bosses closely resembling those in the choir vault of Norwich Cathedral, carved by John Everard *c.* 1472 and possibly by the same hand. Above the wall ribs are carved heads of kings and queens. Today the church choir, walled off, is the women's ward, and the original infirmary hall at the west end, also walled off, is similarly arranged for men. Between the two wards is the thus truncated portion of the nave, rendered into a square church of three bays, with the chantry chapel and entrance porch projecting on the south.

If the Norwich hospital faintly recalls such medieval Italian institutions as the Ospedale di Santa Maria Scala of Siena, the late thirteenth-century hospital of St. Mary in Chichester recalls the arrangements in the celebrated Hôtel Dieu at Beaune in Burgundy. St. Mary's, however, is but a miniature and has lost its ancillary buildings, and its more exact counterpart is the hospice of the Heiligengeist in Lubeck in Baltic Germany. Originally of the infirmary hospital type, St. Mary's became an almshouse after the Reformation. Cells, common hall and chapel are here disposed beneath a single roof. It consists of a single large and lofty hall, down the centre of which runs a wide stone-paved passage with cells or cubicles on either side, while the eastern termination is occupied by the chapel, divided from the rest by a light screen. The plan almost duplicates that of the early Egyptian *laura* or Coptic monastery. Before the Reformation, of course, the places of these cubicles would be occupied by the beds of the sick. The predominance of oak here is notable. Solid posts support the open timber roof, the cubicles are separated by screens, and the chapel has stalls with carved miserere seats, canopied sedilia and pews, all of oak.

In the Middle Ages there were fourteen hospitals in York. All that remain are the ruins of St. Leonard's, improbably said to have been founded as early as 936. In its prime it had 200 beds but no resident doctor. What we see now is part of the chapel, ambulatory and entrance passage, Norman and Transitional work.

15

Gothic High Noon

Feudalism was dealt a mortal blow on Bosworth Field in 1485 as the last century of the Middle Ages drew to a close. It coincided with the peak of our endeavour in the world of wrought stone and the Gothic arts, when we achieved a perfect synthesis of structural and aesthetic elements in the Perpendicular style. As J. D. Sedding, the Victorian architect, wrote, "the Perpendicular takes up all that was incomplete in former phases, adding thereto the able disposition of lines and masses, and a higher range of carving and colour decoration, and, in brief, gives every architectural resources its highest and fullest expression."

Its glories are the Lady Chapel of Gloucester Cathedral, Bath Abbey, St. Mary Redcliffe at Bristol, the presbytery of Sherborne Abbey and the magnificent vaulting of its nave, King's College Chapel, Cambridge; St. George's Chapel, Windsor; and the Henry VII Chapel in Westminster Abbey, all flowing with vertical lines and ceiling with almost eastern opulence. Then there are the towers of Wells, Magdalene College, Oxford, and Bell Harry at Canterbury, and the screened and vaulted cloisters of Gloucester, Wells, Canterbury, Worcester and Chester. The fan-vault is one of the wonders of the age, to be developed to degrees of whimsicality, though it has been pointed out that, in the absence of transitional examples, there seems to be no link between the late fourteenth-century fan-vaults in the Gloucester cloisters and the high large-scale fan-work of the Sherborne Vaults of c. 1440. Then there are the lacy stone screens of chantry chapels, the timber 'angel' roofs of Suffolk and the fretted rood screens and lofts of the West Country and the Welsh Marches. And so to the greater colleges of Oxford and Cambridge, where the unity of Perpendicular design is seen to perfection.

There is also something of street architecture, and while most town houses are still of timber, often with bracketed corner-posts of elaborate design and carving, and with long continuous ranges of windows; they do frequently occur in stone. The high street of Glastonbury is graced by two elegant stone buildings. The Tribunal, described as "newly built" for a sessions house and gaol in 1517, is fairly simple. The upper storey is broken by a slightly projecting oriel window, of four lights with a canted light in each side, separating two-light windows at each end. The doorway has a four-centred arch, and above it is a panel carved with Tudor arms and rose, while to the right is a continuous range of four two-light windows, each four-centred in a square head. The building is terminated with a moulded cornice and parapet. Lower down the street is 'The George', originally a monastic hostelry for pilgrims built by Abbot Selwood *c.* 1480. This is three-storeyed and far more elaborate, packed with movement and studiously unsymmetrical, one half differing from the other though the building is flanked by hexagonal buttresses. On the left a bay window runs over the full height while the right-hand portion is divided into three and two-light windows. All the windows have traceried heads, and there are panels over the entrance archway. The whole is surmounted with simple crenellations or battlements.

Such buildings conformed to what had become our national style, the first essentially English architectural and artistic expression to be seen in this country and here alone. Happily, monasteries and castles apart, none of them lies in ruins, though there are a few substantial houses, abandoned after damage sustained in the Civil War or by later fires, that are of some interest, among them Wingfield Manor, Derbyshire; Bradgate Park, Leicestershire; and Cowdray House, Sussex.

Wingfield, towering above a steep escarpment, is a little earlier in date and indeed is another example of the transition from castle to manor house. It was begun by Ralph, Lord Cromwell, in 1441, a foundation confirmed by the money-bags carved over the gateway, for the noble lord was Treasurer of England. Besieged in the Civil War, the house was dismantled on the orders of another, more sinister, Cromwell. The gateway leads onto two quadrangular courts. There are remains of the roofless banqueting hall emblazoned with the Shrewsbury arms and quarterings and lighted by an octagon window and a line of

Gothic mullioned windows, and beneath it, intact, is an aisled and rib-vaulted undercroft. There is also part of the chapel, adjoining an apartment with another rich Gothic window, and there are guard chambers and a high embattled tower. It was here that a later Earl of Shrewsbury held Mary Queen of Scots in custody, her suite of apartments being, traditionally, those on the west side of the north court.

The ruins of Bradgate lie in the Triassic landscape of the Charn-wood Forest beyond the outcrops of rock, the cedars and the ancient twisted oaks. Begun by Sir Thomas Grey, first Marquis of Dorset, towards the close of the fifteenth century and com-pleted by his son before 1510, it was among the earliest great houses to be built without fortifications, as it was among the early houses to be built of brick. What remains are four towers, part of the chapel with the alabaster tomb of the founder, portions of the kitchens and other fragments. This was the birthplace and home of that ill-fated girl who was for nine days Queen of England, Lady Jane Grey. It was in one of these towers that Roger Ascham found her reading Plato's *Phaedro* while the rest of her family were out hunting. She was then 14, and four years later she was to die in the Tower of London.

Cowdray House was begun in 1492 for the Earl of Southamp-ton, whose initials are carved in the stone ceiling of the entrance porch, and it has remained in ruins since a fire of 1793. It was built on the quadrangular plan with a gatehouse in the middle of the west range. The three-storeyed gate-house with turrets is intact, but it is the east range that is the most impressive. Here the great hall is lighted by tall pointed windows with traceried heads, while the rooms about them have later generous windows with transoms and mullions. The almost square hall porch, crenellated like the rest, has octagonal buttresses and, over the entrance arch, a mutilated carving of the arms of Henry VIII. There were later alterations here, made some time before Queen Elizabeth's pro-longed visit in 1591 with all its attendant junketings. There were two long galleries with frescoes, and the hall and staircase were similarly frescoed with the story of Tancred and Clorinda from Tasso.

An event of far-reaching significance in the first half of this sixteenth century was largely responsible for a massive wave of secular building and the introduction of new ideas. This was the separation of the State from the Church of Rome and the Dissolution of the Monasteries. The story is a familiar one. The matrimonial entanglements of Henry VIII and the condemnation by the Papal Court, the Anti-Papal Legislation of 1532 and the Act of Succession two years later, securing the Crown to the off-spring of Anne Boleyn, were the harbingers of the coming storm. The continued existence of the monastic orders, owing allegiance to Rome, would have constituted a danger to the royal supremacy, and since a precedent in monastic suppression had already been established in alienating the estates of monastic houses for the endowment of Wolsey's colleges at Oxford and Ipswich, it was not difficult, with the enlistment of the shrewd legal mind of Thomas Cromwell, to make a clean sweep. Cromwell sent his commissioners or agents on tours of inspection of the monasteries throughout the kingdom. The evidence of these visitations was presented in a vast document called the *comperta*. Undeniably there were some lapses in monastic life, but the formidable indictment of a decadent monachism as here presented was largely based on a mass of venomous exaggeration compiled by unscrupulous agents. The end came with the surrender or dissolution by Acts of Parliament and attainder in the years 1536–9. With the exception of the cathedral priories and a few others selected for episco-pal status, the monasteries were systematically ransacked and levelled. The iconoclasm was extended not only to the buildings and their art contents but to the destruction or filching of priceless manuscripts and incunabula, plate and vestments. (In 1547 it was the turn of the collegiate foundations, hospitals, gilds and chantries).

Let Glastonbury serve as a single example of what happened. This was perhaps the most venerated and venerable site in all Britain and the meeting-place of British and English influences and traditions. Cromwell's agents battened their eyes on the splendid abbey and estate and decided it was ripe for plucking. They wrote off to Cromwell: "We assure your lordship that it is the goodliest house of that sort that ever we have seen ... a house mete for the kinges magjesty and for no man else; which is our great comfort. . . . The house is greate, goodly and so pryncely that as we have not seen the lyke; with 4 parkes adjoynyng ... a great mere well replenished with greate pyke, breme, perche, and roche; 4 faire manour places belonging to the late abbott, the furthest but 3 myles distant, beyng goodly mansions."

The king's men pounced. The saintly old Abbot Whiting was quickly tried on trumped-up charges of being in possession of treasonable literature against the king's marriages and of concealing treasure, and, with five of his monks, he was hanged on Tor Hill. Even before the trial Cromwell had assessed the loot in his memoranda. There was 11,000 ounces of plate, besides the gold, the furniture and "the rich copes". In ready money there was over £1,100 (at least £35,000 in today's currency), and the annual revenue was assessed at £3,500 (or almost £110,000 today). What happened to the vast invaluable library? There is extant a catalogue of the library made in the thirteenth century, so rare and antiquated in script that the monks of the day could not read them. By the time that Leland saw the library in Abbot Whiting's time it had swollen into a veritable treasure-house. Hardly any Glastonbury books are known today. The abbey was granted to the odious Edward Seymour, Duke of Somerset, but shortly afterwards it became the quarry of all the neighbouring country. Of the great church, the alleged burial place of King Arthur and Guinevere, only fragments remain, and of the conventual buildings nothing but that remarkable kitchen.

The bulk of monastic estates were sold or leased or given away as marks of favour, and in many instances the conventual buildings were converted into desirable residences, but the church was almost invariably pulled down, the ruins serving as a stone quarry. Of over 800 monastic houses that were dissolved there is hardly a trace of a third of them, while about another third have fairly substantial remains. Among the best preserved of those converted into private houses are Lacock Abbey, Forde Abbey, Buckland Abbey and Milton Abbey. Some such houses have themselves fallen into ruin, among them Titchfield Priory in Hampshire. This was a Premonstratensian monastery until King Henry gave it to Thomas Wriothesley, Earl of Southampton, who as Lord Chancellor of England had been able to secure a great deal of monastic loot for his grateful monarch. Wriothesley lost no time in converting his new possession to domestic use, but his splendid Tudor house, called Place House, fell into disrepair in the eighteenth century and most of the stones were carted off. What chiefly remains is a lofty gate-house built through the nave of the monastic church to give ingress to a courtyard where the cloister had stood. Designed by Thomas Bartewe, who remodelled

the presbytery of Winchester Cathedral and later designed forts
for the king, and completed in 1540, this has a compact grouping
of six lofty towers, embattled, with two-light mullioned windows,
and larger transomed and mullioned windows in the gate-house
proper. A letter written to Wriothsley mentions that Bartewe
had told the writer "that smoke shall not be avoyded by the
chymneys of your chiefe lodgings if the steple stand"—so the
church tower had to come down.

The Dissolution of the Monasteries and the cessation of all their
activities released a vast body of architects and masons and diverted
them to the provision of houses for the new owners of the monastic estates and other *nouveaux riches*. Extremely few new churches
were built over the remainder of the sixteenth century, but the
aftermath of the Dissolution was remarkable for a spate of private
building. This was the age of what has been called the Tudor
Renaissance, the age of Hampton Court, the rose-tinted Compton
Wyniates, East Barsham Manor and Layer Marney with its eight-
tiered towers shot with glass. It is a mistake to assume that the
Gothic idiom in architecture ended abruptly with the early years
of this century. It did not do so any more than did the medieval
forms of art and literature. For some time building was carried
on by men trained in the Gothic tradition, even though they now
frequently worked under foreign artists trained in the classical
tradition. Yet while the Tudor mansion still embodied the hall-
house plan, often as part of the quadrangular plan introduced
during the Middle Ages, it introduced many new features.

The end of the feudal system and the later law by which the
great landowners were enabled to break the ancient entails on
their estates brought about a new way of living which was
reflected in a new domestic architecture. The great hall was no
longer needed for entertaining, feeding and even sleeping large
bodies of retainers, and it now absorbed less space, while greater
privacy was obtained by grouping many apartments round the
hall nucleus of the house. Large windows, generally mullioned
and transomed into many lights, were designed for amenity as
much as for show. Staircases were given more prominence, and
among new features were the central tiered porch and the long
gallery. The gallery reached its peak, of course, in the Elizabethan
house, largely due to the fashion of displaying portrait paintings,
but it derived from the covered passages which connected the

various half-detached portions of a medieval house, and it already appeared in a fairly developed form in the first half of the sixteenth century. The winged *E*-shaped plan popularly associated with the Elizabethan period also appeared. Yet the disposition of buildings was still markedly medieval, and traceried stone or brick panelling appeared side by side with the classical trappings of antiquity. The transition from Gothic to Renaissance was a gradual process, and what is often referred to as Gothic Revival is clearly Gothic Survival.

The gate-houses of Leez Priory in Essex, though essentially Tudor in character, are still dominated by the medieval past. After the Dissolution the Augustinian priory became the property of Lord Rich, who pulled down the monastic buildings and erected a mansion in their place. Here he followed the claustral plan, with outer and inner courts, each with a monumental gate-house. These gate-houses are almost all that remain of the mansion, which was razed to the ground in 1753. Both are of brick. The outer gate-house has a broad flat arch in a square head, with moulded shields in the spandrels, set between polygonal turrets. Above the entrance is a single square-headed window. The only enrichment lies in the trefoiled corbel friezes and angle pilaster strips on the turrets and the banded or moulded brick in the battlements. The door is markedly Gothic, with cusped tracery filling the heads of the panels. The inner gate-house, tall and narrow, also has polygonal turrets and battlements but is a little more ornate. Above the pointed arched entrance are two transomed and mullioned windows, one above the other, with a pediment over the upper. Trefoiled corbel friezes also appear here, but they are combined with diaper and chequerwork patterns in the brick, and there are lavishly moulded chimney-stacks.

The use of brick and diapering was based on French practice. Tudor brick was generally red in colour though the tone varied with the quantity of iron in the clay, so that it might turn out a pale biscuit or a deep purple. Bricks which were more deeply burned in the kiln became purplish and even black and were then employed for diapering in the prevailing red or yellow material. By the middle years of the sixteenth century what is now called 'English Bond', in which the bricks are laid in alternate rows of headers and stretchers, was almost universally adopted, though there were irregularities of pattern, as may be seen at Leez Priory.

Our brickwork of the period, together with our later Georgian
brick, plum and magenta-coloured, is as fine as any in Mantua
and Cremona, Bruges or the Hanseatic cities. Decorative work
on brick houses was largely confined to carved and moulded
brick and to terracotta, which, unknown in the Middle Ages,
was introduced into England by Italian craftsmen and was rarely
used after the first half of the sixteenth century (though the
Victorians revived it).

Terracotta work at its most elaborate is to be seen at Layer
Marney, Essex; East Barsham Manor, Norfolk, and Sutton Place,
Surrey. One of the last instances of its use is that which dis-
tinguishes Great Cressingham Manor in Norfolk, for many
years a farm and now derelict. The house was probably built by
John Jenny, *c.* 1545, replacing a property which had belonged
to the Benedictines of Norwich. It lies beyond a castellated gatehouse, but it retains only half of its south façade. This is severely
simple in its lines, with a flat front broken only by turret-like
angle buttresses with jutting roofs and an identical central buttress, from which rises a brick chimney stack with octagonal
shafts and moulded bases. The windows are simple and squarish
with transoms and mullions. A moulded frieze divides the upper
and lower storeys, and this combines an interesting motif with a
Gothic trefoil and a Renaissance leaf ornament. The entire wall
of the upper storey is covered with tall narrow traceried panels
in rust-coloured terracotta, and each of these panels contains a
monogram or a hand clasping a falcon, the initials of the builder
and his wife and the Jenny family crest. The lower storey was
originally covered with plaster in imitation of stone but is now
cement rendered and mutilated. Great Cressingham Manor is a
hybrid and it represents the Tudor swan song of Gothic art.

The most astonishing hybrid of the period was the royal palace
of Nonsuch in Surrey, "the emblem of Tudor pride, the ostenta-
tious product of a new and vigorous race", as Ralph Dutton has
put it. Henry VIII imported craftsmen from all over Europe,
though the work was mainly done by Italians, to build this vast
and flamboyant plaything, of such scale and character that it
lived up to its name. Charles II gave it to his mistress, the Countess
of Castlemaine, by whom it was dismantled. Not one stone of it
remains, but we may see it through the pages of Samuel Pepys'
Diary, for he was there during its last days. There were two courts,

one of which was built by Lord Lumley after the King's death. There was a gate-house with a clock turret, and a great banqueting hall three storeys high, with eight rooms, well windowed, on either side. The lower storey was of stone, the upper timber-framed, the timbers and panels between them richly gilded and painted and covered with ornamental scales of slate. There were two great towers, extravaganzas five storeys high, and in each the upper storey but one billowed out, and the whole, like the clock tower, was capped with a dome or cupola. The walled garden was divided into alleys and segments and rounds, and there were fountains and marble pinnacles or pyramids. Here at least the Renaissance was writ clear for all to see. Henry never outdid this gesture of pageantry and showmanship, unless it was in his setting for the Field of the Cloth of Gold.

One more ruin may be noticed, Biddulph Old Hall in Staffordshire, built by Francis Biddulph in 1588. It lies on the edge of Biddulph Moor, once the home of a wild dark people, the 'Biddlemoor men', probably a pocket of ancient Celts driven up there at the time of the Saxon invasions and remaining isolated there over the centuries. The house survived less than a century, for it was destroyed in the Civil War after a siege of 1643. There is little that can readily be identified, but there are fragments of the hall and other apartments, all with transomed mullioned windows, and there is an octagonal tower with an ogee-shaped dome.

England now lay on the threshold of a new era. The changes in ideas of education and the dissemination of the classics, together with an enormous stylistic revolution spreading across the Continent, were about to create a new architecture. It could no longer be said that we had a national style.

16

Renaissance or Decline?

The Elizabethans were civilized and secular, exuberant and fussy, and their great houses were like them, often built on plan as medieval castles but interpreted in terms of Elizabethan chivalry, with lofty walls and angle towers and a raised central block representing a keep, and wholly tricked out with the classical details that had at last reached England. They were confident that they were creating a Brave New World. Courtier and artist alike were now inspired by Greeks and Romans, Castiglione's *Courtier* and Plutarch's *Lives* were the text-books for the art of good manners and accomplished living, and Philip Sidney, Essex and Fulke Greville became the popular embodiments of the new ideal. Hence the immediate success of *Hamlet*. They even went to heaven in style, and their peacock-bright funereal monuments, as richly garnished as bridal cakes, distinguish—or clutter—our parish churches.

This was a many-faceted world, impressive in its splendours of court life, the gay courage of its adventures and the riches of its arts. It was the age of Shakespeare, Marlow, Sidney and Spencer, of Tallis, Byrd and Dowland, and of Nicholas Hilliard, that incomparable miniaturist. It was an age of panache and fantasy, qualities that readily crystallized in the architectural scene. Longleat and Burghley, Montacute and Kirby, Hardwick and Wollaton, these are among our national achievements. Many such houses derive from Serlio and Renaissance Italy, from Flanders and the Low Countries, though the principles were often misunderstood and extravagantly misapplied. Within, there was a panoply of stained glass, oak panelling, tapestry and pendanted plaster ceilings like clusters of stalactites, while gargantuan bulbous buffets were heavy with such masterpieces by local craftsmen as the Gibbon Salt.

Despite the preponderance of completely new houses, the substantial buildings and spacious layout of medieval castles presented
opportunities for adaptation and extension that were too good
to be ignored. The castles of Wardour, Carew, Dudley, Sudeley,
Raglan, Ludlow and Kenilworth were all given face-lifts, and
this earlier period was markedly medieval in spirit if not in physical detail. The Queen granted Kenilworth to Lord Robert Dudley
in 1563, the year before she created him Earl of Leicester, where
she first visited him in 1565. Dudley built the four-square gatehouse still named after him (and still inhabited), its porch having
pilasters and shell-topped niches and bearing his initials. He also
modernized the medieval keep, but his main additions, now called
Lord Leicester's Buildings and in ruins, were the ranges on the
east side of the inner court with three canted bay windows in the
façade. He had his father's work on Dudley castle as a precedent,
not to be slavishly copied but as a hint of what could be introduced in the way of Ionic doorways and elegant transomed and
mullioned windows lighting high and spacious apartments. All
this, with a lavish garden layout, was done in the early seventies,
and with deliberation, for the Queen's seventeen-day sojourn
there with a retinue of thirty-one barons, her court ladies and
some 400 servants. With the aid of Sir Walter Scott and some
contemporary chronicles one can easily conjure up those days of
fete and festival such as England had never seen before and will
probably never seen again. As to the truth of the relationship
between the Queen and the ambitious, fawning Robert Dudley,
we shall never know, but it is at least certain that Elizabeth was
sufficiently mistress of her own soul to avoid the snare of marriage,
leaving the earl in the unenviable position of *cavaliere servente*.

Meanwhile Sir Henry Sidney, the great Elizabethan President
of the Council of Wales fitted a Renaissance house into a corner
of the fortress of Ludlow, with a great hall and highly decorated
state apartments, and he built the existing gate-house adjacent to
the keep. At Raglan Lord Worcester's deeper coffers allowed him
to build a grand Elizabethan mansion. He raised the height of his
hall and topped it with a large cupola, and he added a lofty oriel
and a three-tiered porch. At the south end of the hall was a
panelled drawing-room, and above this was the earl's private
dining-room (formerly, of course, the lord feasted on the dais
of the hall with the retainers below him in the same apartment).

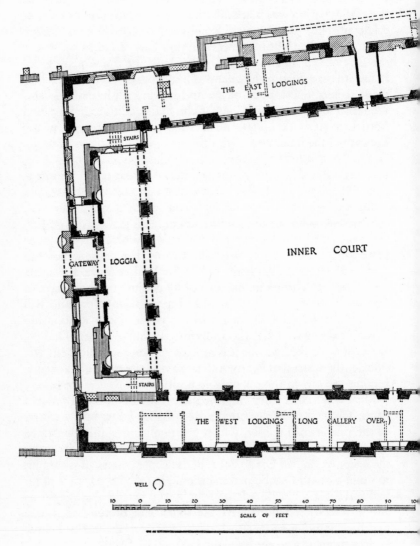

THE EAST LODGINGS

INNER COURT

GATEWAY LOGGIA

STAIRS

STAIRS

THE WEST LODGINGS (LONG GALLERY OVER)

WELL

SCALE OF FEET

Kirby Hall (*courtesy of the Department of the Environment*)

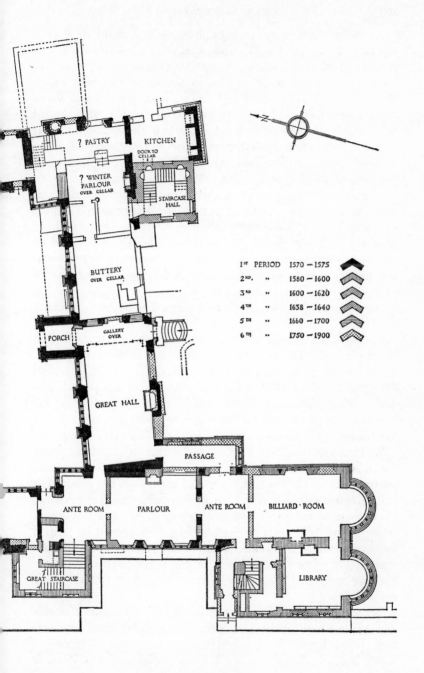

? PASTRY   KITCHEN

DOOR TO
CELLAR

? WINTER
PARLOUR
OVER CELLAR

STAIRCASE
HALL

BUTTERY
OVER CELLAR

PORCH   GALLERY
OVER

GREAT HALL

1ST PERIOD 1570 — 1575
2ND, ,, 1580 — 1600
3RD ,, 1600 — 1620
4TH ,, 1638 — 1640
5TH ,, 1660 — 1700
6TH ,, 1750 — 1900

PASSAGE

ANTE ROOM   PARLOUR   ANTE ROOM   BILLIARD · ROOM

GREAT STAIRCASE   LIBRARY

Next to the dining-room was the long gallery, and long it was, 126 feet, with a great bow window at the end of it. Like Kenilworth and most of Ludlow, this too is in ruins, and a broad fireplace with two standing figures in the stone surround stands islanded on high, for floor and ceiling have gone. Lord Worcester's son built the brick gazebo outside the old walls, he set up a marble white horse with waterworks in the Fountain Courts and he set up figures of Roman emperors in round-headed niches of brick which were lined with cockle-shells in geometrical patterns, of which there are some mouldering remains.

The second half of the century did away with compromise and brought the first fully matured fruits of the Renaissance. The shell of Kirby Hall in Northamptonshire, now in the custody of the Ministry of Works, has the dream-like quality of an Elizabethan masque. It was begun by Sir Humphrey Stafford in 1572 but it was shortly afterwards purchased by Sir Christopher Hatton, the Queen's beloved Lord Chancellor, who with an eye to receiving his royal mistress made more lavish plans. The house is generally attributed to John Thorpe, the brilliant architect of so much of this period, but there is no reliable documentary evidence though it appears that Thorpe's son Thomas was chief mason there. There is extant a folio of plans, elevations and architectural drawings by John Thorpe for many houses of the period, and one of Kirby bears the inscription "Kerby whereof I laid the first stone 1570". In general, however, the folio may be regarded as a reference book rather than as a record of Thorpe's own work.

Kirby is quadrangular in plan, and in the principal range the porch leads into a screened passage, with hall and living-quarters on one side and kitchen, buttery and pantry on the other. The hall at least is still roofed and has a beautifully canted oak ceiling, the timbers carved with classically derived foliage and mouldings, rising to the full height of the building. It is lighted by refined full-length windows divided into regular rectangular lights and separated by giant fluted pilasters, and in an angle are two screen-like bay windows. The general impression is one of rhythmic vertical flow.

What is so marked here is the prodigality of classical motifs. The three-tiered porch is a riot, the round-headed entrance flanked by Ionic fluted pilasters, the storey above having a round-headed window with a broken pediment (an addition of

1638) and flanking Corinthian columns projecting on leaf-carved brackets. A balcony to this window is supported on bold brackets immediately above the entrance arch. The upper stage of the porch is a dummy with nothing behind it, a piece of confectionary embodying cartouches, shell devices, roundels and foliage and rising to a screen of short Corinthian pilasters, itself finally crowned by a Dutch gable played off by flaming ball ornaments on either side. Sir John Summerson has shown that the ornament here derives from Serlio, from a treatise by Hans Blum and from the title-page of John Shute's *Chief Grounds of Architecture, 1563.*

Other notable features at Kirby are the two staircases contained in projections in the range overlooking the garden, each consisting of four straight wide flights surrounding a rectangular central newel. The long gallery, and the adjective is highly appropriate, runs the full length of the west wing, on the first floor, with windows looking both ways, that is into the court and over the garden. The principal rooms have semi-circular bow windows on the south. The garden elevation has dormer windows in Dutch gables with obelisks, and the two-storey wing has gables to match though they are merely ornaments. Raised terraces were among the features of the Elizabethan garden, and both terrace and garden here have been reconstructed by the Ministry of Works.

In the middle of the seventeenth century Inigo Jones was called to design the north range with an arched loggia. It is interesting to recall that the mason in charge at that time was Nicholas Stone, the distinguished sculptor, whose tombs and effigied monuments are among our major artistic achievements in the second half of the seventeenth century. The walls of the forecourt are pierced by high stone cartouched arches which are contemporary with this northern range of the 1640s.

The fashion for dispensing with gate-houses in favour of simple arched gateways can be seen as early as 1583 at Holdenby House, also in Northamptonshire, another seat of Sir Christopher Hatton and similarly consecrated to Gloriana. Of this magnificent country house (where, incidentally, Charles I was arrested by Cornet Joyce) absolutely nothing remains but the massive arched gateways, one on each side of the courtyard, almost but not quite identical and surmounted with arabesques.

Another house of the period which lies in ruins is that at

14

Moreton Corbet in Shropshire, which, like the later Hardwick Hall, though far different, may owe something to Vitruvius and his contemporaries. Here in 1579 Sir Andrew Corbet built a sumptuous classical range to the south of a medieval castle keep, and he altered the old gate-house to some semblance of uniformity, achieving a striking combination of old and new elements much as did his friend Sir Henry Sidney a few miles away at Ludlow. It is not very substantial and is simple in plan, two storeys and attics, with generous rectangular windows, moulded cornices and friezes, pedestal columns, and with Dutch gables crowning the elevation.

It is time, however, to journey across into Derbyshire to the birthplace of that remarkable woman Elizabeth of Hardwick, or 'Building Bess' as she was called, who by her last marriage became Countess of Shrewsbury. The massed towers of Hardwick Hall dominate this landscape, but barely a stone's throw before it lie the ruins of the Old Hall, where Bess was born in 1520. In her old age she began to modernize this house, but on the death of her husband she abandoned the project and began to build the new Hardwick. What remains of the Old Hall is the gaunt skeleton, lofty and almost four-square, with roofless walls and empty but still mullioned windows silhouetted against the sky through the dark walls. One cranes one's neck to see the remnants of coloured plasterwork, the hunting scenes of one chamber and the mutilated figures of Gog and Magog in Roman armour over the mantelpiece of another chamber.

Opposite looms the great glittering mansion which Bess built in 1590–7 to designs by Robert Smythson, author of the monstrous Wollaton and much else, which for all its outward severity and angularity is one of the climaxes of the Elizabethan age, as essentially English as a Shakespeare play. The prodigality and size of its vast windows render it 'more glass than wall' as the old jingle goes, and among its conceits are the initials E and S perforated in the stone parapets of each tower. The interior is all pageantry, its long receding gallery tapestried and hung with portraits, and its great chamber or state room hung with a monumental frieze of coloured plaster depicting forest and hunting scenes.

Bess of Hardwick had already engaged in vast building enterprises at the first Chatsworth, Bolsover, Worksop and Oldcotes.

Bolsover comes within our purview for it is one of the most fantastic ruins in these islands. It stands high on a lofty promontory of the same ridge from which Hardwick rises and it looks over a precipice to a slice of Derbyshire grey with colliery smoke, contrasting vividly with the dramatic belvedere itself. It was begun and probably planned by Robert Smythson in 1613, but since he died in the following year much of the credit must go to his son John and, no doubt, to his patron Sir Charles Cavendish, the younger son of Bess of Hardwick, a dwarf, a gallant soldier and a philosopher who corresponded with Descartes.

The keep of Bolsover, though massive and squarish with angle turrets and a staircase tower, is merely symbolic of martial strength, for it is commodious, well windowed and filled with luxurious amenities. Empty, though still habitable, it is rich in vaulted and painted ceilings, with lacquered panelling and, in the Star Chamber, with paintings of the Twelve Caesars. There is a Pillar Parlour, a Marble Closet, a Heaven Room and an Elysium Room. The hooded chimneypieces of local stone and Derbyshire marble are ornate and French in feeling, though probably designed by John Smythson with the aid of some of the currently published source books. Even though the interior of this building is arranged in the manner of a tower house it contrives to be theatrical and has a mysterious obsessive quality. And immediately in front of it is a small raised forecourt with battlemented pavilions and, in the centre, a Venus fountain.

A terrace has been built along the top of the wall above the precipice, and ranged along it is the other wonder of Bolsover, the Riding School added by Sir Charles's son, William, the Cavalier Marquis, later Duke of Newcastle, who here trained his steeds in the ballet of the *haute école* and who wrote a treatise on horsemanship. There is nothing else quite like it in England, though one recalls the later Riding School at Hovingham Hall in Yorkshire, and the mind associates it with the Spanish Riding School attached to the Hofburg in Vienna. The building dates from about 1629 and is Italian Baroque in character, roofless, empty and ghostly. It is a remarkable building, 170 feet in length, its main entrance with voussoirs and a broken pediment approached by a perron or double stair. Among its curiosities are the rounded buttresses or stays or shafts, resembling cannon and clamped, hanging, to the wall, for they rest on nothing and they support nothing. These shafts are heavily rusticated, and indeed the entire façade has such vermiculations, an obsession at Bolsover for they are even extended to the wooden door leading from the keep onto the garden wall. There is some mystery about the authorship of this Riding School. It is certainly by John Smythson, but the seventeenth-century George Vertue in his notebooks categorically states that the Duke of Newcastle's architect here, as at Welbeck and Nottingham, was Samuel Marsh. More likely Marsh was the chief mason.

There is, strangely, yet another ruin which was the product of John Smythson[1] and his patron Sir Charles Cavendish, Slingsby Castle in Yorkshire's North Riding. It was begun in the 1620s and despite the late date is still of Elizabethan type, It was a castle in name only and was a substantial and impressive house. It is oblong, of two storeys and a vaulted basement, with four corner wings or projections continued at their corners by turrets. It is now a gaunt broken skeleton retaining some of its cross windows (one mullion, one transom) with pediments, the upper pediments of eyebrow type. The vaults of the basement rooms are generally of tunnel type, but in places they stand on short octagonal piers resembling those in the Bolsover keep.

Yet another castle in name only was begun by the Elizabethans and completed by the Jacobeans. Lulworth Castle amid the plantations and groves of Dorset reflects equally with Bolsover the medieval chivalry of Spenser's *The Faerie Queene*. It is a big angular block, battlemented, with circular angle towers, but it has the classical trappings of the period. A balustraded flight of steps leads up to the entrance porch, where the archway is flanked by pairs of Ionic columns, and between each pair is a shell-headed niche and, above it, a swagged cartouche. Surmounting the cornice of the porch are the standing figures of two Roman centurions. In the main façade above the porch is a featured wheel window patterned geometrically into seven tangent circles, now devoid of glass. The remaining windows are paired arched lights with lion masks beneath them. Elsewhere there are arched niches filled with statues of knights and ladies.

Lulworth was begun in 1588 by Henry Howard, second Viscount Bindon, and completed in 1609 by the third Viscount. It

[1] For the Smythson family and their work see Mark Girouard, *Robert Smythson and the Architecture of the Elizabeth Era* (London, 1966).

was the home of Mrs. Fitzherbert during the short year of her first marriage to Edward Weld, and in 1830 it was lent for six months to the exiled Charles X of France. The house was gutted by fire in 1929 and is now a melancholy and strangely affecting shell where sycamores have taken root in the roofless space formerly covered by the central tower. The Welds, like the Howards, were Catholics, and a fascinating adjunct of the estate is the Catholic chapel of 1786, built to resemble a mausoleum, with sash windows, because of the prevailing penal laws against Catholics, with a dainty Ionic interior like a miniature Pantheon.

A few years after the building of Lulworth John Thorpe was planning a strange house for Sir Thomas Georges at Longford in Wiltshire. The design of Longford Castle, begun in 1580, appears to have been influenced by Sir Thomas's Swedish wife who wished the house to be modelled upon Tycho Brahe's castle of Uranienborg. Still inhabited, this is a triangular building with round towers at each of the three angles. We are not immediately concerned with this, but it is to the point that in 1593 Sir Thomas Tresham built a triangular lodge in the grounds of his seat Rushton Hall in Northamptonshire. Now Tresham, knighted by Queen Elizabeth at Kenilworth in 1576, had been brought up as a Protestant, but in 1580 he was converted to Roman Catholicism by his friend the Jesuit Father Campion, and for harbouring this recusant priest he suffered, off and on, seven years imprisonment. "The most tyme I employe in studie ys in divinitie," wrote Tresham. In Rushton Lodge he embodied symbolically the doctrine of the Holy Trinity. This Trinitarian fantasy is a miniature but perfect product of Elizabethan Baroque, a study in ginger-brown and pinkish grey, intact but empty and in the custody of the Ministry of Works. It is a remarkable monument, a by-product of the Jesuit Counter-Reformation and a translation in stone of the mystical verse of the period. But Tresham was also a mathematician, and some may see his buildings as studies in Euclid.

In plan the lodge is an equilateral triangle, of three storeys, each floor converted internally into a regular hexagon, with three windows on each side on each floor, these being in the shapes of trefoils, crosses and triangles. Each side has a crocketed gable rising to three-sided tapering obelisks. Below the gables a frieze with a continuous Latin inscription runs round the entire building, each side bearing thirty-three letters. The symbolism of the Trinity interwoven with the trefoil which was the heraldic badge of the Treshams, is carried on in the windows. Over the entrance is a triangular pediment enclosing the Tresham arms and the motto *Tres Testimonium Dant*. Everywhere there are Christian symbols, the cross, monogram and nails, the Agnus Dei, a chalice, the seven-branched candlestick and the pelican. The monument is animated by a religious frenzy, and this, at least, redeems it from a possible charge that it is a picturesque folly. Inevitably the name of John Thorpe is linked with it, but this seems highly improbable, and it would appear that Sir Thomas Tresham worked out his own design with the professional supervision of Richard Stickells, Clerk of the Works at Richmond, who aided him in his other projects.

Before Tresham had finished his lodge in 1595 he had embarked upon another project at Lyveden in the same county. This, known as the New Build, was intended as a secondary residence, and as Rushton Lodge symbolized the Trinity so Lyveden New Build was an interpretation of the Passion. It was never completed, and it stands roofless and glassless in the middle of solitary empty fields. In plan it is a Greek cross, of two storeys and basement, with a bay window over two storeys at the end of each arm, one bay containing the entrance. Each arm forms a square, and the four equal arms enclose a square central space. Above the first-floor windows is an entablature carved with elaborate emblems of the Passion. Above the upper floor runs another entablature incised with inscriptions from the Vulgate. On each of the three floors are three rooms, again symbolic of the Trinity. It might be seen as a substantial garden pavilion, an adjunct to the manor house close by, and indeed there are meagre traces of a garden layout, including a long raised terrace and canals enclosing a 'water orchard'.

The brilliance and pomp of the great Elizabethan and Jacobean houses are but faintly reflected in the sturdy but simple vernacular domestic architecture of the yeomen. Some such houses of the period stand derelict or are put to farming use, but few are significant enough to deserve notice here. An exception is Wycoller Hall in a remote and romantic watery setting with a plethora of clapper and clam bridges on the south-western Lancashire-Yorkshire border. The roofless ruin is late sixteenth-century, a

long low house with a crumbling tower, many-mullioned windows, and a hall in which a great semicircular fireplace has stone
seats built round its curved back. It was abandoned in 1819, and
it was a ruin when Charlotte Brontë came here, later to meta-
morphose it into the 'Ferndean Manor' of *Jane Eyre*. Until recent
years it was smothered by sycamore and elder, but a local society
has now taken it under its wing. Nearby a derelict house has a
beautiful ogival-arched porch. This is a haunting corner of
Elizabethan England that has died.

There is little further to detain us—in the way of ruins, that is—
in the period between Inigo Jones and Christopher Wren. In
the Cotswolds that stout cavalier Sir Baptist Hicks began to build,
in 1613, his country seat at Chipping Campden. The house did
not survive the Roundheads' onslaught in the Civil War, but one
windowed wall survives together with the gateway and some
delicious pavilions. The gateway is intact with fancy tapering
gables above the archway and its flanking walls, and the engaged
lodges, one on either side, have ogee-shaped roofs. Behind,
isolated in the meadows, are two pavilions that are quite finicky
in their ornament, for they are surmounted with flaming onion-
shaped urns and twisted barley-sugar chimneys. This quiet corner
with the grouped gateway and lodges, almshouses and stately
Perpendicular 'wool' church is an eye-catcher. But Campden is a
place of rare quality, its high street a miracle of domestic architecture from every age, though one must single out the Gothic
house, *c.* 1380, of William Grevel, "the flower of the wool
merchants of all England", the fourteenth-century Woolstaplers'
Hall and the arcaded market hall of 1627.

Two years after the launching of Campden House, the house
of Houghton Conquest near Ampthill in Bedfordshire was begun,
designed for the Countess of Pembroke, sister of Sir Philip
Sidney. This was the 'House Beautiful' of Bunyans' *Pilgrim's
Progress*. It was not designed by Inigo Jones, as is sometimes
claimed, though it certainly may be identified with an associate
or at least a contemporary follower. It is, or was, for it was dismantled in 1794, an *H*-shaped house of Jacobean type, of brick
with stone dressings. One elevation had three loggias tiered one
upon the other, and there seem to have been some affinities with
Kirby Hall, but there were extensive alterations here about 1685.
According to a publication of 1827 Sir William Chambers made

further alterations about 1765, but this could be due to a con-
fusion with Chambers's work at nearby Ampthill House, since
Houghton Conquest was frequently known under that name.

Of the Wren period was the house designed or completed by the
Dutch Captain Wynne for Lord Craven at Hampstead Marshall
in Berkshire, but nothing remains but eight splendid gateways of
1685. Each gateway has piers of brick with stone decorations,
with shell-headed niches and topped with ornamental stone
urns. They now stand lost and forlorn in a park denuded of both
house and garden, and in this they recall the earlier solitary gateways of Holdenby. The mysterious Wynne or Winde designed
the lost Buckingham House on the site of Buckingham Palace,
the most splendid private house in London, with a grand double
staircase frescoed by the Venetian Bellucci. He also worked for
Lord Craven on Combe Abbey in Warwickshire.

Before the eighteenth century was fully launched we were
introduced to the masterpieces of Christopher Wren, Nicholas
Hawksmoor and John Vanbrugh, to St. Paul's Cathedral, the
Royal Hospital at Greenwich and the palace of Blenheim,
achievements without peer in Europe. Our earliest ruin of the
new century lies in a fold of the hills on the Isle of Wight. It is
Appledurcombe House begun by Sir Robert Worsley in 1710
and completed by Sir Richard, who made a collection of works
of art in Italy and wrote a history of the Isle of Wight. The
architect is unknown but the garden was laid out by 'Capability'
Brown. The gardens have gone and so have some of the follies,
though there is a battered obelisk, and the Freemantle Gate in
later Grecian taste survives intact. It was an attractive house of
warm stone subtly stained pink with lichen, and though most of
it stands it is a mournful wreck, or was until the Ministry of
Works recently took it over. Before that, rooks flew through the
house, through the gaping broken windows with their finely
moulded wooden shutters on the inside, and the park was over-
grown with anemones and Star of Bethlehem. In the centre of
the garden front the entrance doorway, flanked by lions, is contained within a giant frame of Corinthian columns supporting
an entablature, and above the door is an oeil-de-boeuf light with
swags and festoons, a hint of the Petit Trianon. The three-storey
house is surmounted with a balustrade, and there are projecting
two-storey wings. The windows throughout are divided by

Corinthian or Composite pilasters. The south front has a colonnade, recently drooping with Virginia creeper but now this has almost certainly been swept away by the restorers. Plasterwork and Italian paintings were stripped in 1855, when the house became a school and then, for a brief space, a monastery.

We must leave it to the reader to decide whether we are justified in including Vanbrugh's Seaton Delaval, set just a little way from the Durham coast but on the edge of the coalfield, for though only a few years ago it was a blackened derelict hulk it has now been cleaned up and is in part habitable (though, in fact, it is not). It was begun by Vanbrugh in 1718 for the extraordinary and violent Delavals. This was the last of Vanbrugh's great houses, and while it still shows Vanbrugh to be a man of the theatre and a master in the disposition of mass and volume it tends to retreat from the full-blown Baroque of Blenheim and Castle Howard. Yet somehow it has a more Piranesian flavour, and it is still a dramatic essay in megalomania. Its scale is awesome, vast forecourt, colossal porticoes, the Doric front lifted on a high flight of steps, Cyclopean columns and blocks of stone and massive rustications. In its former dereliction it recalled Bolsover in distant Derbyshire. The wings are of extreme length, one of them housing the stables, as spacious and immaculate as the aisled chapels of a church. These wings are colonnaded, and the long perspective of arches reminded Sir Sacheverell Sitwell of "the ruined stables and granaries of Moulay Ismail, at Meknes, in Morocco".

The eighteenth century saw the triumph of the classical orders, representing, as Miss Olive Cook has so shrewdly put it, "the imposition of the temple architecture of an extinct Mediterranean civilisation upon the house design of a northern people". There are still surprises and valid artistic achievements and true genius in this century of James Gibbs, William Kent, Robert Adam, James Wyatt, John Nash and many lesser men of talent whose work represents the late fulfilment of the classical Renaissance in England, often combined with the large-scale landscape gardening which was also an entirely English product, made possible by the wealth of a squirearchy that has all but vanished.

We could, it is true, indicate a handful of ruins of indifferent to middling worth in this period. We could point to Gibside in Durham, where the hall, orangery and so-called banqueting house are all ruinous, though James Paine's chapel of 1760 with

Ionic portico and perron has been rescued. Or to John Nash's own home of East Cowes Castle on the Isle of Wight, built in 1798 and dismantled in 1950, a grey and black turreted castle with palms growing through the roof of the glass conservatory, the remains of an octagon library, the winter garden and long gallery where wild strawberries and toad-flax are, or were, rooted into the paving. East Cowes heralds the eclecticism of the nineteenth century and, it may be, the loss of our artistic integrity. But we have already exceeded our brief and we dare go no further.

Index